D1345721

The Grid

The Grid

The Decision-Making Tool for Every Business (Including Yours)

Matt Watkinson

BUSINESS
BOOKS

13 5 7 9 10 8 6 4 2

Random House Business Books
20 Vauxhall Bridge Road
London SW1V 2SA

Random House Business Books is part of the Penguin Random House group of companies
whose addresses can be found at global.penguinrandomhouse.com

First published by Random House Business Books in 2017

www.penguin.co.uk

A CIP catalogue record for this book is available from the British Library

ISBN 9781847947949 (hardback)
ISBN 9781847941879 (trade paperback)

Typeset in 11.2/15 pt Minion Pro by Jouve (UK), Milton Keynes
Printed and bound by Clays Ltd, St Ives plc

Penguin Random House is committed to a sustainable future
for our business, our readers and our planet. This book is made
from Forest Stewardship Council® certified paper.

For my dad, who taught me how to learn.

Contents

Author's Note

On one level, this is a straightforward business book. The grid is a tool to help you make better decisions. It provides a structure for identifying both issues and opportunities within existing businesses, and for putting new business ideas to the test – all with no prior experience necessary. But its underlying motive is deeper than that.

Most of us have a professional ambition of one kind or another. Some dream of working for themselves, others to rise within the ranks of their employer. Many love their job just as it is, but want to broaden their knowledge. Pursuing and achieving these goals can be immensely rewarding and fulfilling.

This book aims to help you towards those goals – whatever they might be – by improving the decisions you'll make along the way. In doing so, its true aim is to contribute to your success and well-being as an individual, and those of society as a whole.

The mathematician George E. P. Box once remarked, 'Essentially, all models are wrong, but some are useful.'[1] He rightly believed that models can never represent the complexity of the real world, but that they are valuable anyway. They bring structure to our thinking, and help us tame that complexity. They illuminate the problems we seek to solve.

In the grid, I hope you will find a model that's a little less wrong, and a little more useful than the alternatives.

Matt Watkinson
26 December 2016

Acknowledgements

I'd like to take this opportunity to thank the following: my wife Louise for her tireless support, encouragement and understanding. Patrick Walsh and Carrie Plitt, whose input on the early ideas was invaluable. Nigel Wilcockson at Random House for commissioning and editing the book.

My dear friend, confidant and 'minister for brevity', Ben Smith. Whatever I have done, he has always found a way to make it better. Natalie Malevsky, who has been part of this journey from the start and has never lost enthusiasm for the project. My family John Watkinson and Howard Watkinson. Arthur Nurse, who created the beautiful icons, Peter Kremmer and the team at Dekoratio for graphic design work, and Panos Damaskinidis.

My thanks to the following for their feedback and insight: Csaba Konkoly, Walter Kiechel, Alex Bromage, Ian Storrar, Diana McKenzie, Shelley Stanford, John Maddigan, Mikael Reichel, John Syfret, Cat Funk, David Pinder, Sionade Robinson, Marco Seiler, Rory Sutherland, Andy Puddicombe, Anna Berger, Janina Rustige, Philip Rowley, Emma Honeybone, Edd Read, Tim Leake, Scott Redick, Bruce Lampcov, Thomas Eriksen, Anne Heinung, Nick Livesey, Clive Stevenson, John Sills, Adam Bice, Mark Simpson, Marc Provissiero, Lorna Morris, Roland Geeraedts, Nigel Pepper, Bernard Grenville-Jones, Bonnie Austin, Sam Aborne, Kristin Peck, Don Spetner, Per Sjöfors, Mica Vaipan, Matthias Bader, Arif Haq and Will Sansom at Contagious, Kal Patel, Deborah Dolce, Tamar Cohen, Tim and Anthony Pask, and Rob Isaacs.

To Nicole Parsons for the inspiration.

To the members of my Buddhist community, whose guidance and encouragement were invaluable: Kim Upton, Sean and Liz Ruiz and all of the Lotus Lions District in Beverly Hills.

To friends who supported and distracted in equal measure: Hans Mills, James Cooper, Adam Davis, Will Skjøtt, Megan Butler, Ben Wall, Draža Jansky, Raph Colson, Brooke Wescott, Jono O'Connor and countless others.

Finally, to the hundreds of authors from whose work I learned so much.

Introduction

'As you can see, Mr Watkinson, we really have no choice but to operate,' the doctor said, pointing to a fuzzy-looking scan on the screen.

'On which one?' I asked.

'Both.'

I'd been training hard for a few months – lifting weights, cycling
and running – when my knees had started to hurt. Eventually the
pain was bad enough that I'd had to stop exercising altogether and
had ended up at the surgeon's office. He booked me in for an arthro-
scopic procedure the following week, on both knees.

Six months later it was clear the surgery hadn't fixed the problem.
I was still in pain and couldn't exercise. I saw physiotherapists and
osteopaths, I squashed my lower half with a foam roller. Nothing
made any difference. In a final attempt to get help I called Nicole
Parsons, a local sports rehabilitation expert.

She listened patiently to my woes, then unpacked some high-tech
equipment from her bag: a ruler, a camera and a clipboard with some
blank stick figures on it. After taking photos and making some meas-
urements, she sketched over the top of the stick figures and presented
her diagnosis.

The problem, she explained, had nothing to do with my knees: my
muscle groups were imbalanced, from my shoulders down to my feet.
This meant my hips were out of alignment with my knees, so when I
moved my legs, the bones and joints were pulled all over the place,
hence the pain. Using an approach called the Egoscue Method, she

prescribed exercises to rebalance my muscles and resolve my postural issues.[1] Her approach worked. With regular sessions and sticking to the programme, I was soon up and running again.

As I lay sprawled on her mat, it struck me that this situation was similar to what I experienced at work. People would make a decision in one part of a business, without realising how it might impact another; we'd identify a problem and try to fix it without identifying the root cause, often making matters worse. Everyone jumped straight to specialist surgery – nobody looked at the whole as Nicole had done. I wondered whether learning more about her approach might help my work and asked her for some book recommendations.

Surprised at my interest, she recommended a book called *Anatomy Trains*, which explains how the body's muscles are connected into one system.[2] I ordered the book that evening, oblivious to how my knee surgery and that conversation with Nicole would lead to the book you're now reading.

These events coincided with an exciting time in my professional life. About two years earlier, working as an independent designer, I'd arrived at the conclusion that the way we approached making products, services and customer experiences better could be dramatically improved.

We gathered data and tested our work endlessly with customers, but didn't use any robust principles to interpret our findings and guide our decision-making. Results were hit and miss. My father, an engineer, had drummed into me from an early age that first principles were the correct starting point for decision-making. What were the first principles in experience design? I wondered.

I believed that a set of simple principles would help us to consistently make better decisions, in less time and at less cost, so I set about trying to identify what those principles might be. After three years of research, I arrived at ten principles that could be applied to improve the experience of using any product or service. A year or so later *The Ten Principles Behind Great Customer Experiences* hit the shelves.[3]

The book was well received, and I have heard from readers around the world who are using the principles to improve their businesses. As I hoped, the guidelines proved to be universal, and the book won the CMI's Management Book of the Year in 2014.

For me, the best thing about this development was that clients now wanted my involvement at earlier stages in their projects. Rather than helping to execute decisions that had been made weeks or months before, I was being asked to help shape new ideas and to advise on more strategic matters.

Seeing first-hand the difficulties involved in making decisions about starting, growing or rescuing a business was fascinating. Most clients didn't have a robust way of evaluating their options and generally didn't know whether they were making good or bad decisions. Opportunities were missed. The time and money wasted were astronomical.

It was around this time I met Nicole and her anatomy textbook and came to the full realisation that whenever something is composed of interconnected parts – whether it's a body or a business – its overall behaviour can't be determined by looking at those parts in isolation. When you're dealing with a system, analysis will only get you so far. You need synthesis in equal measure.

But this wasn't what was happening in practice. People weren't basing their decisions on a 'space-station view' of the business, where cause and effect were visible and the behaviour of the whole could be seen. They were making them at ground level, where their department or expertise formed a horizon line that they couldn't see beyond. That's deeply problematic. When decision-makers look at each part of a business in isolation they usually aren't aware of how individual decisions can add up to unintended and undesirable outcomes.

If instead we could look at a business as a whole, we'd make better decisions and stack the odds of success much more in our favour. With this idea lodged in my mind, I began researching what leading business thinkers had to say on treating a business holistically. Surprisingly little, it turned out.

Academic business books tend to be specialised, because

academics themselves are usually specialists: they therefore don't pay much attention to holistic thinking. The same is true for books written on a specific subject: they go into detail about their area, but do little to explain it within the context of the whole. (My first book is guilty of this too.) Books written by entrepreneurs tend to be overly anecdotal and it isn't always clear how their lessons could be applied to other businesses. Many books mention in passing that a business is an interconnected system, but few explore the implications of this.

There are models, matrices, frameworks and approaches for every single aspect of a business, but none fit together, and they frequently contradict each other. This helps explain why many businesses I work with shun theory altogether. With so many frameworks, each slicing and dicing things in a different way, clients have no way of knowing which ones to use, and even if they do, most models can only ensure that one aspect of the business works well, not that it works overall.

This, to me, was another big issue. As with my work on customer experience, there wasn't a simple, universal set of principles to help people structure their thinking when making decisions – whether strategic or tactical. This makes structured team discussions almost impossible and leads to silly mistakes, because as we drown in detail we lose sight of the basics.

Seeing these two issues – reductionist thinking and a lack of simple principles to follow – present themselves so often in businesses of all shapes and sizes, I realised that what we needed was a better way to make business decisions, and I set myself a brief to come up with something to make our lives a little easier.

That 'better way' should allow decision-makers to see their business as a whole, whilst helping them to identify actions that would improve its overall success. It should work for any and every business; be simple to understand; and, most importantly, it should be pragmatic.

The result, after thousands of hours of research, plenty of sleepless nights and over 150 iterations, is a tool that I call 'the grid'.

The Grid

The grid is a simple tool for making better decisions, whoever you are and whatever the size or shape of your business. As I've readily admitted, there's no shortage of methods, tools and frameworks out there, so you'd be forgiven for questioning the need for another. There are, however, some things that make the grid different, and a bit special.

It allows you to think in wholes

Business thinking has always been based on an analytical approach: breaking things down into small pieces, then studying them in isolation. The problem is that everything in a business is interconnected – the whole doesn't behave like the sum of its parts.

Because most frameworks are based on this traditional, reductionist view of the world, they don't show us how our actions affect the business as a whole, so we make decisions that have unintended consequences. We might cut production costs in the hope of making a bigger profit, but accidentally make our products less desirable by reducing their quality. The net result is that we sell fewer units and become less profitable, not more. We might make changes to our brand designed to appeal to new customers, but end up alienating existing customers and cause them to leave.

The grid treats a business as a single, interconnected system that is inseparable from its environment. It gives you the entire picture, allowing you to manage conflicting goals, consider trade-offs and make decisions that improve the overall success of the business, all of which are skills that separate the great from the good.

Other sciences have embraced a systems-based view of the world: physics, mathematics, biology and ecology; even economics is moving in this direction.[4] It's time business thinking did too. The grid isn't just a shiny new model; it's the envoy of a modern, holistic approach to management, decision-making and strategy that will surely come to dominate our discipline too, as it has others.

It sees the world in motion

Every business is in a constant state of flux. The environment is always changing – sometimes a lot, sometimes a little – and so is the business itself. Unfortunately, most analysis tools treat the world as if it were standing still, rather than constantly moving.

It doesn't matter what our strengths and weaknesses are today. It matters whether they are getting stronger or weaker, and what they will look like tomorrow. Unlike most tools, which force you to take a 'snapshot' of the current situation, the grid helps you to identify what is changing, and why. It sees the world as dynamic and constantly changing, and helps you to make decisions based on the direction in which you're travelling, not your current location on the map.

It is universally applicable

There are plenty of books on how to build a start-up or administer a global empire, and thousands of industry-specific books too; but there are very few that tackle the fundamentals that underpin all of them.

By going back to the most basic elements of running a business, the grid will be your friend whatever size, shape or age your venture. It is also a useful tool for organisations outside the immediate realm of business, such as non-profit organisations and government. You can even use the grid to help guide individual career decisions.

It is a tool for teams or individuals

I described the book to a friend as being written with two audiences in mind: people who don't know enough and people who know too much. Most of us know too much about one thing and too little about another – we are part expert, part ignoramus, and even the brightest among us make simple mistakes. That's why pilots and surgeons use basic checklists before they take off or stab you with a scalpel.

On top of that, while our idiosyncrasies and partial views of the world make collaboration and teamwork so essential and rewarding, they also make it infuriating. When we believe our perspective is correct, we end up at loggerheads with people who see the world differently.

This is where the grid comes into its own. It allows anyone and everyone to consider an issue, or the likely impact of a decision, from all the perspectives that matter. It allows finance to see the marketing view of the world, and vice versa. It allows people from different disciplines to have structured conversations in language everyone understands, using a common reference point. It will force you to consider different points of view, turning teamwork from an aspiration into a reality. If you're working solo, the grid will help you resist the temptation to ignore the stuff you don't find fun or sexy, but which plays a decisive role in the success of your venture.

It is complementary to existing ways of working

Because the grid is primarily a tool to help you structure your thinking and assist in decision-making, it doesn't require any kind of formal 'adoption'. You just work your way through it as and when you need to, either by yourself or with your team. This makes it a natural complement to other popular ways of working, such as the lean start-up movement, where the grid can be used to form hypotheses to validate.

Book Structure

The book is structured in two parts: 'fast track' and 'deep dives'.

Fast track

Part One gives you everything you need to start using the grid. The first chapter introduces the grid and how it is constructed from basic principles. The second introduces another level of detail. The third shows how the grid is used in practice, considering three scenarios: creating a new business, product or service; evaluating an existing business; and making a strategic decision.

Deep dives

Part Two takes a deeper look at all the topics, with a chapter dedicated to each box of the grid. It makes sense to read them in sequence – especially if you are starting a new venture – but if a topic from Part One leaps out at you, then get stuck in with an à la carte approach, reading just the topics that interest you. If you're really short on time there is also an executive summary at the end of the book (pp. 261–79) that condenses each deep dive into a few pages.

You can also download a copy of the model from my website: www.matt-watkinson.com.

Welcome aboard!

Part 1
Fast Track

1 Constructing the Grid

When I explain the grid to someone for the first time I sketch it out on paper, talking it through step by step. Seeing it build up gradually helps them to take it in, and to realise that its simplicity isn't at the expense of its power. With that in mind, I'm going to talk you through it as if we were sitting together with the notepad in front of us.

There are three things that make for a successful business.

The first is **desirability**. If people don't want or need what you offer, you have a fundamental problem.

The second is **profitability**. If people love what you provide but it costs more to make than you can sell it for, you won't be around for long.

The third is **longevity**. There's no point making a fortune today if you lose it all tomorrow. If you make $100 a day, the more days you make those $100 the better. Furthermore, people are reluctant to buy from a business that might not be around to support that purchase in the future.

These three goals are interdependent. Desirability without profitability doesn't work, and you can't have longevity without the other two. A smart business decision is one that increases all three, or takes an informed view about the trade-offs between them: a little less desirability for a massive profit hike might be OK, but take that too far and you compromise your longevity when your customers swap to an alternative.

The real difficulty is that you must make decisions about these three goals while the landscape is constantly changing. A business is like a boat floating on the ocean, with currents moving it one way and the wind blowing it another. One minute the water is calm, the next huge waves are crashing over the bow. To keep a boat on course you must consider these factors when navigating. The same is true with business decision-making, where, broadly speaking, change is experienced within three distinct categories.

What **customers** want and how they behave can change. Since without customers you don't have a business, paying attention to these changes is paramount.

Market conditions can also change. New rivals emerge, categories grow and decline, new government regulations come into effect, any of which can impact your success.

Finally, the **organisation** – the business itself – is always changing. As your business develops, you will find that your capabilities, strengths and weaknesses change. Maybe you have a larger workforce and more cash than you used to, but you aren't as nimble as you once were, for example.

Now for the interesting part. We've got three goals: **desirability**, **profitability** and **longevity**. We've also got three changing layers: the **customer**, the **market** and the **organisation**.

Because everything in a business is interconnected, each layer can affect each goal: a change in competition can affect our profitability for example, or a change related to our customers might make our products less desirable.

To illustrate this, we draw a table with a column for each of our goals – desirability, profitability and longevity – and a row for each kind of change – customer, market and organisation. This gives us a grid with nine boxes, each containing a factor that affects our success, and which when considered together gives us a holistic view of the enterprise. Together, these nine boxes determine the success or failure of every business.

So, what's in the nine boxes? Let's take it a column at a time, starting with desirability.

	desirability	profitability	longevity
customer	WANTS & NEEDS		
market	RIVALRY		
organisation	OFFERINGS		

Desirability

There are three factors that determine desirability: the **wants and needs** of the customer, the **rivalry** we face in the market, and the **offerings** that our organisation creates. Let's consider a few scenarios.

If your customers' wants and needs change, but your offerings stay the same, it's reasonable to expect desirability to go down.

If you face a brilliant new rival, you can expect that to have an impact too. A change in rivalry can also be to your benefit, though. A competitor's misstep can make your products more desirable than before.

Finally, if customers' wants and needs and the rivalry you face both stay the same, but you work to improve your offerings, you can expect desirability to go up.

I use the term 'offerings' to reflect the breadth of things that an organisation creates: as well as the product or service itself, there's also the brand and overall experience of being a customer – all of which affect desirability. Also, since you will often use the grid to decide where to make sacrifices, 'offerings' seems appropriate!

	desirability	**profitability**	longevity
customer	WANTS & NEEDS	REVENUES	
market	RIVALRY	BARGAINING POWER	
organisation	OFFERINGS	COSTS	

Profitability

It's no surprise that the **revenues** from your customers and the **costs** your organisation incurs affect your profitability, but what about that middle box, **bargaining power**? It's often overlooked, but is absolutely crucial to success.

Every business is sandwiched between its customers and its suppliers. Your suppliers would happily charge you twice as much for half the goods because that would increase their profits. Your customers naturally seek the best deal for themselves too. This means you're not just in competition with your rivals, there is also a competitive element to your relationships with suppliers and customers too. Whoever has the most bargaining power gets the best deal overall.[1]

Bargaining power is important because without it your profitability will be squeezed by customers driving down prices, suppliers driving costs up, or both. When you are in a powerful position you get to squeeze back, reducing your costs by driving a hard bargain with suppliers, or increasing your prices if your customers have little option but to stick with you.

As you'll see, though, exploiting your power can be dangerous. If used too much it creates resentment, which can ultimately bring you down. More on that later.

	desirability	**profitability**	**longevity**
customer	WANTS & NEEDS	REVENUES	CUSTOMER BASE
market	RIVALRY	BARGAINING POWER	IMITABILITY
organisation	OFFERINGS	COSTS	ADAPTABILITY

Longevity

Without customers, you don't have a business. The more customers you have, and the longer you keep them, the more chance you have of surviving and prospering. That's why a growing and/or committed **customer base** is a goal for businesses the world over.

Moving down a row, a desirable, profitable product that nobody can copy makes for a rosy future indeed. Swedish giants Ikea and Tetra Pak made their founding families billionaires by creating inimitable aspects to their businesses, the former with an ecosystem that is extraordinarily difficult to copy in its entirety;[2] the latter by patenting an aseptic milk carton.[3]

The easier something is to imitate, the more intense competition becomes and the less profitable it is likely to be in the long term. **Imitability**, then, plays a significant role in determining the longevity of our business.

Finally, an organisation's ability to adapt directly determines whether it will survive into the future. Eventually a huge (and often hugely unexpected) change will land on the doorstep of every business – think digital downloads for the music industry or search engines for Yellow Pages.

When it does, if you've engineered **adaptability** out of the business you'll be ruined in no time. All too often, in the pursuit of a short-term profit, organisations sacrifice their adaptive capacity and recognise the problem only when it's too late. Returning to our nautical metaphor, a boat that's firmly anchored in place can't move when the weather changes and so ends up at the bottom of the sea.

Immediate Conclusions

Now that I've given you a whistle-stop tour of the grid, let's see what basic conclusions can be drawn.

Every box matters

To begin with, you can see that every box matters. If any one of these nine perspectives is forgotten, ill-considered or ignored, it can lead to decisions that will derail a successful business, or ensure a new one never gets off the ground.

Success is not guaranteed by excellence in one or two areas, it emerges from all nine boxes on the grid. Naturally, at times some take on greater significance than others, but missing a box entirely can spell disaster.

Imagine launching a wonderful product only to realise that a more powerful rival can not only copy it, but do it better. All you've done is given them proof that the opportunity exists, and your hard work has gone to waste because of one box – imitability.

Worse still, imagine incurring all the costs of building a polished product, just to realise that it doesn't fit with your customers' wants and needs, or that it won't create sufficient revenue to enable you to make your money back. It's heart-breaking stuff and it happens every day, not because people aren't smart or hard-working, but because it's easy to miss simple things. All nine boxes matter, and if you ignore one you're in trouble.

A change in one causes changes in the others

Another important conclusion is that change in one box causes change in the others. If left unchecked, a change in your customers' wants and needs will affect the size of your customer base and your revenues. If you become easier to imitate, it will cause an increase in rivalry and reduce your bargaining power. Cost-cutting through efficiency gains usually comes at the expense of adaptability, and so on.

Earlier, I mentioned that business thinking generally focuses on reduction and analysis: splitting problems down into smaller and smaller pieces, and exploring them in exhaustive detail. Now you can see that the real challenge isn't analysis at all; it's synthesis. Decision-making isn't about optimising one area at the expense of the others. It's about keeping these nine elements in balance; picking your battles to win the war.

General knowledge matters

Since success emerges from all nine boxes on the grid, there are implications for the skills you must develop as an individual. For small-business owners, entrepreneurs and CEOs, general under-standing has always been invaluable – but the grid reveals that it is equally important for everyone else too.

In a world where everyone is a specialist, performance improve-ments come less from greater competencies and more from better co-ordination; less from deepening our expertise, and more from broadening our general knowledge. The larger an organisation grows, the more acute the issue becomes.

It's not how great you are at your job that defines your overall success, it's the latent impact of your expertise on the other areas of the grid. To build a successful business you need to make sure that all nine elements work to reinforce, rather than undermine, each other.

You must keep the ends in mind, not just the means

Many topics critical to business success are missing from the grid. Hard factors, like processes and technology; and soft ones, like people and culture. These are essential considerations and occupy the major-ity of many a decision-maker's day-to-day activities. Why do they not have their own, clearly labelled presence on the grid?

Because these factors are instrumental to the success of the busi-ness rather than the direct cause of it – they are the means rather than the end. The grid aims to provide a more robust way to think about them.

For example, a common consideration for a business is deciding whether to invest in a new technology. You can evaluate that decision from the perspective of every box in the grid: Will it reduce your costs? Does it affect your imitability? How might this technology enhance your offerings? Does it make you more or less adaptable?

As you can see, the technology itself does not directly determine your success – its impact manifests itself through the boxes of the grid. A technology that saves you money may be a poor investment if it compromises your customer experience or ability to adapt in the future.

The same is true for the impact of an organisation's culture on the success of the business, since this too reveals itself through the nine boxes. Organisations typically emphasise some elements of the grid over others: prizing revenue growth over profit; taking an aggressive approach to rivalry; or obsessing over brand appeal rather than commercial viability. For others, their culture can ensure that they fail to adapt when the environment demands it of them. Again, the grid provides a means to view the impact of an organisation's culture from above and consider its impact on the business as a whole.

Far from being dismissive about people, the grid is a tool to help you work together more effectively, sharing perspectives and solving problems as a team. It can also set staffing discussions in a broader context, helping to make more robust cases for decisions around recruitment and how human resources are deployed.

Behind every element of the grid there is the expertise, talent and judgement of people. They create the customer experience, come up with proposition ideas and make decisions about the brand. They manage suppliers and control costs. Rather than being nowhere on the grid, they are everywhere. They are not on the grid as individual items because their impact is pervasive.

2 The Elements of the Grid

The next step towards using the grid is to get more specific: it's one thing knowing that a customer's wants and needs are important; it's another entirely having a structure to identify precisely what they are.

This chapter introduces three elements within each box of the grid. Many will be familiar, and there's no need to commit them to memory or keep track of them. You only need a basic understanding of each to get started.

I finish with two case studies that show what can happen if any of these elements are mismanaged. These reinforce the two themes of the book: that every element matters and that a change in one affects the others.

	desirability	profitability	longevity
customer	**WANTS & NEEDS** ● values & beliefs ● goals ● barriers	**REVENUES** ○ revenue model ○ price ○ volume (qty & freq.)	**CUSTOMER BASE** ○ awareness ○ acquisition ○ retention
market	**RIVALRY** ○ category ○ territory ○ alternatives & substitutes	**BARGAINING POWER** ○ with customers ○ with suppliers ○ rules & regulations	**IMITABILITY** ○ legal protection ○ durable advantages ○ competitor lag
organisation	**OFFERINGS** ○ proposition ○ brand appeal ○ customer experience	**COSTS** ○ fixed costs ○ variable costs ○ capital expenditure	**ADAPTABILITY** ○ cash position ○ scalability or capacity ○ complexity & rigidity

Desirability

Wants and needs

A customer's *wants and needs* are underpinned by three factors:

- Customers choose products and services that reflect their **values and beliefs**: riding a Harley, for example, or believing that a camera with more megapixels is better than one with fewer.
- Every product or service is also a means for customers to achieve their **goals**: losing weight, learning another language, or arranging a meeting, for example.
- **Barriers** are obstacles preventing customers from achieving their goals or from adopting your product or service. Examples might be the skill required, or products they already have that are incompatible with yours.

	desirability	profitability	longevity

customer

WANTS & NEEDS
- values & beliefs
- goals
- barriers

REVENUES
- revenue model
- price
- volume (qty & freq.)

CUSTOMER BASE
- awareness
- acquisition
- retention

market

RIVALRY
- ● category
- ● territory
- ● alternatives & substitutes

BARGAINING POWER
- with customers
- with suppliers
- rules & regulations

IMITABILITY
- legal protection
- durable advantages
- competitor lag

organisation

OFFERINGS
- proposition
- brand appeal
- customer experience

COSTS
- fixed costs
- variable costs
- capital expenditure

ADAPTABILITY
- cash position
- scalability or capacity
- complexity & rigidity

Rivalry

Three elements determine the *rivalry* you face, and how it might be changing:

- Your **category** – the kind of product or service you sell – determines the basic requirements you must meet to be competitive. How easily rivals can launch a business in that category, and whether it is growing or declining in popularity, will also affect the intensity of the competition.
- Your **territory** – where your business is located and the geographical area you cover – impacts the size of your opportunity and the rivals you face.
- Finally, within your chosen field there will always be **alternatives and substitutes** – other options customers use to judge the desirability of your offering. Alternatives are direct rivals, like competing airlines. Substitutes are indirect rivals, like a domestic airline competing with a train service.

	desirability	profitability	longevity

customer

WANTS & NEEDS
- values & beliefs
- goals
- barriers

REVENUES
- revenue model
- price
- volume (qty & freq.)

CUSTOMER BASE
- awareness
- acquisition
- retention

market

RIVALRY
- category
- territory
- alternatives & substitutes

BARGAINING POWER
- with customers
- with suppliers
- rules & regulations

IMITABILITY
- legal protection
- durable advantages
- competitor lag

organisation

OFFERINGS
- ● proposition
- ● brand appeal
- ● customer experience

COSTS
- fixed costs
- variable costs
- capital expenditure

ADAPTABILITY
- cash position
- scalability or capacity
- complexity & rigidity

Offerings

Your *offerings* consist of these interconnected elements:

- The product or service **proposition** is the concept the customer is buying into. For it to be desirable, customers must have clear, obvious reasons to choose it over alternatives.
- The expectations and associations people have about a business – its **brand appeal** – affects the desirability of all its products and services.
- The **customer experience** is also important. If your website is confusing, staff are impolite or returning damaged goods is difficult, desirability will suffer – no matter how good your product.

	desirability	**profitability**	longevity
customer	**WANTS & NEEDS** ○ values & beliefs ○ goals ○ barriers	**REVENUES** ● revenue model ● price ● volume (qty & freq.)	**CUSTOMER BASE** ○ awareness ○ acquisition ○ retention
market	**RIVALRY** ○ category ○ territory ○ alternatives & substitutes	**BARGAINING POWER** ○ with customers ○ with suppliers ○ rules & regulations	**IMITABILITY** ○ legal protection ○ durable advantages ○ competitor lag
organisation	**OFFERINGS** ○ proposition ○ brand appeal ○ customer experience	**COSTS** ○ fixed costs ○ variable costs ○ capital expenditure	**ADAPTABILITY** ○ cash position ○ scalability or capacity ○ complexity & rigidity

Profitability

Revenues

Creating a profit requires *revenues* from customers. Three considerations must be borne in mind:

- The mechanism by which you make the money, your **revenue model**: choosing between selling your services for a fixed price, or charging by the hour, for example.
- You must also decide the **price** – not leaving profit on the table by undercharging, or losing customers by setting the price too high.
- Finally, you need to consider the **volume** – the quantities people buy, and the frequency with which they buy them.

	desirability	**profitability**	longevity
customer	**WANTS & NEEDS** ○ values & beliefs ○ goals ○ barriers	**REVENUES** ○ revenue model ○ price ○ volume (qty & freq.)	**CUSTOMER BASE** ○ awareness ○ acquisition ○ retention
market	**RIVALRY** ○ category ○ territory ○ alternatives & substitutes	**BARGAINING POWER** ● with customers ● with suppliers ● rules & regulations	**IMITABILITY** ○ legal protection ○ durable advantages ○ competitor lag
organisation	**OFFERINGS** ○ proposition ○ brand appeal ○ customer experience	**COSTS** ○ fixed costs ○ variable costs ○ capital expenditure	**ADAPTABILITY** ○ cash position ○ scalability or capacity ○ complexity & rigidity

Bargaining power

Your *bargaining power* also affects your ability to make a profit.

- Deals with strong buyers can leave you with thin margins, so it's important to consider your **bargaining power with customers** and how it might be changing.
- Your **bargaining power with suppliers** is equally important. If your business becomes too dependent on a particular supplier, they can turn the screw on you – growing their profits at the expense of yours.
- Governments introduce **rules and regulations** for many reasons, but a major driver is to protect society by controlling the power of organisations.

	desirability	**profitability**	longevity
customer	WANTS & NEEDS	REVENUES	CUSTOMER BASE
	○ values & beliefs	○ revenue model	○ awareness
	○ goals	○ price	○ acquisition
	○ barriers	○ volume (qty & freq.)	○ retention
market	RIVALRY	BARGAINING POWER	IMITABILITY
	○ category	○ with customers	○ legal protection
	○ territory	○ with suppliers	○ durable advantages
	○ alternatives & substitutes	○ rules & regulations	○ competitor lag
organisation	OFFERINGS	COSTS	ADAPTABILITY
	○ proposition	● fixed costs	○ cash position
	○ brand appeal	● variable costs	○ scalability or capacity
	○ customer experience	● capital expenditure	○ complexity & rigidity

Costs

An organisation incurs *costs* in three basic categories:

- **Fixed costs**, like rent or staff salaries, stay the same regardless of production volumes.
- **Variable costs** depend on production volumes – like the raw materials or packaging you need to make and sell your product. A car manufacturer will have high variable costs, a software provider will have low variable costs.
- **Capital expenditure** refers to longer-term investments, like a factory or equipment purchase. These are treated differently to routine operating expenses since their impact on profitability is spread over the useful life of the asset.

	desirability	profitability	longevity
customer	**WANTS & NEEDS** ○ values & beliefs ○ goals ○ barriers	**REVENUES** ○ revenue model ○ price ○ volume (qty & freq.)	**CUSTOMER BASE** ● awareness ● acquisition ● retention
market	**RIVALRY** ○ category ○ territory ○ alternatives & substitutes	**BARGAINING POWER** ○ with customers ○ with suppliers ○ rules & regulations	**IMITABILITY** ○ legal protection ○ durable advantages ○ competitor lag
organisation	**OFFERINGS** ○ proposition ○ brand appeal ○ customer experience	**COSTS** ○ fixed costs ○ variable costs ○ capital expenditure	**ADAPTABILITY** ○ cash position ○ scalability or capacity ○ complexity & rigidity

Longevity

Customer base

The size of your *customer base* – the number of customers you have – relies on three factors:

- People can't become customers unless they know you exist, so raising **awareness** is your first consideration.
- Awareness should lead to **acquisition** – new customers joining your business. There's no customer base if people won't buy what you're offering.
- Finally, your customer base won't grow if existing customers leave at the same rate as new ones join. **Retention** – keeping hold of the customers you have acquired – is crucial for most businesses.

	desirability	profitability	**longevity**
customer	**WANTS & NEEDS** ○ values & beliefs ○ goals ○ barriers	**REVENUES** ○ revenue model ○ price ○ volume (qty & freq.)	**CUSTOMER BASE** ○ awareness ○ acquisition ○ retention
market	**RIVALRY** ○ category ○ territory ○ alternatives & substitutes	**BARGAINING POWER** ○ with customers ○ with suppliers ○ rules & regulations	**IMITABILITY** ● legal protection ● durable advantages ● competitor lag
organisation	**OFFERINGS** ○ proposition ○ brand appeal ○ customer experience	**COSTS** ○ fixed costs ○ variable costs ○ capital expenditure	**ADAPTABILITY** ○ cash position ○ scalability or capacity ○ complexity & rigidity

Imitability

The ease with which a rival can copy you – your *imitability* – dramatically impacts your longevity. You can make yourself less imitable in three ways:

- You can seek **legal protection** – using patents, trademarks and copyright to stop rivals from copying you.
- You can build **durable advantages** that are challenging to imitate – such as a unique cost structure or product ecosystem.
- Finally, you can create **competitor lag** – leaving your rivals trailing as you make advances, or forcing them to make difficult trade-offs that delay them from acting.[1]

	desirability	profitability	**longevity**
customer	**WANTS & NEEDS** ◯ values & beliefs ◯ goals ◯ barriers	**REVENUES** ◯ revenue model ◯ price ◯ volume (qty & freq.)	**CUSTOMER BASE** ◯ awareness ◯ acquisition ◯ retention
market	**RIVALRY** ◯ category ◯ territory ◯ alternatives & substitutes	**BARGAINING POWER** ◯ with customers ◯ with suppliers ◯ rules & regulations	**IMITABILITY** ◯ legal protection ◯ durable advantages ◯ competitor lag
organisation	**OFFERINGS** ◯ proposition ◯ brand appeal ◯ customer experience	**COSTS** ◯ fixed costs ◯ variable costs ◯ capital expenditure	**ADAPTABILITY** ● cash position ● scalability or capacity ● complexity & rigidity

Adaptability

An organisation's *adaptability* ultimately determines its chances of survival in the long run:

- If you run out of cash, you cannot continue to operate the business. The stronger your **cash position**, the greater the scope of options you can pursue.
- Your **scalability or capacity** can also be a major constraint. Operating at full capacity leaves you with no room to plan for the future, and if your business cannot scale it cannot grow.
- Finally, **complexity and rigidity** within a business make changing direction agonisingly slow, if not impossible.

Case Study: The Ultimate Wheelchair

To tie every element together, let's look now at two examples – one that comes from a start-up, and the other one drawn from a large, existing business.

Several years ago, I became involved with a project to create a brilliant product – an upmarket wheelchair. At the time, most wheelchairs were ugly and poorly designed, and there was an opportunity for a state-of-the-art model without rival.

The company did its research and learnt about the shortcomings of existing products on the market. Most were ungainly pieces of machinery that looked like relics from a bygone era, especially compared with the sleek designs we see for bicycles or even office chairs. There seemed to be little genuine innovation by established players, and the market therefore looked ripe for a fresh entrant with a design-led philosophy.

As the project progressed, however, rather than keeping a laser focus on customers' wants and needs, the company's mission became to build the best possible product with no compromises whatsoever. Starting with the technology and working backwards to the product, it was decided that the chair would have many configurable options and that each chair would be made to measure from carbon fibre.

In the quest for perfection, one of the UK's most advanced carbon-fibre manufacturers was approached to help with a prototype. The wheelchair company was a minnow compared to the well-funded motor-racing teams the manufacturer was used to dealing with, so it found itself voluntarily entering into a situation where it had no bargaining power. It then had to switch suppliers to find a firm that approached the project as a partnership. By this point, however, costs were already mounting.

Poor supplier selection, and an overly ambitious proposition, meant a high selling price if they were to cover their costs. Rather than establishing a target price at the beginning of the project, and constraining the product features and costs to meet this figure, they allowed the price to creep inexorably up and up as the product developed.

By the time it was launched, the proposition was beyond the reach of most potential customers. An upmarket wheelchair is one thing, a wheelchair that costs as much as a car is quite another. Most potential customers simply couldn't afford it. Working out a product's price by marking up costs is a classic mistake many make, and one that I will address later.

Because manufacturing costs were so high, there was no way the product could be sold by retailers or a distribution network without pushing the price from obscene to insane: there wasn't enough margin to go round.

As a workaround, they decided not to hire a showroom but instead to offer demonstration visits. The problem, though, was that some potential customers were reluctant to have these take place in their homes, meaning that on one occasion a demonstration ended up taking place in an office car park. Given that this was a high-end, expensive item, it was hardly the premium customer experience you'd expect.

It wasn't only the price that turned out to be problematic. The product could only be sold in the EU, where it met regulations. Large markets like the USA, Asia and Australia were out of the picture because their regulatory requirements were different, involving separate – and expensive – approval processes. Despite thousands of fans on Facebook and keen media interest, actual demand for the product never materialised.

The company aimed to sell one wheelchair per week – an almost impossible task considering the unfortunate combination of high price and small territory. Two years after launch just a handful had been sold.

This example (mapped onto the grid overleaf) shows a cascade of problems, resulting in a product that didn't fit customers' wants and needs.

	desirability	profitability	longevity
customer	**WANTS & NEEDS** ( ) values & beliefs ( ) goals (5) barriers	**REVENUES** ( ) revenue model (4) price (9) volume (qty & freq.)	**CUSTOMER BASE** ( ) awareness (10) acquisition ( ) retention
market	**RIVALRY** ( ) category (8) territory ( ) alternatives & substitutes	**BARGAINING POWER** ( ) with customers (2) with suppliers (7) rules & regulations	**IMITABILITY** ( ) legal protection ( ) durable advantages ( ) competitor lag
organisation	**OFFERINGS** (1) proposition ( ) brand appeal (6) customer experience	**COSTS** (3) fixed costs (3) variable costs ( ) capital expenditure	**ADAPTABILITY** (11) cash position ( ) scalability or capacity ( ) complexity & rigidity

Figure 1 An illustration of what went wrong at the wheelchair start-up, showing the key elements involved.

The root of the problem was an overambitious proposition (1) and selection of a powerful supplier (2), which created high production costs (3).

High costs meant a high price (4), an insurmountable barrier to most potential customers (5), leaving no margin for retailers or distributors and damaging the customer experience (6).

Regulation was a significant challenge (7), limiting the territory where the product could be sold (8).

The combination of high price and small territory led to low sales volumes (9) because they couldn't acquire enough customers (10).

The net result was running out of cash, and needing more and more outside investment to keep the business afloat (11).

Case Study: The Volkswagen Emissions Scandal

We may never know the full truth behind 2015's emissions scandal, but this much we know for certain: in the US Volkswagen has admitted modifying the software in certain diesel engines to cheat on emissions tests, with dire consequences. Here is how the situation unfolded.

Customer values have changed over time towards lessening the environmental impact of their motoring, as concerns over climate change have grown and emissions regulations have been tightened. This has created the opportunity for new categories and alternatives to emerge – hybrid and electric cars like the Prius and Tesla Model S. These four elements of the grid are highlighted on the diagram below.

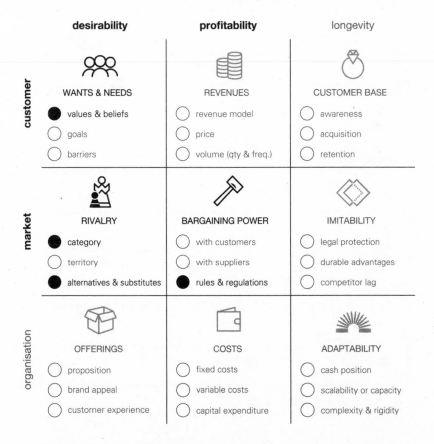

Figure 2 Customer values and emission regulations have changed, leading to the emergence of new categories and alternatives.

Volkswagen had big ambitions to become the world's largest carmaker by 2018.[2] To achieve this, they set themselves the goal of tripling sales in the United States.[3] To help them get there, they rejected the hybrid approach in favour of the 'clean diesel' engine, which they believed gave cars a compelling combination of low emissions and high fuel economy without sacrificing performance.[4] A strong proposition – so far so good.

To bring their proposition to market, Volkswagen invested heavily in developing the EA 189, a diesel engine that would be used not just in Volkswagens but across many brands in the group, including Audi, SEAT and Skoda.[5] This would provide economies of scale, spreading the fixed cost of developing the engine across a much larger number of units – also good.

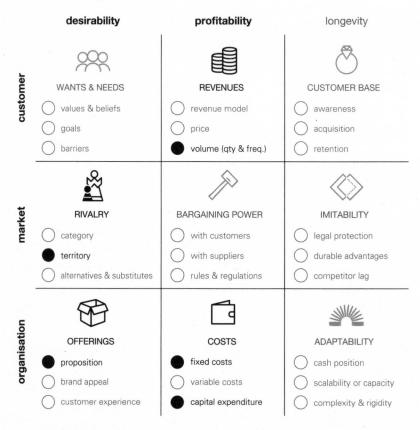

Figure 3 Volkswagen's ambition is to triple sales volumes in a clear territory – the USA. They invest heavily in their clean diesel proposition, creating an engine that can be used across many brands to spread the fixed cost. These considerations are highlighted on the grid above.

Around 2008, Volkswagen faced a challenging situation. The new engine that they had developed couldn't meet pollution regulations in certain countries, including the United States, without being uncompetitive on certain absolutely key value metrics like fuel economy and performance.[6] This conundrum left the company with four choices:

Option One

They could market an inferior proposition that complied with regulations at the expense of performance and fuel economy. This product might not be as compelling as alternatives, so might sell in lower **volumes**.

Option Two

They could add extra pollution-control technology, such as Mercedes' BlueTEC solution, which would cause their **variable costs** to increase.[7]

Option Three

They could change their strategy completely, effectively abandoning their clean diesel **proposition**.

Option Four

They could ignore the **regulations** and decide instead to cheat. This would mean that their proposition could remain intact, extra costs could be avoided and their strategy could continue largely unchanged.

We can see these various strategic options plotted on the grid overleaf.

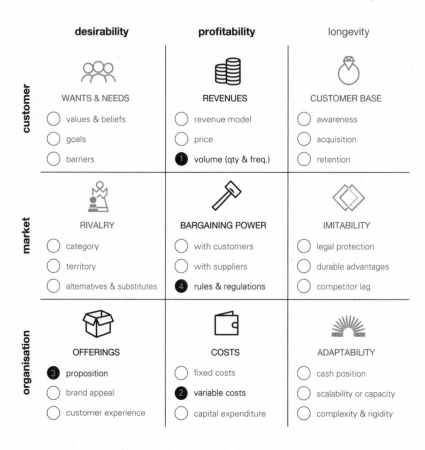

	desirability	**profitability**	longevity
customer	**WANTS & NEEDS** ○ values & beliefs ○ goals ○ barriers	**REVENUES** ○ revenue model ○ price ● volume (qty & freq.)	**CUSTOMER BASE** ○ awareness ○ acquisition ○ retention
market	**RIVALRY** ○ category ○ territory ○ alternatives & substitutes	**BARGAINING POWER** ○ with customers ○ with suppliers ❹ rules & regulations	**IMITABILITY** ○ legal protection ○ durable advantages ○ competitor lag
organisation	**OFFERINGS** ❸ proposition ○ brand appeal ○ customer experience	**COSTS** ○ fixed costs ❷ variable costs ○ capital expenditure	**ADAPTABILITY** ○ cash position ○ scalability or capacity ○ complexity & rigidity

Figure 4 Volkswagen's strategic options mapped onto the grid. Should they sacrifice (1) volume, (2) variable costs, (3) their proposition or (4) the regulations?

Volkswagen picked option four and developed a 'defeat device' for the engine that detected when it was being tested and switched into a low-emission mode, only to spew up to forty times the approved level of some pollutants during normal usage.[8]

The plan worked brilliantly for a while, but ignored a golden rule, especially in the social media age – 'If you don't want anyone to know, don't do it.' When it surfaced that eleven million vehicles contravened emissions regulations, the repercussions were catastrophic.[9]

The scandal dramatically changed customers' beliefs about VW's clean diesel proposition. It impacted the ownership experience for existing customers, whose cars needed to be upgraded or bought back by VW.[10] It didn't do their brand any favours either.

Affected models were withdrawn from sale, reducing revenue.[11] Prices of other products were reduced in a bid to win over hesitant consumers.[12] Thousands of cars were stuck at ports, unable to be sold, dramatically increasing inventory costs.[13] Variable costs also rocketed because each affected car had to be put right or bought back. Add to that the cost of lawsuits and fines from customers and authorities around the world.

At the time of writing, Volkswagen have set aside $18 billion to resolve the crisis, resources that could have been rather more advantageously deployed elsewhere.[14] The scandal has tarnished the entire diesel category in the US and given a free ride to alternatives, who now have one fewer rival to worry about in the short term.[15]

As I stated at the outset, a business is an interconnected whole where changes in one area can affect another. In this case, altering some lines of computer code came with an estimated $18 billion price tag.[16] It also highlights the dangers inherent in short-term, reductionist approaches to decision-making. There is a simple alternative. The grid helps us consider the impact of our decisions on the whole business. The next chapter shows how to do this in practice.

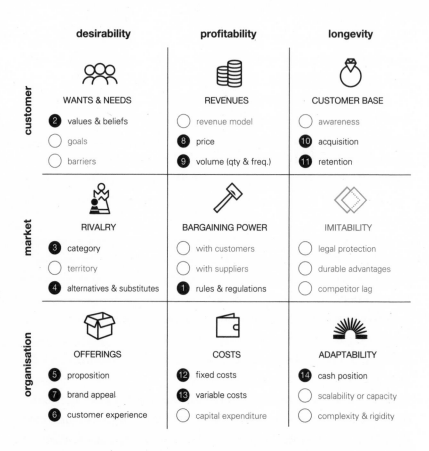

	desirability	profitability	longevity
customer	**WANTS & NEEDS** (2) values & beliefs ( ) goals ( ) barriers	**REVENUES** ( ) revenue model (8) price (9) volume (qty & freq.)	**CUSTOMER BASE** ( ) awareness (10) acquisition (11) retention
market	**RIVALRY** (3) category ( ) territory (4) alternatives & substitutes	**BARGAINING POWER** ( ) with customers ( ) with suppliers (1) rules & regulations	**IMITABILITY** ( ) legal protection ( ) durable advantages ( ) competitor lag
organisation	**OFFERINGS** (5) proposition (7) brand appeal (6) customer experience	**COSTS** (12) fixed costs (13) variable costs ( ) capital expenditure	**ADAPTABILITY** (14) cash position ( ) scalability or capacity ( ) complexity & rigidity

Figure 5 Volkswagen decided to cheat emission regulations (1) with catastrophic consequences for other elements of the grid.

The scandal permanently altered customer beliefs about the product they had bought (2), it tarnished the entire diesel category in the US (3) and it gave alternatives a free ride while the affected cars were withdrawn from the market (4).

When the scandal broke, their clean diesel proposition lost its appeal (5); it affected the ownership experience for existing customers, who now had to go through an upgrade or buy-back programme (6); and the brand's reputation was damaged (7).

Prices were lowered across the board to stimulate demand (8) as sales volumes went into decline (9). With the products withdrawn from sale and a buy-back scheme offered for existing customers, both acquisition and retention were affected (10,11).

Volkswagen had the one-off fixed costs of the fines and lawsuits from regulators and other aggrieved parties (12). They also faced increased variable costs as each vehicle sold had to be upgraded, and new diesel vehicles were fitted with a costly alternative pollution-control technology (13). They set aside $18 billion to resolve the crisis, a significant but manageable proportion of their cash reserves (14).

3 Using the Grid in Practice

This book has two central themes. First, success emerges from *all nine boxes* in the grid. Second, a change in one area of the grid will affect another. But how do you use this insight in practice? How does it help us make better decisions?

This chapter demonstrates how the grid can be used in three situations: starting a new venture, reviewing an existing business, and thinking through a decision. Before you dive in, though, let me restate what the grid really is, and what it's for.

The risk with any model is that it turns us into template zombies – more concerned with ticking boxes than with the outcome.[1] To avoid this, you need to remember that the grid is just mental scaffolding: an instrument to help structure your thinking. Print it when needed, scribble on it, discuss it with colleagues, decide what to do next, then toss it away.

If customer groups will be affected differently by a decision you plan to make, try running the implications for each segment through the grid separately. If you've got different brands, propositions or territories, you could run them through the grid separately too, but you don't have to. How you use it depends on the decision you are trying to make. The aim is to support your thinking, not create a rigid process.

It's best just to try it out and see what happens. If you're seeing a situation with greater clarity and ideas are popping into your head; if you're feeling more confident, have noticed a flaw in your plan, or have discovered a new opportunity, don't overthink it – the grid is doing its job.

The same is true for how you keep track of your thoughts as you go. Mark elements in red, amber or green. Use ticks, crosses, SWOT (strength, weakness, opportunity, threat) or even longhand notes. Put a line through things that aren't relevant. Again, the important thing is to find an approach that works for you. There are some example worksheets as suggestions at www.matt-watkinson.com.

Scenario One: Starting a Business

Sensational stories reinforce a mystique about entrepreneurs. Founders are fearless risk-takers with nerves of steel; unshakeable visionaries with ideas that will prove sceptics wrong; intuitive masters who know they'll win out in the end.

Grains of truth perpetuate the myth. There is risk, uncertainty and luck involved in getting something off the ground; having a vision and empathic understanding of what customers want is immeasurably valuable; and some do seem blessed with the intuition to create great businesses.

But we hear the crazy stories because they are so unusual. They are the exception, not the rule. What don't make the headlines are the thousands who have come unglued taking excessive risks, pursuing a vision others didn't share or following their intuition all the way to ruin.

The successful entrepreneurs I know don't fit the swashbuckling persona. They are diligent and open-minded. They listen to their customers. They are constantly learning. They are confident but humble. They sweat the boring details. When their assumptions turn out to be wrong, they change their minds. For those who can adopt such a mindset, the grid will be a valuable ally. Here's how it can help shift the odds in your favour.

A successful business is a unique configuration of the elements within the nine boxes on the grid. While it's easy – and fun – to spend time only on the elements you're comfortable with, it's all for nothing if this means you miss something crucial that will cause you problems later. A logical approach when starting out is to consider each element in turn, beginning with your customers' wants and needs, then working down each column until you've covered all the bases. It helps to ask yourself three questions for each element.

1. What assumptions am I making?

Basing decisions on incorrect assumptions can send you down the wrong path, so you must clarify your assumptions for each element of the grid. Just listing those assumptions as hypotheses to test is half the battle already won. If you're not aware of the hypotheses you're making, you can't know if they're right or wrong.

2. How can I test my hypotheses?

Once you've listed your hypotheses – such as 'Demand for our category is growing' or 'Existing alternatives are difficult to use' – you should test them.

Take inspiration from Innocent smoothies, who started in earnest after the founders ran a stall at a music festival. They put out two bins labelled 'YES' and 'NO' for people to put their empty cups in, with a question above asking: 'Should we give up our jobs to make these smoothies?' With a full YES bin at the end of the weekend, they got to work on building their business.[2]

Michael Bloomberg is another great example. He was so hungry for feedback on his ideas he'd buy hot drinks from the deli opposite Merrill Lynch at 6 a.m., head into the office and offer them to anyone who could spare a minute to share their thoughts.[3]

If you have a question about customers' wants and needs, get out there and speak to them. Build a prototype of your product and see if it works. Mystery-shop your rivals. Get quotes from possible suppliers to understand the costs. While these things all require effort, none are difficult, and time spent here will pay dividends. The hardest part is knowing which questions to ask – the deep-dive chapters will help you here.

3. Do the parts fit together?

As you continue around the grid, keep zooming out to consider the whole, checking that the parts fit together. This is the 'whack-a-mole' stage of the project, where you must establish if the overall configuration makes for a viable business. You may need to rejig the proposition to reduce costs, or aim for a larger territory to get volumes up so the sums work, for example.

Ultimately this means returning to the three overarching goals:

- Does our research suggest that our offering will be desirable?
- Based on our estimates, can it become profitable?
- If it takes off, will our business be able to survive into the future?

If you've been through each box on the grid, and you're comfortable with the answers to these final questions, great! If not, revisit your ideas until you are. It doesn't have to be perfect. It doesn't even need to be close – no initial idea will tick all the boxes, and some factors may not become relevant until a later date. You just don't want to waste your time on something fundamentally flawed.

Scenario Two: Reviewing an Existing Business

Once a business is up and running, it's natural to seek ways to improve it. Many want to grow their revenues, margins and customer base, but that won't be everyone's goal. Some, like the firms profiled in Bo Burlingham's *Small Giants*, have chosen to be better rather than bigger.[4] Others just want to make ends meet doing something they love.

Whatever your goal, the logical starting point is understanding where you are now: your current strengths and weaknesses; areas of uncertainty or change and those of relative inactivity or stability. By providing a structured way to analyse a business, the grid helps you identify which areas need work – and how they're affecting the business as a whole.

Your metrics could show room for improvement in the customer base, for example – while awareness and acquisition are both healthy, your retention might be declining. Or perhaps upcoming rules and regulations mean your costs might change and you need to increase your prices.

The grid's hierarchy allows you to work methodically from box to box, rooting out the elements that need improvement. As with the new-business scenario, the simplest way to do this is to work around the grid, assessing each element in turn.

Once you've isolated the areas of opportunity, you can focus your attention on solving well-defined problems instead of throwing ideas at the wall and seeing what sticks. In practice, people naturally follow their noses and home in on their weak spots, then prioritise which areas to tackle first.

Recently, for example, I was asked to help a services firm that was experiencing some financial difficulty. When the CEO and I sat down with the grid to analyse the business, we quickly eliminated costs, bargaining power and imitability as major problem areas, then, after some back and forth, rivalry too – we'd revisit that another day. The immediate problem was simply that not enough revenue was coming in because of low sales volume, and something had to be done before the business ran out of cash.

Looking at the client's data together, we saw some odd patterns. First, satisfaction was high, yet repeat purchasing was extremely low. Second, while the firm was generating enough leads to be potentially very successful, few of them resulted in sales.

Tackling the retention issue first, we realised that repeat purchasing was low because little attempt was made to resell services to existing clients. The business sold one-off projects, rather than an ongoing service, for no other reason than that's what they'd always done. Changing their pitch from one-off projects to a biannual 'check-up' was a minor adjustment to their proposition that could yield big returns.

Turning our attention to those low conversion rates, we looked at the customer experience and saw that most leads went cold during the proposal stage. Prospects were excited after initial conversations, but usually didn't get back in touch after they'd received a proposal.

Here we found a real problem. Proposals were long, full of technical jargon and didn't mention the valuable outcomes of what was on offer. It's no wonder people weren't getting back to the company: they probably weren't reading past the first couple of pages.

This was one area where an immediate improvement could be made. The company therefore set about changing the proposal format at once, reducing it to a couple of jargon-free pages that emphasised the benefits of their services. Once they'd done this, they could take another run through the grid and find their next priority area.

There are several recurring themes in this example that are worth mentioning.

First, there will always be several angles of attack for improving a business. You should prioritise those that will offer the greatest returns. You can't prioritise until you have a view of the business as a whole.

Second, a business typically has entrenched ways of working that go unexamined, simply because they have always been done that way. Just as a fish doesn't know it's swimming in water, we often can't see problems that are immediately obvious to others. The grid helps reveal these issues because it forces you to consider every aspect of the business.

Third, issues can originate in unexpected places, and instinctive, superficial analyses are often wrong. In the case of the business above, improving the customer experience was a more potent leverage point than increasing awareness. Driving more traffic to the business wouldn't have helped much, yet this would have been a common reaction for many in a similar position.

Finally, I've usually found that most people can solve their own problems once they have a structured approach to follow. By giving teams a common language and reference point to structure discussions, the grid helps people collaborate more effectively and work methodically through issues. It's really exciting to see in action.

Scenario Three: Thinking Decisions Through

Businesses are typically not short on ideas, new projects to pursue or decisions that need to be made. Many of these will arise from reviewing the business in the previous scenario. Next, the grid can guide you towards the best outcomes.

In *Good Strategy Bad Strategy*, Richard Rumelt defines a strategy as a 'cohesive response to an important challenge', and suggests that it consists of three elements. First, a *diagnosis* that defines the challenge. Second, a *guiding policy*, or broad approach, to overcome that challenge. Finally, there must be *coherent actions* to carry out that policy.[5]

Defining the challenge requires identifying the grid elements that you want to improve, for example: *increase sales volumes, improve customer retention*, or *reduce fixed costs*.

Your *guiding policy* is your idea for how you might make those improvements: *spend more on advertising, improve the customer experience* or *outsource manufacturing*. Then, once you have an idea, you use the grid to evaluate each option's overall impact: which elements will improve, which might get worse, and whether the net result would be favourable. You can consider a variety of scenarios when doing this: best case, worst case and most likely.

Finally, your *coherent actions* are the next steps to implementing that policy or gathering further information to help you decide a route forward.

This process is straightforward in practice:

1. Identify which box or element you want to improve.
2. Come up with a range of possible solutions.
3. Run each possible solution through the grid to assess the overall impact on the business.
4. Choose the best route forward, and decide the next steps to implement the plan.

To conclude the chapter, here is a real-world example.

On a crisp autumn day, I sat down with Tim and Anthony, brothers who have grown a successful business renovating exclusive London properties. Over the years they've built an enviable reputation for fine craftsmanship and attentive customer care – standards that reflect their close involvement in each project.

As the business has flourished, their workload has grown exponentially. There simply aren't enough hours in the day to manage every project with such deep personal attention, run the business and plan for the future. This unmanageable workload is their *important challenge*, to use Rumelt's language. They agree that the logical route forward is to hire a project manager to oversee day-to-day work, but they want to be sure they've thought this idea (or *guiding policy*) through.

It's an emotional talking point for them. They are excited about their potential if they can devote more time to pursuing new opportunities, but are understandably nervous about handing over the reins to someone else. They've spent years building a reputation; they don't want to lose it overnight. Once the kettle has boiled and the tea is brewing, we sit down with the grid to see what comes up.

We start by revisiting the challenge, which lies in the adaptability box, specifically *capacity* – they can't grow the business with their current limitations, and there is no contingency if something goes wrong. Hiring a project manager would free them up to focus more on strategy and pursuing new opportunities. But how would this solution affect the other boxes?

Moving across a column, we start to think about how a new hire could affect profitability. The obvious impact would be an increase in fixed costs, but Anthony (who looks after the accounts) is not concerned about whether they can afford it. Looking through the revenues and margins on their projects for the last few years, it becomes apparent that only a small increase in sales would be enough to maintain their current profitability and there is plenty of cash in the bank. With the extra capacity, and the brothers free to focus on growing the business, they expect that revenue and profit would increase.

Whilst we're scanning the revenue box, I ask whether having a dedicated project manager might allow them to charge a higher price since it might bring with it the promise of a more tailor-made service – possibly a better one, too. They hadn't considered this – their focus had been mostly on the cost side of the equation – and they make a note to research customer opinions after the meeting – their first *coherent action*, sticking to Rumelt's terms.

Returning to the costs box, they think aloud about whether an experienced manager might bring more to the table than just freeing up their time. Could a hire with the right experience improve their operations? The right candidate might be able to reduce project costs by minimising rework or implementing more efficient processes.

They make a note that these skills could form part of the job description, and agree that it might be worth paying more than they had first intended to secure a top-flight manager charged with reducing the variable costs across all future projects. They could even consider working this into a bonus package. Another next step.

Having looked at revenue and costs, the discussion turns to bargaining power. Their business relies heavily on a network of subcontractors, specialising in everything from installing audio-visual equipment to making bespoke staircases. Over the years the brothers have built close relationships with two suppliers in particular, and it is only now that they consider how this new hire might affect them.

I ask how these powerful suppliers might react to having a new sheriff in town. If they don't get along, could it affect the quality of their work, the customer experience or their brand's reputation?

This isn't something they'd thought of, but they quickly propose a solution – to let their key subcontractors know what they are planning, and to involve them in the hiring process. This simple decision will reduce any friction in the transition, and is a powerful gesture of goodwill. Action number three.

Finally, we arrive at the offerings box. The brothers are most concerned that the new hire is a good ambassador for their brand and delivers the kind of experience that has built their reputation. If these elements are adversely affected it will reduce their positive word of mouth, and with it new referrals.

As we mull over options to mitigate these risks, Tim suggests that they formulate a plan for a gradual handover before the hiring process begins, to make sure that the quality of the overall experience – their key selling point – isn't affected by the transition. Action four.

When we break for lunch everyone is feeling more confident. By working our way through each box, a lot of the heat has been taken out of the discussion, everyone has aired their ideas and concerns in a structured way, and a clear route forward has been agreed.

The sums add up, the responsibilities for the new role are taking shape, and their idea to involve their partners in the hiring process should minimise any risk of a backlash. Not bad for a couple of hours' work. A basic summary of our discussion is mapped onto the grid opposite. As you can see, even quite a simple decision can spread its tentacles across many elements of the grid.

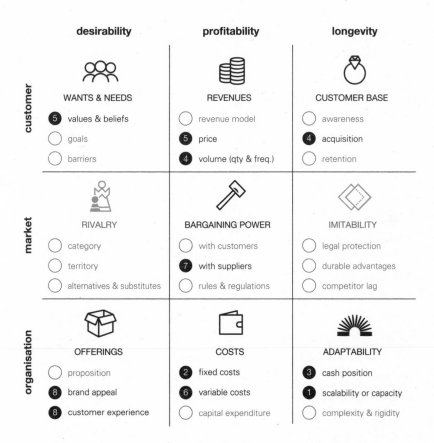

Figure 6 Assessing the impact of hiring a project manager using the grid.

1. The requirement for a project manager is being driven by adaptability – the business cannot scale any further, and the brothers have no contingency or time to plan for the future.
2. The hire will increase their fixed costs.
3. The business has plenty of cash – they can comfortably afford to make the hire.
4. The new project manager will free them up to sell more, acquiring new customers and increasing volumes to offset the extra costs. The result should be more profit, not less.
5. Nobody knows whether a dedicated project manager will allow them to charge a higher price, so they make a note to research customer opinions.
6. The right person might help them cut variable costs; a candidate with strong process management and cost-control skills is a smart idea.
7. A new boss could cause friction with their suppliers. They decide to involve their key subcontractors during the hiring process, to smooth the transition.
8. Their big concern is that their new hire delivers on their brand's reputation and creates the experience their customers expect. They plan a gradual handover before they hire to make sure their offerings aren't affected.

Part 2

Deep Dives

Deep Dives

So far we've been snorkelling in the shallows, looking down on the grid from above. Now it's time to strap on our scuba gear and head down into each box, to see what's going on in more detail. What follows is a chapter for each of the nine boxes, working through the grid column by column.

Before you read them, I'd encourage you to print out the grid (see www.matt-watkinson.com) and try using it in practice. When you come to an element where there is uncertainty, a knowledge gap, or weakness, head straight to the corresponding deep-dive section. You might, for example, conclude that the proposition is an issue; customer barriers are not well understood; or that pricing is a concern.

Reading the topics of most value first is the most effective use of your time. With this in mind, I've structured the deep dives as nine individual essays (recommended further reading for each is listed on pp. 281–8). There is cross-referencing between them – it's unavoidable considering the holistic nature of business – but I've kept it to a minimum so you can take an à la carte approach.

If, however, you are starting a new business, product or service from scratch, I'd encourage you to work through these deep dives in order. The most common cause of new business failure by far is no market need.[1] Understanding the desirability column will help you towards the product–market fit that eludes many new ventures. You can then consider how best to profit from that offering, and how to sustain the business into the future.

	desirability	profitability	longevity
customer	**WANTS & NEEDS** ● values & beliefs ● goals ● barriers	**REVENUES** ○ revenue model ○ price ○ volume (qty & freq.)	**CUSTOMER BASE** ○ awareness ○ acquisition ○ retention
market	**RIVALRY** ○ category ○ territory ○ alternatives & substitutes	**BARGAINING POWER** ○ with customers ○ with suppliers ○ rules & regulations	**IMITABILITY** ○ legal protection ○ durable advantages ○ competitor lag
organisation	**OFFERINGS** ○ proposition ○ brand appeal ○ customer experience	**COSTS** ○ fixed costs ○ variable costs ○ capital expenditure	**ADAPTABILITY** ○ cash position ○ scalability or capacity ○ complexity & rigidity

Deep Dive One: Wants and Needs

The world's most exclusive cheese comes from a farm near Montreux in Switzerland. For a few weeks each year, the cows graze on the Alpine meadows when they are flowering, which gives their milk a unique taste. This milk is then heated over a wood fire and left to age for the whole summer. The result is a cheese so exclusive that it's not even for sale.

The farm's owner, Jean-Claude Biver, never accepts payment for his produce. Instead, he gives it away to friends, family and a handful of his favourite restaurants.[1] M. Biver can afford to be selective since making cheese is his hobby. His business is making watches.

In 1981, M. Biver and his partner bought the rights to the Blancpain name for 22,000 Swiss francs (about $15,000). Although Blancpain had not made a watch for a decade, he saw potential – it was officially the world's oldest watchmaking brand. A decade later the Swatch Group bought Blancpain for $43 million.[2]

After M. Biver joined the board, Swatch tasked him with running Omega, another luxury brand. With Biver in charge, sales nearly tripled.[3] Then, after a brief retirement, he took the reins at Hublot, where sales increased fivefold in three years. How does he do it? In an interview with watch magazine *Revolution*, he explained his simple philosophy:

First, start with the king. Who is the king of Hublot? Immediate answer – the customer.

If you want to serve a customer, you must know his history, where does he come from, how was he educated, what does he like, what does he hate, what is his religion, what is his passion, what is his hobby, what is his character, how wealthy is he, how generous is he. All this, we have to know. The more we know, the better we can serve him.

Hublot has a king who loves polo, who loves cricket, who loves sailing, who loves football, who loves Formula One, who loves music, who loves Coachella, who loves to have tattoos. So, are we going to do that? OF COURSE! If the king likes it. We are going to follow . . . We have got to adapt to the taste of our king. And that's it! It's not more difficult than this.[4]

Understanding the customers' wants and needs is fundamental to the success of any venture. How can you create products they desire if you don't know what they want? Yet few take the time to understand them as deeply as Jean-Claude Biver. In fact, it's common for businesses to ignore them altogether. The number-one cause of start-up failure is 'Building a solution looking for a problem'.[5]

To truly understand your customers there are three things you need to know:

Who are they? What are their **values and beliefs**?
What are they trying to achieve? What are their **goals**?
What is standing in their way? What **barriers** do they face?

Many come unglued worshipping just one part of this trinity – creating products that appeal to the customer's self-image but don't get the job done; or that meet their functional needs, but are impossible to adopt. Understanding your customers' wants and needs takes all three perspectives.

Values and Beliefs

In the 1950s, scientist Curt Richter performed experiments on rats that would cause outrage today. He put the rodents in an escape-proof bucket of circulating water, forcing them to swim indefinitely, and timed how long it took them to drown – usually about fifteen minutes.

He then repeated the experiment, only this time, just as the poor rats gave up, he saved them and allowed them to recover, then threw them into the bucket again. This time, however, the rats didn't give up after fifteen minutes. They powered on for *two and a half days* before drowning.[6]

When they believed they were destined to drown they gave up quickly. But when they believed they would be saved, they summoned incredible stamina. Their beliefs had a profound effect on their behaviour – a characteristic not unique to rodents. The products we choose, the brands we love, the people we hang around with, the food we eat, all reflect our beliefs and values.

Our beliefs matter because they determine what we find pleasurable. As Paul Bloom explains in *How Pleasure Works*, 'The enjoyment we get from something derives from what we think that thing is. For a painting, it matters who the artist was; for a story, it matters whether it is truth or fiction; for a steak, we care what sort of animal it came from.'[7] If our prized Van Gogh turned out to be a fake, we'd toss it in the trash, however beautiful the scene – our pleasure stems from our beliefs about who painted it. What we believe and what we find desirable are inseparable.

We cling to our beliefs stubbornly, even when there is ample evidence to the contrary. We like to avoid *cognitive dissonance* – stress caused by the internal inconsistencies between our beliefs and actions, between two contradictory beliefs we might hold, or by information that conflicts with our world view.[8]

We also prefer to seek out information that supports our existing beliefs and downplay whatever contradicts them, a phenomenon known as the *confirmation bias*.[9] We've all heard someone say 'I'll believe it when I see it!' But in fact, the opposite is true. *We'll see it when we believe it*. As more of our news comes from social media sites like Facebook, whose algorithms are designed to show us content it thinks we will like and share, it is quite literally becoming the case that we only see what we already believe.

As the Hungarian physicist Eugene P. Wigner remarked, 'People do not build their beliefs on a foundation of reason. They begin with certain beliefs, then find reasons to justify them.'[10] As such, to truly understand our customers' wants and needs, we must start with their values and beliefs. Only then can we design offerings to suit them or understand any sticky beliefs we must overturn in order to succeed. To bring structure to the task, we consider several perspectives.

The customer's identity

We all have beliefs about the kind of person we are – an internal narrative that defines our sense of self. One of my friends is an ice-hockey fanatic. Another is a vegan. Another sees herself, first and foremost, as a mother. Ask someone what they do for work and some will reply with their profession – 'I'm a lion tamer.' Others with their employer – 'I work for the police.' These answers reflect how these people see themselves. These aren't mere facets of their personalities – they are the essence of their being.

When choosing a product or service, what it says about us – how accurately it reflects our self-image – tends to hold more sway than any other consideration.[11] We often choose functionally inferior products that better express our identity over functionally excellent ones that don't; or more expensive products that say the right thing about us over cheaper ones that conflict with our self-image. The first step to understanding your customers is to consider *how they identify themselves* and how we can reflect that image through our offerings.

Coca-Cola's 'Share a Coke' campaign did this quite literally, replacing the logo on the bottle with names – like Dave, Sarah or John – an idea that came from a simple 151-word brief. The results of the campaign were mind-boggling: 150 million bottles sold; 998 million impressions on Twitter; and 730,000 glass bottles personalised through an e-commerce store in the UK alone.[12]

The first step towards understanding our customers' wants and needs, then, is to know exactly who they are. However, when asked about their customers, many reply in general terms: 'SMEs', 'Fortune 500 companies' or 'global telcos'. These are organisations, though, not people. Is your actual customer the CMO? The founder? The janitor?

Creating a product or service with real people in mind – people you might know or could at least recognise – makes it much easier to unearth their wants and needs. With real people in mind – mountaineers, veterinary surgeons, goths – we're far more likely to create products that are in tune with their needs. We should also identify not just the primary customer, but the surrounding stakeholders whose needs are important – the end user, the buyer and various gatekeepers along the way – and consider their needs separately.[13]

The customer's values

Once we know who our customer is, we turn our attention to their values – what they care about, and the principles or standards they subscribe to. Are they eco-conscious? Will only the best do? Are they a stickler for good service? A friend sums up his buying mentality with one sentence – 'Buy once, cry once.' He appreciates quality goods that last a lifetime and is willing to pay for them.

Since its launch in 1997, the Toyota Prius has been a hit, especially in Japan and the USA. With sales exceeding the five million mark, it is still in production twenty years later.[14] Its success is the result of it becoming a four-wheeled expression of green values.[15]

Furniture brand Vitsœ have a cult following because they epitomise the design excellence and attention to detail that their customers appreciate. Their ethos – 'Living better, with less, that lasts longer' – strongly resonates with their customers' values.[16] We can't make our offering mirror customer values unless we know what those values are.

In 1957, a team of agricultural researchers at Iowa State College proposed another reason why understanding customer values is so important – they affect a customer's likelihood of adopting new technologies. The model that emerged from this research – the technology adoption life cycle – has remained in use since, with little modification.[17]

Their model suggests five distinct groups. First come the *innovators*, who love technology and are excited by new developments. Next are the *early adopters*, who have a vision for how it might give them an advantage over their competition. Then come the *early majority*, who wait until the product is proven in practice. Then the *late majority*, who want to buy from an established market leader when costs have come down. Finally, you have people like my dad – the *laggards* – who upgrade with extreme reluctance. Combined, the early and late majority account for about two thirds of the market.[18]

Each of these groups behaves differently: early adopters seek huge opportunity and are comfortable with some risk. The late majority are cost-conscious and risk-averse. The innovators are passionate about advances in science and technology; the laggards don't care.

There's no point pitching an unproven, early-stage product to customers where risk-averse behaviour is encouraged and rewarded, however large the potential benefits. This explains why start-ups that target big companies often fail.[19]

I fell into this trap a few years ago when pitching a new software product to a bank. They loved the idea and we got all the way to the purchase order stage, at which point their procurement and legal teams got involved, bringing proceedings to an abrupt halt. One comment from their lawyer is etched in my mind: 'Risk-taking is inevitable in business if you want to innovate and improve, we get that. But our policy is to structure the contracts so we don't assume any of that risk ourselves.'

We failed because of a mismatch in values and rewarded behaviour. For all the bluster about innovation, two thirds of the market aren't especially keen on it, and many have processes in place to stop it happening.

When developing business-to-business offerings, it's therefore important to bear in mind that it may not be your target customer's values that matter (as an individual), but rather those of the organisation as a whole.

The customer's social groups and communities

Whether it's a team-branded sports shirt or an exclusive networking group, products or services that strongly express our social group (or one we aspire to) have a magnetic appeal.[20]

An example is private club Soho House, which restricts membership to professionals in creative fields. Their website explains, 'Unlike other members' clubs, which often focus on wealth and status, we aim to assemble communities of members that have something in common: namely, a creative soul.'[21] (And wealth and status, in my experience.) Identifying customers' social groups not only helps businesses create a desirable offering, it makes marketing that offering easier, since there is then a way of targeting them.

Understanding your customer's identity, values and social group is only half the battle, however. You also need to understand what they believe about your product category and brand, and how their past experiences have shaped their learned behaviours.

Understanding beliefs about the category

We form beliefs about product categories: *the more megapixels a camera has the better*; *organic food is healthier that non-organic food*; *all banks are the same*. We don't have the time or energy to become experts in everything from loft insulation to whisky – our beliefs help us take short cuts.[22]

Violating category expectations, or worse still, not appearing in a clear category at all, can doom a product to failure from the outset, something I cover in detail in the next chapter. For now, it's worth pondering what beliefs the customer has about the category. You may want to change them, but you can't do that until you know what they are.

Understanding beliefs about your brand

In 2011 Aston Martin released a small city car called the Cygnet – a rebadged Toyota iQ with a few styling tweaks that contradicted almost everything we associate with the Aston Martin brand. Hoping to sell 4,000 a year, they halted production after fewer than 150 sales.[23] The product flopped because it violated customer's beliefs about the brand – a basic mistake.

Once customers form beliefs about a brand, it's difficult to change them. We can avoid running into difficulties down the line by making sure our communication with customers creates realistic beliefs from the outset, then actively considering the beliefs customers have about our brand when making decisions. I cover brand appeal in more detail in Deep Dive Three: Offerings (see pp. 101–21).

Understanding the effect of past experiences

Opposite a friend's apartment is a parking meter where people take an age to get their ticket. One day I went out to see what the issue was. Simple: the cancel button on the machine is grey, and the pay button is red. People put their money in then automatically press the grey button, to find their coins returned. Confused, they put the money back in and do the same thing again – a phenomenon known as a *strong habit intrusion*.[24]

Over time we build up whole libraries of these learned behaviours, allowing us to do as much as possible on autopilot, whether it's looking for the shopping basket in the top right corner of a website, or driving on a particular side of the road. Violating these learned behaviours in a bid to differentiate oneself is a tactic that seldom ends well.

Our past experiences inform our beliefs. This is one reason why a reliable, consistent service is crucial. A bad first experience may affect customers' expectations so adversely that they never come back, or leave you facing an uphill struggle to win them over again. Don't fall into the trap of thinking you can endlessly iterate your way from a turkey to a smash hit – the first poor experience forms beliefs in the customer's mind that must then be overcome. The best advice: get the execution right first time, or very right the second time.[25]

Changing beliefs

When I proposed to my wife I knew exactly which engagement ring she wanted. She pointed at it in the Georg Jensen store – wink, wink, nudge, nudge. But why give a diamond ring at all? It's not the long-standing tradition you might think. The idea gained popularity through one of the most successful advertising campaigns in history.

Faced with declining sales in the late 1930s, De Beers turned to advertising agency N. W. Ayer to transform the American public's perception of diamonds – to make them synonymous with romance, eternity and betrothal. They wanted men to believe that the measure of their love was best expressed through the size and quality of the diamond in the ring they used to propose with.

The advertising agency approached their task with zeal, even lecturing high-school girls on the importance of the diamond engagement ring. Their slogan – '*A diamond is forever*' – captured the essence of their campaign. In 1967 they repeated the trick in Japan, where only 5 per cent of brides received a diamond ring. Fourteen years later that number was up to 60 per cent.[26] In many parts of the world the diamond engagement ring is now an unquestioned tradition.

As De Beers demonstrated, beliefs and perceptions can be changed. In fact, our progress often depends upon it. The question is, how can we do that most effectively?

In *The Business of Belief*, Tom Asacker likens this process to getting customers to cross a footbridge that spans a deep chasm.[27] Instead of pushing them across by yelling at them or using logical arguments that fall flat – your fear of heights is irrational! – you should encourage them to follow your lead, so they gently inch their way across. Asacker suggests a two-pronged approach.

First, you start with what's already there – their existing desires and feelings. You need to know what will motivate them to cross. 'People are drawn across the bridge of belief by their anticipation of a better experience and a better life,' he writes. 'Effective leaders ignite people's imaginations by painting vivid, compelling, and personally relevant pictures – ones that move them.'[28] De Beers did this brilliantly, tapping into men's desires not only to express their love, but to demonstrate their status and success in life.

Second, you have to do everything you can to make them feel comfortable and safe, providing reassuring evidence that the bridge is steady and secure.[29] De Beers excelled here too, making sure that diamonds were featured in romantic movies and feeding pictures of celebrities and royalty wearing diamonds to magazines. Surrounded by evidence from their role models that the diamond was the ultimate symbol of romance, customers eagerly followed suit.

Goals

In the late sixties, Japanese firm Hitachi introduced the Magic Wand, a vibrating mains-powered massager, designed to help relieve back pain. Customers, however, had other ideas. Much to their consternation, Hitachi had created a smash-hit sex toy, still described as the 'Rolls-Royce of vibrators' over fifty years later.[30]

Other products have succeeded in similarly unintentional ways. Timberland work boots became fashion items; the Range Rover became a city status symbol; the Hammond organ – originally designed as a low-cost alternative to a church pipe organ – achieved great success as a jazz and rock instrument. As a back massager, the Magic Wand is OK, but as a sex toy it's a market leader. The product itself hasn't changed, what changed was *the goal the customer had in mind.*

Every product or service should be thought of as a means for the customer to achieve an objective. As marketing professor Theodore Levitt remarked, 'People don't want to buy a quarter-inch drill. They want a quarter-inch hole.'[31] For your offering to be useful it must satisfy a customer's goal, even if it's not the one originally envisaged – as the Magic Wand demonstrates.

It is easy to lose sight of your customers' goals over time. If you design, manufacture and market drills all day, it's easy to forget that the customer's goal is to make a hole, not own a drill. The danger is that this narrow vision can blind you to the threat of new rivals, and to exciting opportunities you might pursue.

To help stop this from happening, you can consider customer goals from three perspectives: the *super objective*, the *subtext* and the *success criteria*.

The super objective

A few years ago, I realised that actors could teach me a thing or two about understanding customer wants and needs, since to play a character well you must *become* that person – think like they think, and feel as they feel. This led me to the Stanislavsky system – a method used by actors to bring greater depth to their characters – where I discovered techniques that were more useful than anything I'd seen in business literature.

I learned to start by understanding the nature of a character – or rather, in this context, a customer – by uncovering their *super objective*, an overarching goal that drives all their other behaviour.[32] A customer's immediate goal might be to buy some bathroom scales, but the scales are a means to achieving a higher-level goal – losing weight or monitoring progress on an exercise routine. Going up another level, a possible *super objective* might be to increase their sense of self-esteem: to feel better about their body image. It's an insight that could help develop a better product.

Discovering your customer's super objective opens your mind to a world of opportunities that you can't see at the product level. Many of today's hot products and services have tapped straight into the customer's super objective, often satisfying it in a deeper, or simpler, way.

The aim of purchasing music has always been to listen to it – this is the super objective. The iTunes Store, Spotify and other streaming services have kept this super objective in mind. The record industry, however, was so preoccupied with the format – selling physical units – that they missed the opportunities afforded by the Internet. Listening to music is the real goal. Ownership of physical units – perhaps even ownership in general – was just a means to that end.

Similarly, the super objective of reading a book is to learn from or enjoy the contents. By focusing on this super objective, Amazon created the Kindle, rather than being blinkered by the physical format of the book. In these examples the super objectives seem obvious. But that didn't stop the majority from ignoring them.

Super objectives don't change often, if at all, making them a stable platform from which to work. There are also far fewer super objectives than low-level goals, making them easier to document and a great starting point for any customer segmentation work.

To uncover super objectives, start with obvious customer goals and keep asking 'Why do they want to do that?' until you reach their overarching goal. Then, having bleached your brain of existing products and services, imagine all the wonderful ways you could satisfy this higher need.

Always try to keep the customer's super objectives in mind, and acknowledge that your product is just a means to an end. If you see a new rival offering that taps directly into the customer's super objective, take the threat seriously.

The subtext

It's common for people to say one thing, think something else and do another thing entirely. We have some things we feel comfortable talking about and some we don't, which throws a spanner in the works when it comes to customer research. If people don't say what they think, and don't do what they say, how can we hope to know what they want? The second technique I stole from the Stanislavsky system helps us here.

The secret is to consider the *subtext* – to ask *what is our customer thinking but not saying?*[33] *What goals don't they feel comfortable mentioning?* If you can understand their subtext – something important to them that they don't openly discuss – you can create more compelling offerings.

One example is Lloyds Pharmacy's Online Doctor. This UK business offers specific services for health issues we don't feel comfortable talking about – erectile dysfunction, hair-loss treatment or emergency contraception, for example.

As the website says, 'These conditions can be hard to talk about face to face with your GP, but our online service provides a safe and discreet way to get the treatment you need.'[34] They emphasise the subtle packaging in which the medication arrives and the absolute confidentiality of the service, which are as important to the customer as getting the right treatment.

By considering the subtext around these issues – *I want to avoid embarrassment* – they created a hit service, scooping a host of healthcare awards.[35] Many reviews reveal just how important subtext can be, some customers even saying that they'd rather sit at home in pain indefinitely than go to the doctor about their problem. Their goal may be to get better, but the *subtext* of avoiding embarrassment is too heavy for them to use their regular doctor.

If anything, subtext is even more pronounced in business-to-business offerings. Saving face, looking great in front of the boss, earning a bonus, avoiding accountability or building an empire are often the real goals hidden in the subtext; and as I learned early on in my career, ignoring these things, or worse still mentioning them, doesn't typically end well.

Success criteria

Once you've established the super objective and subtext, the final perspective is the customer's intended *outcome and success criteria.*[36] In other words, *how do you know if the customer has achieved their goals successfully?* Unlike the super objective or subtext, which can sometimes feel a bit abstract, the outcome and success criteria should be as explicit and tangible as possible.

Some example outcomes and success criteria for customers of this book might be:

- I feel more confident in my business decision-making.
- I have learned some practical techniques that I can use to make better judgements.
- I gained valuable knowledge about fields that are not my specialism.
- Reading the book felt like a good use of my time.

Don't get too hung up on documenting them in a formal way, just note them down – as many as you can – you can manicure, consolidate and measure them later. The point of the exercise is to get your brain firing with as many thoughts as possible about what your customer is trying to achieve, so these hypotheses can be tested, validated and used as the basis for developing your products and services.

The acid test

To wrap up this section, here is a sneaky question that reveals how well you understand your customers' goals:

If your product or service is the answer, what is the question, and who is asking it?

Answering this question forces you to do three things: one, to see your offering as a solution to a problem the customer has; two, to frame that opportunity concisely; and three, to know exactly who you are targeting.

Gather answers from people both inside and outside the business. If you have wildly diverging responses, or struggle to find a clear answer, it's a sure sign that customer goals warrant further investigation.

Barriers

Barriers are obstacles that prevent customers from achieving their goals or adopting your product. Most businesses are so focused on product benefits that they forget about barriers entirely, leaving an open goal for those who can recognise and dismantle them. These barriers can be grouped into three categories: the operational; the experiential; and the financial.

Operational barriers

The Airbus A380 'superjumbo' is a brilliant airliner which offers a fantastic flying experience, but its sheer size means it can only land at a few airports. The engines are so far apart that they can cause blast damage to runway lighting; powerful tractors are needed to tow them around specially widened taxi lanes; and extra support vehicles are needed to load passengers and supplies into the upper deck. All told, London Heathrow set aside $220 million to accommodate the behemoth.[37]

With only a limited number of appropriate routes for the A380, it's clear why most carriers choose smaller planes that can be used more flexibly and yield returns more easily. Airbus say they will never recoup the $25 billion invested in the project, and with orders dwindling, may have to end production in 2018.[38]

As the Airbus story illustrates, operational barriers can limit the success of an otherwise excellent offering. Let's look at the most common operational barriers, any one of which can be powerful enough to stop new customers in their tracks.

Installation

If getting started with a product or service is difficult it deters custom-ers. Cumbersome registration and account-creation processes, installing drivers and software – these obstacles turn us off. A major reason cloud-based computer systems have become so popular is that hardware and infrastructure become someone else's problem.

In addition to being aware of the time and effort needed to get started, it's important to be mindful of any process changes or add-itional equipment that your offering requires. These can be a greater burden on the customer than you anticipate, and can derail otherwise promising products.

Compatibility

Before Apple and Google entered the smartphone market, BBM – BlackBerry's instant messaging product – was a huge success and a major draw to the brand. But when customers started moving to more desirable iPhones or Android phones, rather than open BBM up to those new platforms, BlackBerry kept it restricted to their own devices, erecting a barrier to millions of potential users. This strategic own goal was the final straw for co-founder Jim Balsillie, who had been campaigning to open the platform. When the board approved a plan to keep the service closed he resigned and sold all his stock in the company.[39]

Contrast this with WhatsApp – another instant messaging product – who recognised that as the competitive landscape changed, dismantling barriers had become crucial to success. Unlike Black-Berry, WhatsApp made their product available in as many languages and on as many platforms as possible.

When BlackBerry eventually opened BBM to other devices it was too late. At the time of writing, WhatsApp has more than a billion active users, more than ten times BBM's remaining user base.[40] Find-ing ways to make your product compatible with the technologies or equipment your customer already has will make it much easier for them to adopt it.

Competing technologies

The twilight zone between two technologies – one mature and stable yet showing its age, the other fresh and full of promise but not quite up to standard – can be a difficult time. The early days of digital cameras and the current transition to electric cars are good examples.

Nobody likes to back the wrong horse, so when it comes to technology standards the customer will often wait, or go with the technology they expect to triumph. This can erect an insurmountable barrier if your solution is based on technologies customers expect either to fail or to have a short shelf life, however well your product or service performs.[41]

Functional risk

As obvious as it sounds, customers consider the risks of adopting a product that might fail to deliver. Your product must work if you want people to buy it.

Medical start-up Theranos had an incredible promise – a technological breakthrough that allowed hundreds of blood tests to be run from a pinprick, rather than needing whole vials. Their test results would be faster, more accurate and cheaper than traditional methods.

Captivated investors poured more than $400 million into the business.[42] Founder Elizabeth Holmes was showered with awards and became the youngest self-made female billionaire in history.[43] Pharmacy chain Walgreens launched a partnership and began incorporating Theranos Wellness Centers into their pharmacies. There was just one problem – their miracle technology didn't work.

After an investigative report in the *Wall Street Journal* questioned the company's claims, the whole operation came off the rails.[44] By mid-2016, less than a year after the article appeared, the picture could not have been more different.

Holmes had been banned from the blood-testing business for two years, although it is understood that she is appealing this decision.[45] Forbes had revalued her net worth from $4.5 billion to zero.[46]

Walgreens had severed all ties with Theranos, which is currently subject to a criminal investigation over claims they misled investors.[47] This extreme example illustrates a simple point – the product or service has to work.

Distribution and network effects

It ought to go without saying that a customer cannot buy a product or service that is not physically available to them. You must choose the distribution channels that make your offering as convenient and accessible as possible.

A more challenging barrier to overcome is one where the value of the product stems from the number of people using it – in other words, where it depends on the creation of a network. Launching a messaging app or social network is difficult because in the early days there will be few people to talk to. The same is true of marketplaces like Airbnb or eBay, where you need a critical mass of hosts and guests or buyers and sellers for the product to take off. I explore this topic is more detail in Deep Dive Eight: Imitability (see pp. 229–34).

Experiential barriers

Of all the barriers, perhaps the biggest is the potential customer's inertia, risk aversion and unwillingness to experiment. It might seem obvious, but to encourage customers to adopt our products we need to make the adoption experience as pleasant as possible. Here are some perspectives to consider.

Trialability

Experiencing a product's benefits first-hand – perhaps with a free trial period, sample or in-store demonstration – eliminates risk for the customer.[48] How we make those benefits as observable as possible during the trial is also key to encouraging the customer to commit.[49] The higher the price, or the more unusual the offering, the more important trialability becomes.

Training and expertise

Customers aren't always aware that they have the problem your product solves, or simply aren't expert enough in the domain to choose the product that is right for them. This is a golden opportunity for marketers to move beyond shovelling product information at customers and instead start playing an active role in educating customers in both the merits of their particular product and how to choose within the category. In a world where supply outstrips demand in just about every market, becoming an ally in the customer's decision-making is a huge opportunity.

There are two approaches you can take to doing this. One is to go beyond describing the features of a product to also communicating the specific benefits they bring. The other is to provide educational content that actually helps the customer learn about the category. Rucksack-maker GORUCK do an outstanding job on this, explaining not just the features and benefits of their bags, but also explaining the construction techniques, choice of materials, the reasoning behind design decisions, and which products work best in a given scenario.[50]

Once we have chosen a product, for most of us picking up the instruction manual is an admission of defeat, not a logical starting point. The prospect of a steep learning curve can be enough to put us off, especially with technology products.[51] The aim should be to move customers from novice to intermediate as quickly as possible, then allow them to advance at their own pace.

Strong fallback options

If an exciting new product doesn't work as expected, rather than persevere we often go back to our tried-and-tested solutions. Strong fallback options create a barrier since the customer has little incentive to keep trying if the new service doesn't immediately perform well. When there are strong fallback options, adoption may be an uphill battle unless the new offering is significantly better, reliable and easy to use.

Learned behaviours, mental models and the MAYA principle

As I explained on pp. 66–7, over time we build up libraries of learned behaviours and mental models about how the world works. When challenged by new ideas, we instinctively want to reject them in favour of what's already familiar to us. Going against the grain of an existing habit or convention can make products difficult to adopt.

The legendary modernist designer Raymond Loewy, who designed everything from logos and cigarette packets to trains, buses and refrigerators, observed: 'Our desire is naturally to give the buying public the most advanced product . . . Unfortunately, it has been proved time and time again that such a product does not always sell well. There seems to be for each individual product . . . a critical area at which the consumer's desire for novelty reaches what I might call the shock zone . . . It is a sort of tug of war between attraction to the new and fear of the unfamiliar.'[52]

In response, he targeted what he called the MAYA stage – shorthand for *Most Advanced Yet Acceptable* – a zone where the product has sufficient novelty to be attractive, but is not so radical as to be unfamiliar.[53] Determining the MAYA stage for your product or service may make it easier for others to adopt; pushing past it, even if it makes logical sense or is technically possible, may turn customers away.

Financial barriers

NetJets were the first to market with the concept of 'fractional ownership'[54] for air travel – allowing individuals or businesses to buy a share in a private jet rather than owning it outright, spreading the costs of purchase and maintenance across multiple parties. They have led the market since, boasting a global fleet of more than 700 planes.[55] They succeeded by removing a financial barrier that stood in their customers' way: their customers wanted to fly privately, but costs were either prohibitive or couldn't be justified.

To be clear, reducing financial barriers is not simply about reducing the price. You should always find the optimum price for your product from the outset, rather than just discounting to get a sale – something I cover in Deep Dive Four: Revenues (see pp. 123–43). Reducing financial barriers can be about making the price point accessible, or helping the customer feel comfortable paying it.

Cutting the up-front cost using a clever revenue model, or allowing the cost to be spread over multiple payments, can make higher prices accessible without denting the customer's cash flow. This is common practice for big-ticket items.

You can also reduce the cost of switching and minimise any financial risk that the customer faces. Simple things like reassurance that transactions and financial data are secure can make a big difference in getting the customer over the line, as does a clear, effortless returns policy for online shopping.

Bringing it all together

The easiest way to think about the impact of adoption barriers is to work through each category and assign a rating: Not Applicable/Red/Amber/Green.[56] You can also do the same for your closest rival's offerings and see where the differences lie. To give an example, let's look at the adoption barriers facing PowaTag, a mobile payments app that made headlines when it flamed out in 2016 despite raising close to $200 million in funding.[57]

The PowaTag solution worked by having the user install an app on their phone, then scan a QR code (a kind of square barcode) using the phone's camera. The app would then process the transaction using credit card details the customer stored in the app during registration.

Retailers could show these codes on their website, printed advertisements or the product itself to allow customers to buy straight from a catalogue or magazine, or to reorder a product that had run out by scanning the packaging. Audio waves could also be used to raise awareness of a purchase opportunity – either emitted by beacons in stores or embedded in the soundtrack of adverts. A table showing the barriers consumers faced would look something like this:

Operational Barriers	Rating	Notes
Installation	AMBER	Consumer must download app, create account and store credit card details before they can use the product. Solutions already integrated into the phone's operating system or hardware would not face this barrier.
Compatibility	GREEN	App works on both major smartphone platforms iOS and Android.
Competing technologies	RED	Smartphone manufacturers are embedding an alternative NFC (near-field communications) technology in their products for mobile payments, which already has growing support at retailers. Apple Pay, Android Pay and Samsung Pay are based on this technology.
Functional risk	AMBER	Scanning a QR code can be hit and miss. Alignment and background lighting both affect success rate when scanning.
Distribution and network effects	RED	To drive consumer adoption requires massive adoption and support by retailers otherwise there is nowhere to use the app. Retailers will only adopt the technology if there are sizeable benefits to them, or if their customers demand it.

Experiential Barriers	Rating	Notes
Trialability	RED	Without widespread adoption by retailers, consumers will struggle to experience the value proposition first-hand.
Training and expertise	GREEN	The app does not require any specialist skills to use and the consumer does not require any expertise, other than to understand the technology and what it is for.
Fallback options	RED	Consumers have a variety of means to make payments. Traditional e-commerce checkouts, debit, credit and contactless smart cards, or cash.
Learned behaviours, mental models/ MAYA	RED	Scanning a code with the camera is not a familiar purchasing model. Using the camera on a phone to scan a code on a laptop screen or tablet is an unusual way to buy something. Products like Shazam have familiarised consumers with scanning audio files to trigger an action but not to purchase in a retail environment.

Financial Barriers	Rating	Notes
Upfront cost	GREEN	The app is free.
Switching cost	GREEN	There is no switching cost per se.
Financial risk	AMBER	Powa is not a well-known consumer brand. Some consumers may feel uncomfortable storing their card details in an app that is not from a trusted brand.

Figure 7 A table showing the barriers facing PowaTag customers.

You can see that PowaTag faced several problematic barriers: a competing technology endorsed by powerful brands, a network effects problem, limited trialability, clear fallback options, and an unfamiliar mental model.

However well the solution worked in practice, these adoption barriers go a long way to explaining the misfortune of the business and its struggle to raise funds from venture capitalists who deeply understand these types of technologies and markets. PowaTag's funding came instead from an investment fund more closely associated with equity and fixed-income markets.[58]

An alternative strategy using the same or similar technologies might have led to a viable business – perhaps the technology could have been licensed to other brands to embed in their own apps to avoid the network effect barrier – but as a mainstream mobile payment standard, such high adoption barriers were likely to put a QR-code solution out of the running.

The product that is easiest to buy and use generally wins. If customers are likely to face high barriers to achieving their goals or adopting your product, you must identify ways to dismantle them.

Key Questions

Values and beliefs

- How do customers describe or identify themselves?
- What values do your customers want to express through their product choices?
- What beliefs need to change for your offering to succeed? How will you do this?

Goals

- What are your customers' super objectives?
- What hidden goals or subtext does your customer have?
- How do you know if your customer has achieved their goals successfully? What are their success criteria?

Barriers

- What equipment does your customer already have that you must work with? Does this make a barrier? What ways of working might your offering impact?
- Can you reduce the effort required to get customers started with your product or service?
- What financial barriers stand in your target customer's way? Can you find a way to dismantle them?

	desirability	profitability	longevity
customer	**WANTS & NEEDS** ○ values & beliefs ○ goals ○ barriers	**REVENUES** ○ revenue model ○ price ○ volume (qty & freq.)	**CUSTOMER BASE** ○ awareness ○ acquisition ○ retention
market	**RIVALRY** ● category ● territory ● alternatives & substitutes	**BARGAINING POWER** ○ with customers ○ with suppliers ○ rules & regulations	**IMITABILITY** ○ legal protection ○ durable advantages ○ competitor lag
organisation	**OFFERINGS** ○ proposition ○ brand appeal ○ customer experience	**COSTS** ○ fixed costs ○ variable costs ○ capital expenditure	**ADAPTABILITY** ○ cash position ○ scalability or capacity ○ complexity & rigidity

Deep Dive Two: Rivalry

What are your earliest memories of competition?

My first are of board games – Connect Four or Cluedo – and racing my brother on the Scalextric track. I also played sports from a young age. I was a good runner as a kid, and rowed as a teen until it became ultra-competitive. I lost interest at that point – rowers are an obsessive bunch.

School life was also intensely competitive. Incarcerated at boarding school, we competed for the best grades, competed on the frozen sports field, and competed for places at universities. I competed with my best friend to see who could care less. We were both dismal disappointments.

These early experiences give us ideas about competition that stick. There are winners and losers on the sports pitch, and the purpose of competition is simply to beat our opponents. In academia, excellence exists within the crisp confines of a syllabus. There is, however, something we don't acknowledge about these activities: both are as *cooperative* as they are competitive.[1]

In sport, rivals first agree on the rules of play; cheating upsets fans and competitors alike – just ask Lance Armstrong. For school tests to be consistently graded, the correct answers must be agreed up front. But neither constraint applies to commercial competition – at least not to the same degree.

If sports were like business, nobody would cry foul if you turned up to a boat race with a hovercraft – that's innovation. Taking to the football field with a hundred men would be deemed a scale advantage.

There are also no right answers. The aim is to invent new rules, and force others to play by them. Intentionally or not, though, we tend instinctively to bring mentalities from these other competitive arenas to business. Two counterproductive approaches are especially common.

One danger stems from the goal simply to be *the best*. Determined to beat our rivals, we respond to every move with one-upmanship.[2] They cut the price, we cut ours more. They add a feature, we add two. The eventual result? A product that nobody wants, less profit, or both.

The other approach is to follow *best practices* – copying the syllabus laid out by the market leader – until everyone's offerings are the same and customers choose almost exclusively on price.[3] Neither approach works well. Instead, we should take our inspiration from the natural world.

Ecosystems contain millions of species that interact, compete and coexist, much as businesses do in an economy. Ecologically speaking, competition is defined as *direct or indirect interactions between species that reduce access to resources needed to survive.*[4] Swapping the word 'species' for 'organisations' gives us a smart definition of competition in business: *direct or indirect interactions between organisations that reduce access to resources needed to survive.*

This makes perfect sense. As in the natural world, competitive interactions may be direct or indirect: they may come from confrontation with members of our own 'species' – rival businesses operating in precisely the same sector – or from changes in demand up- or downstream from us. Also, as in an ecosystem, the intensity of competition in an industry depends on the scarcity of resources – too many suppliers chasing too few customers inevitably threatens our survival.

Finally, if we view the business world less as a competitive sport and more as an ecosystem, we also acknowledge *the possibility of coexistence*. Direct competition – locking horns and fighting – is usually a last resort in the natural world because even the victor suffers. The same is true in business. Head-to-head competition, whilst unavoidable at times, isn't a great starting point.

History's greatest military thinkers share this perspective. As strategy mastermind B. H. Liddell Hart explains, direct assault – whether on ways of thinking, on business rivals or in combat – 'provokes a stubborn resistance'.[5] The more obvious our attack, the more aggressive the defence.

To minimise bruising confrontation, species evolve to use resources in distinctive ways. As Darwin himself explained, 'More living beings can be supported on the same area the more they diverge.'[6]

The giraffe's long neck gives it access to leaves that others can't reach. Some species share territory but feed at different times of the day, avoiding conflict. This is the approach we should bring to the economic jungle – to flourish by *being different*. How do we do this in practice?

The starting point is to form a deep understanding of the competitive landscape. Only then can you decide how best to fit into it. I suggest a three-step process. Start by exploring your **category** – building basic knowledge about the dynamics of your market. Next, identify your habitat – the geographic **territory** that you intend to occupy. Finally, identify your rivals: the remaining **alternatives and substitutes** that must be faced.

You can then position yourself so as to minimise direct confrontation, increasing your chances of success. For existing brands the same three lenses can help to identify current threats and opportunities.

Category

A category is *a class of product or service that the customer understands* – toasters, tablets, tents, that kind of thing. Choosing a clear category is essential for two reasons: first it reflects how customers think; second it gives you boundaries that make competitive analysis manageable.[7]

Category clarity

Consider these two offerings: Renault's Avantime, a two-door MPV (minivan) coupé, and Vodafone's '360', a hardware and software offering that was part phone, part app store, part social network aggregator and part cloud-based address book.[8] They have two things in common: they didn't fit into a product category that customers understood and they both failed.

Customers buy from established categories because it makes life easier. When a product is in a clear category – running shoes, office chairs or garden sheds – we understand what the product is for and how it works, and we usually have a basic idea of how to choose between options. When products fall outside an obvious category, it becomes easier for us to simply reject them – we can't be bothered to figure all that out.[9]

Even if products are extremely innovative or don't really belong in an existing category, it makes sense to market them in familiar terms until consumers and pundits collectively decide that a new term is needed to describe them. The iPhone was marketed as a phone, for example, not as a hand-held nanocomputer. Choosing a clear category is step one.

Category potential

Next, whether it's a new venture or we're already in the market, we must be mindful of our category's potential. There is little point entering a category that is too small or competitive to create a viable business; nor is there much sense clinging to a shrinking market. Savvy leaders analyse categories dispassionately, entering and exiting based on the returns they might generate, rather than being sentimental about product lines or business units.[10]

A basic step, then, is to assess whether our category is growing or shrinking, and the size of the opportunity. To estimate this, we can gather data from research reports, media coverage and the sales figures of existing players in the category. We can also take a bottom-up approach, estimating the market size using population statistics and demographics. A popular metric for tracking category growth is *market penetration* – the number of customers who have purchased from the category as a proportion of the total population, over a given time.[11]

Another approach is to look at complementary categories. A decline in tourism may affect demand for restaurants. Apparently, demand for ping-pong tables in San Francisco goes up and down as the technology sector expands and contracts.[12]

Category entry and exit barriers

There's no point fixing on a category because it's very large if it then turns out that it's impossible to make a profit there. One way to assess the profit potential is to look at the category's entry and exit barriers.

Entry and exit barriers affect supply. If there is nothing to stop new rivals pouring into the category, oversupply will drive down prices and margins. If existing players can't leave because of high exit costs, they will fight to make the category as uncomfortable as possible for new entrants.[13]

An entry barrier is anything that makes it difficult for new firms to join a category: the costs of getting started, the need for high-level expertise, economies of scale, access to distribution, and the challenges posed by regulatory hurdles.[14] The presence of all these in the pharmaceutical industry serves to explain why this sector is largely protected from new entrants. But even just one barrier to entry can prove sufficient to see off competition.

If one of those factors were to change – perhaps a lowering of the cost of entry – it would make it easier for new entrants to join. With more competitors two things can happen. First, existing players need to work harder to stand out. Second, the increased rivalry can cause prices to drop.

A good example of entry barriers in action is the impact of Airbnb on traditional hotels. When Airbnb took off, the hotel industry went to war against them.[15] We see why when we consider Airbnb's impact on entry barriers. Hotels must own or lease dedicated premises, pay staff to operate the business and meet complex regulations – especially for health and safety. Airbnb hosts don't have these costs: anyone with a spare room can get started. By removing this entry barrier, Airbnb have allowed the market to flood with new accommodation options. With lower costs, a host on Airbnb can either undercut hotels on price or make unusually high margins. It's no wonder hoteliers are angry.

Exit barriers, as their name suggests, are those factors that prevent or restrict a firm's ability to leave a category, such as assets that can't be sold easily, or interdependencies with other business units. Airlines, for example, face high exit barriers because they can't ditch their planes overnight. The existence of high exit barriers tends to make existing players more defensive in their category; knowing that they cannot leave easily, they may well be prepared to sacrifice short-term profitability to see off a new arrival, or even employ underhand tactics.

When Virgin Atlantic were given permission to operate from Heathrow Airport, direct rival British Airways did their utmost to undermine them. They launched a secret 'dirty tricks' campaign that included accessing Virgin computer systems, telling Virgin customers their flights had been cancelled and poaching Virgin staff; a strategy that ended in a £3 million payout when they were caught.[16]

Category requirements

Every category has baseline features or 'points of parity'.[17] These are the features that identify a product as belonging to that category, and are the bare minimum for a competitive product. For a car, this might be having four wheels; for a phone, making and receiving calls; for a book, a minimum word count that makes it more than just an article. This sounds obvious, but history is littered with the carcasses of products that missed baseline requirements.

RIM's doomed PlayBook tablet was positioned as a 'professional' alternative to the iPad, yet shipped with no VPN access, no ability to print and, astonishingly, without its own email system. Because it failed to meet these basic requirements, the PlayBook was a disaster. In the end, RIM took a $485 million write-down on unsold stock.[18]

The secret to our success as a species has always been our ability to adapt to our surroundings. Unfortunately, this means features that once delighted are soon taken for granted. Paying attention to how baseline requirements are shifting is essential to remaining competitive.

You can also assemble a list of value metrics that customers use to rank performance in your category. For a novel these might be how well known the author is; how many stars it gets in reviews; how long it is; how easy it is to read; how cool the cover is. For a supermarket, they might be quality of food, range of goods, staff friendliness and atmosphere at the store. This gives an idea of how customers think about the category and so provides a rough starting point for mapping out the competitive landscape.

Territory

Once you've determined your category, the next step is to consider your territory – the geographical area you'll cover.[19]

As a basic requirement, your territory must contain enough demand to create a viable business. One densely populated city might be enough for some; others may need global coverage.

Different territories, whether a neighbourhood, region or country, will also exhibit different characteristics across the rest of the grid. Wants and needs, alternatives, costs, regulations and price points – to name just a few – can all vary by location, so if you're considering expansion, you should revisit the grid for each new territory.

If your business relies on network effects to succeed – if the value of the product depends on the number of people who use it – location can take on special significance, since success is often more likely if we focus on one area at a time, rather than spread ourselves too thinly. I cover this in Deep Dive Eight: Imitability (see pp. 229–34).

Another consideration is your specific location within a territory. If your office is in an inconvenient place you may struggle to attract the best employees or clients may be reluctant to visit. If you're considering renting a retail unit, ask what happened to the business that was there before. If it ceased trading, it could be that its problems were bound up with where it was based. Conversely, if a business is close to key suppliers or customers, there may well be a cost advantage.[20] And of course, location is particularly key for such sectors as retail and hospitality. Here, where you are situated has a crucial bearing on footfall and customer awareness. It may also help express your brand values.

Alternatives and Substitutes

Restricting ourselves to a category and territory limits the rivals we must study, but there will still be many alternatives in the market. How do we decide who our real rivals are? The next step is to choose a position.

Positioning

As Al Ries wrote in his classic book *Positioning: The Battle for Your Mind*, 'Prospects don't buy, they choose ... The merit, or lack of merit, of your brand is not nearly as important as your position among the possible choices.'[21] The key, therefore, is to pin down the reference points customers will use and then decide where your offering sits among them. The most effective way to do this, in my view, is to draw a generic 'market map'. (Mine combines elements from strategist Richard Huntington's value grid and Ray Kordupleski's market map.)[22]

The market map is a simple chart with two axes, one showing 'what you pay', the other 'what you get' – in other words, the customer's overall perception of the quality or performance of your offering. The map is divided into nine positions, as shown below.

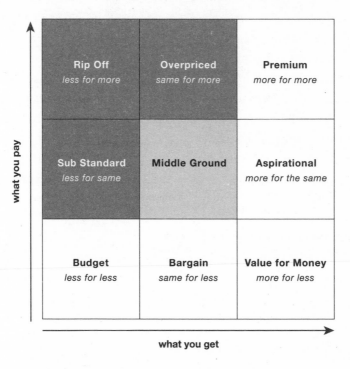

Figure 8 A generic market positioning map.

First, you need to plot the products, services or brands in your category onto the frame. You can start at the bottom with the budget offerings and work your way up; at the top and work your way down; or with one well-known player and arrange others around it – there's no right or wrong way. I've mapped out my wife's perception of women's fashion retailers as an example overleaf.

Once you've mapped out the market, you then need to consider where you fit amongst them – or where you would like to, identifying the specific rivals that customers will use as reference points against which to judge you. This approach offers four key benefits:

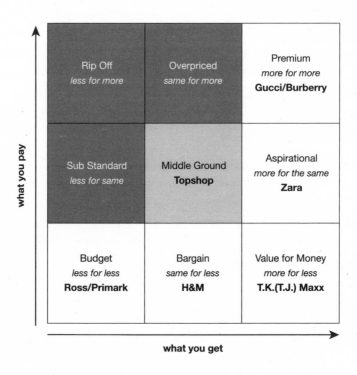

	what you get →		
what you pay	Rip Off *less for more*	Overpriced *same for more*	Premium *more for more* **Gucci/Burberry**
	Sub Standard *less for same*	Middle Ground **Topshop**	Aspirational *more for the same* **Zara**
	Budget *less for less* **Ross/Primark**	Bargain *same for less* **H&M**	Value for Money *more for less* **T.K.(T.J.) Maxx**

Figure 9 My wife's perception of women's fashion retailers.

1. It acknowledges relativity

Your position on the map is relative to others, so can change as rivals come and go. A new budget entrant can push an existing brand up into the middle ground, or a value-for-money offering can make a premium product seem overpriced. By keeping an eye on the map, you can consider how a new entrant might impact your positioning.

2. It forces you to focus on your customer

Where brands are positioned will be highly subjective, which is a good thing since desirability itself is highly subjective. One person's premium is another person's rip-off; one person's value for money is a bargain to another.

This means you can't complete the map without understanding your customers. It forces you to understand their wants and needs.

Asking current and prospective customers which other brands they consider, and how they fit onto the map, can be a revealing exercise. If a business and its customers have different opinions about the brand's position, it raises a red flag.

3. It reveals vacant positions

Mapping out players within a category can highlight which positions are crowded and which are vacant, revealing opportunities for the future. Entrepreneur Jim Jannard is a master at positioning, launching two successful businesses in different positions. Oakley sunglasses was a premium brand that offered 'more for more' – the highest-quality sports sunglasses for a relatively high price. The brand was sold to the Luxottica Group for $2.1 billion in 2007.[23]

RED Digital Cinema, his second major venture, aimed to make professional digital cinema cameras accessible to more film-makers. At the time of its launch in 2007, their first camera cost almost 90 per cent less than some alternatives, yet boasted higher image quality.[24] Renting a rival with equivalent performance for a month could cost more than buying a RED one outright.

Unsurprisingly, this 'more for less' positioning was compelling for many film-makers. A word of warning here, though. The 'more for less' position is by far the hardest to pull off – the clash with customer beliefs is often too great. Many will be suspicious of the quality at such a low price.

4. It helps with marketing and pricing

Success comes from making your offering the obvious, easy choice for the customer. The clearer your position, the easier it is to be chosen. Falling in a grey zone between budget and bargain or aspirational and premium can be a hard sell to customers who are already drowning in choice. Your value propositions and communications should express your position unambiguously.

You can also use the market map to estimate your upper and lower prices from the outset, by considering the prices of the alternatives in neighbouring positions. If you are aiming to create a bargain product, you can identify the products your customers think occupy adjacent positions – in this case budget, middle ground and value for money – and use these to set rough boundaries for your prices.

Pricing should be considered from the very beginning of product development to avoid creating products and services that can never generate returns.[25] I'll explore this in more detail in Deep Dive Four: Revenues (see pp. 123–43).

Sorting the alternatives

So far, I've considered category, territory and basic market positioning, all of which help reduce competitors to a manageable number. Now it's time to address the remaining rivals directly, sorting them into three camps: *alternatives*, *substitutes* and your *own range*.

Alternatives

An alternative is a direct rival that customers will use as a reference point. The Audi A4 and BMW 3 Series are alternatives to a Mercedes-Benz C-Class, for example. Forming a shortlist of alternatives, then determining their strengths and weaknesses using the value metrics you identified for the category, is a logical starting point (see p. 91). If the data is available, you can measure your performance against alternatives by looking at how market share is changing, in terms of units sold, revenues or both.

If this data is not available, you can use a process of elimination to determine the strength of the alternatives. If your revenues or customer base are shrinking, but demand for the category is remaining stable or growing, your rivals are probably affecting you. If you see a significant decline in market share you must revisit the grid and see what is going on – perhaps your proposition needs improving, or awareness has dropped, for example.

Substitutes

A substitute is any offering from outside your category that satisfies your customer's *super objective* (see pp. 69–70). If you are travelling from England to France, substitutes would be the P&O cross-Channel ferry, the Eurostar train or an easyJet flight.[26]

You should be wary of substitutes. It's easy to adopt a product-centric mindset – forgetting the hole in the wall your customer wants and obsessing over the drills you make (see p. 69). This lulls you into ignoring substitutes until it's too late.

As with auditing alternatives, the logical starting point is to short-list the substitutes and determine their strengths and weaknesses. Be sure to consider 'non-consumption' within any list of substitutes – your greatest rival may be customers buying nothing at all.[27]

You can evaluate a substitute category in the same way as your own. Is it growing? If so, is it at the expense of your category? As with alternatives, if you see a major change in the substitutes you face, revisit the grid to consider the scenarios that might unfold.

Own range

Finally, your own products and services can be rivals too. A large range is often a sign that a company has lost its way strategically and is compensating with a scattergun approach. It doesn't know what its customers want, so bombards the market in the hope that something will hit the target.

When taking this approach, businesses suffer for three reasons. First, they inevitably find it expensive to launch new products, which must all be designed, manufactured, stocked, promoted and supported. Second, because they are spreading resources thinly across product and service lines, they find it difficult to be thorough, and quality therefore suffers. Third, customers experience the *paradox of choice*.[28] Overwhelmed by the number of options, they give up or go to a different brand where the range is clearer. Recognising these problems, Steve Jobs slashed the product pipeline by 70 per cent when he rejoined Apple, and set about improving what remained.[29]

The silver bullet test

Markets are chaotic and unpredictable, and in the fog of competition you can lose sight of who your rivals are. To help people stay focused, legendary technologist Andy Grove suggested the 'silver bullet test':

If you had just one bullet in a figurative pistol, whom among your many competitors would you save it for?[30]

Before you go hunting, though, let's think this through. You need rivals as reference points for assessing value – without them it's harder for customers to recognise how great your product or service is. Businesses in emerging categories should welcome rivals who will help establish and grow the market. Some businesses may have avoided head-to-head competition altogether, making this question impossible to answer. Taking these considerations into account, I've reframed the question slightly:

Imagine you have a magic net that can make one competitor's customers your own. Who would you use it on? Who would use their magic net on you?

Your answer to this question will reveal how well you understand the rivalry you face – if you're unclear of your category, territory or position, and the alternatives and substitutes you face there, you'll find answering this extremely difficult. If your team has wildly diverging answers, that should raise a red flag. To help plan for the future, follow this question with another:

Imagine it's three years from now. Who will you use the magic net on?

This helps you distinguish between immediate threats and those on the horizon. If the answers are completely different, don't hesitate to get the gang together and share your concerns.

If answering those questions is still a challenge, strategist Eddie Sung offers an alternative:

If your business shut down tomorrow, where would your customers spend the money they would have spent with you?[31]

This should reveal who your main rival is, a crucial consideration when creating your offering – our next port of call.

Key Questions

Category

- What categories do your products or services belong to? Are they clear to the customer?
- Is demand for the category growing or shrinking?
- What entry and exit barriers exist for the category? Are they changing?

Territory

- Is your territory large enough to support the business you want to run?
- Which territory would offer the greatest demand for your offerings?
- If you were to change or expand your territory, how might it affect the rest of the grid?

Alternatives and substitutes

- What are the direct alternatives your customers will choose between? What are their strengths and weaknesses?
- What substitutes do customers have? Are they a growing concern?
- Is your own range a problem? Can customers easily choose between your offerings?

	desirability	profitability	longevity
customer	**WANTS & NEEDS** ○ values & beliefs ○ goals ○ barriers	**REVENUES** ○ revenue model ○ price ○ volume (qty & freq.)	**CUSTOMER BASE** ○ awareness ○ acquisition ○ retention
market	**RIVALRY** ○ category ○ territory ○ alternatives & substitutes	**BARGAINING POWER** ○ with customers ○ with suppliers ○ rules & regulations	**IMITABILITY** ○ legal protection ○ durable advantages ○ competitor lag
organisation	**OFFERINGS** ● proposition ● brand appeal ● customer experience	**COSTS** ○ fixed costs ○ variable costs ○ capital expenditure	**ADAPTABILITY** ○ cash position ○ scalability or capacity ○ complexity & rigidity

Deep Dive Three: Offerings

In the first deep dive, you got to know your customers and what they want. In the second, you explored the competitive landscape. Now it's time to pull these insights together to define your offerings.

Every offering has three interdependent elements:

- The **proposition** is the concept the customer buys into – a concise expression of what your product or service is, and why it's a good choice.
- The **brand appeal** is the overarching associations people have with your business.
- The **customer experience** encompasses the full spectrum of interactions customers have with you.

These three elements are inseparable. If your proposition is unappealing or your brand doesn't come into consideration, the customer experience is irrelevant. A strong proposition can fail if your brand is weak. A great brand can be destroyed by a poor customer experience.

You can't pick and choose which elements you attend to, and judging the attention each requires can be challenging. It's easy to have a bias towards one area – fussing over the brand and neglecting the customer experience, or obsessing over the proposition but presenting the brand inconsistently – but this is counterproductive. A desirable offering brings all three together.

Fortunately, every successful brand, proposition and customer interaction draws on the same palette of value sources (listed below). There's no need to keep track of them as you go through the list. Instead, think about how they apply to things that you've bought and liked. If your business already exists, smile and nod when your offering's main appeal is mentioned.

Sign value

Anything that expresses the customer's identity – their self-image, values, community or position in society – can be a source of value. The philosopher Jean Baudrillard called this *sign value* because it derives from what it *signifies about them*.[1]

Goods that convey a sense of status or prestige are desirable for this sign value. A black American Express Centurion Card is still just a card that we can use to pay for things (with some pretty juicy perks), but what really makes it desirable is its exclusivity.

Functional value

The second source of value stems from utility – the goals it allows customers to accomplish.[2] You create this value by directly addressing the super objectives, subtext and success criteria that underpin their goals (see Deep Dive One: Wants and Needs, pp. 59–83).

Financial rationales

A brand, product or service can appeal primarily for financial reasons. It might seem a bargain, help us save money or be something we expect will appreciate, such as collectibles or property.

We also use price as a proxy for quality, or find a high price appealing because of what it says about us.[3] Financial rationales don't always dominate, though. Often we simply look for what we think represents good value for money and concern ourselves more with other benefits.

Quality

A reputation for quality is a great source of value, since we expect high-quality products to provide a better ownership experience. They're less likely to break, meaning we won't need to wait around while they are repaired, waste time shopping for a replacement, or feel as if we've wasted our money. Products that boast durability, longevity, accuracy, purity or an illustrious track record often have greater value attached to them than alternatives.[4]

Effort reduction

Most innovations help us do more with less. From self-driving cars to robotic vacuum cleaners, most products and services evolve over time towards effortlessness.[5] Any offering that is more convenient, quicker, easier to use or transport, does a task on our behalf or reduces wait times, derives its value from effortlessness.

A great example is Amazon, whose focus on effortlessness has created incredible value for their customers. One-click shopping, the dash button, same-day delivery – these innovations have effort reduction at their core. Effortlessness isn't just a characteristic of the Amazon customer experience – it's a key pillar of their proposition and brand, and the consistency with which it's evident in everything they do makes for a formidable offering.

Stress reduction

We appreciate courier services that let us track a delivery, or communication apps that notify us when a message has been read, because we hate uncertainty and – more specifically – the stress uncertainty causes. Products that give timely feedback create value because they reduce stress. Similarly, services that prevent us from making mistakes, or are safer to use, combat other sources of stress and create value because of it. Another common cause of stress is feeling that a task is beyond our abilities. Offerings that empower us, either by raising our skill level or by lowering the skill required, are also highly valued.[6]

Sensory pleasure

The way things smell, taste, look or sound, as well as their tactile qualities, can be a huge source of value.[7] Apple is a good example. Whether it's the click wheel on the original iPod, the touch interface for the iPhone or their beautiful packaging, the sensory experience of an Apple product is central to their appeal and the brand's association with design excellence.

Social pleasure

We are wired for social interaction: without it we go insane.[8] Offerings that allow us to connect and interact with others, or that give us a sense of belonging, create huge value. We are also more likely to buy from a friend than from a stranger. Employees who build personal relationships with customers can add great value.

In the same vein, products that are endorsed by others are typically more appealing. Nothing attracts a crowd like a crowd. We look for *social proof* that a product or service is good, based on reviews or recommendations. Building credibility through testimonials, endorsements and media coverage is an important part of the marketer's repertoire.[9]

Control

Few motivators are more powerful than feeling autonomous – we want to feel in control.[10] Giving customers greater control over when and where they interact with you; what things look like; or how much they spend can increase desirability. The opposite is also true. Gadgets with short battery lives annoy us because we have less control over when we can use them and for how long.

Emotional appeal

Finally, the value of an offering often comes down to how it makes us feel. A relaxing massage, the thrill of skydiving or the sense of accomplishment from achieving a goal all demonstrate how a positive emotional response creates value. Remember, too, that reducing negative feelings – anger, frustration, fear or guilt (as we reach for another cookie) – also makes a huge difference.

We'll see these value sources in action as we explore the three elements of every offering.

Proposition

The bedrock of any successful business is a strong product or service proposition. If people don't want what we're selling, it's a fundamental problem, but how do we know if we're likely to succeed or not?

In *Crossing the Chasm*, Geoffrey Moore suggests capturing our proposition in a simple structure,[11] which I've adapted slightly to fit the language of the grid. It may not show you *how* to market your product or service, but it does provide clarity as to what the proposition really is:

For – *target customer*
Who has – *goals*
Our product or service is a – *category*
That unlike – *specific alternative(s)*
Provides – *compelling rationales*

Examples of this sentence in action might be: 'For *wealthy travellers*, who want to *fly privately*, NetJets is an *aviation company* that – unlike *owning a plane outright* – provides *the freedom and flexibility of jet ownership, with less hassle and cost*.'

'For *dachshund fans* who want to *express their love of the breed*, *devotedtodachshunds.co.uk* is an *online retailer* that – unlike *Amazon* – *exclusively sells sausage-dog-themed products*, making it *easy to find accessories they'll love.*'

If you've worked through the first two deep dives on Wants and Needs (pp. 59–83) and Rivalry (pp. 85–99), you will be familiar with the first parts of this formula. What you should therefore seek to pin down now are your *compelling rationales*.

You might decide, for example, that one of the benefits you offer is effort reduction, because you offer an express service with no wait times. Another might be that your service is more reliable or accurate than your competitor's. There are plenty of options to choose from, so let's look at some ways to narrow these rationales down.

Your rationales must be relevant to the customer

Creating features that are irrelevant to the customer or which improve aspects of a product that are already good enough leads to apathy and indifference. You strengthen your proposition by finding aspects of existing offerings that a) the customer cares about, and b) aren't yet good enough.

Canon and Nikon have been the market leaders in digital SLR cameras for years, incrementally improving their products with each new version they bring to market. As anyone with a DSLR knows, though, these cameras are often left at home because they're a pain to lug around – they require too much *effort*.

While Canon and Nikon were stuck in an arms race with one another, other manufacturers used advances in technology to make smaller cameras with comparable image quality. Sales of these 'mirrorless' cameras are going up; sales of DSLRs are going down. The market leaders in mirrorless cameras are Sony, Olympus and Fujifilm.[12] At the time of writing, Canon and Nikon have yet to make serious inroads into the market.

Your proposition should be distinctive

If your combination of benefits is the same as that of your rivals – especially if they already dominate the market – you're unlikely to succeed. A strong proposition is distinctive.

A good example is Google's Android operating system. Their main rival, Apple, offers a premium-priced product in a sealed unit. Android offers a free, open-source product that does the same job: very distinct rationales from Apple's. Google Plus, on the other hand – their floundering social media offering – wasn't distinctive enough to lure customers away from Facebook and suffered as a result.[13]

Your proposition must outperform rivals and industry norms where it matters

Eliminate rationales that don't involve making a *noticeable* improvement on what already exists. Rationales are based on comparative strengths, not absolutes. If there is not sufficient contrast to rival offerings or industry norms, you cannot expect the customer to choose your product.[14]

Tesla have done a great job here, emphasising areas where they outperform alternatives: a growing number of autonomous driving features, zero emissions, the best safety of any car ever tested in America, and lower maintenance and fuel costs, all of which track back to the sources of value we mentioned earlier.[15]

Your rationale should be focused

Another theme that underpins most successful propositions is *focus*. You can't be all things to all people, or outperform alternatives on every rationale. For a product or brand to succeed, it should be the obvious choice when a certain need arises. That won't happen if your rationales are too diffuse, so you should always set out to focus your attention on a small number of them.

A final word of warning

If you can't complete Moore's statement for your proposition, your team can't agree on a common version, or your customers don't buy into it, devote all your energy to resolving this issue before moving forward. You've got to make sure you're making the *right thing* before you worry about making the *thing right*.

Brand Appeal

What words come to mind when you think of the following three brands?

Shell
McDonald's
Rolex

For my part, I associate Shell with *oil*, *drilling* and *Arctic*; McDonald's with *burgers*, *junk food* and *yellow*; Rolex with *watch*, *Swiss* and *luxury*.

The website brandtags.com has taken this game to the next level. Described as a 'collective experiment in brand perception', it shows site visitors a logo and then asks them to tag it with the first word that pops into their head. The site has collected more than 1.7 million tags across hundreds of brands. The more common the association, the larger the text of the tag.

Chevron's three most prominent tags are: *gas*, *oil* and *evil*. Aston Martin's are *James*, *Bond* and *car*.[16]

This site reveals some simple truths about how branding actually works. First, a brand is just a collection of associations that people have with a business. Second, those associations are formed in two ways: *inside out*, through marketing and communications; and *outside in*, through customers' real-world experiences and word of mouth.

Aston Martin's main associations were built *inside out*. The tie-up with the Bond movie franchise was a strategic decision on their part. Chevron's association with *evil*, on the other hand, is not part of their official messaging. Neither, I suspect, is the US Postal Service's number-one association – *slow*.

These brand associations map directly to the categories I discussed at the beginning of the chapter:

- Many relate to **sign value**, describing the social group, behavioural standards or image associated with that brand, like *Swiss*, *evil*, *exclusive* or *cool*.
- Some describe a **function** or close association with a category or product, like *aeroplane*, *bank* or *car*.
- Many reflect associations with **quality** or **financial value**: *crap*, *rugged*, *expensive* or *cheap*.
- The rest describe **experiential** factors: tags like *hassle*, *friendly*, *comfortable* or *exciting*.

The first step to building an appealing brand is to choose a distinctive set of associations you will actively promote from the sources of value given at the beginning of the chapter. You don't need associations in every category; you can use just two or three.

Lush cosmetics, for example, are associated with their strong ethics, and equally strong-smelling stores. American car insurer GEICO is associated with a category (car insurance), a financial rationale (cheap) and an experience (easy), as their tagline suggests: 'Fifteen minutes could save you fifteen percent or more on your car insurance.'[17] The clearer you are on these associations and the more consistently you communicate them, the better.

Once you've decided on your associations, you must make sure that every proposition and customer experience (and decision in general) reinforces rather than undermines them. Gaps and incongruities between the brand image and the brand reality rarely go unpunished, as the following examples illustrate.

Case study: scandalous chocolate

In 2006, according to Rick and Michael Mast, they were making chocolate from scratch in a Brooklyn apartment, selling bars at a local flea market.[18] Fast-forward to the present and the brothers are operating a small empire of boutique stores, where bars can cost over $10.

From the outset, food blogger Scott Craig doubted their story. In an exposé, he pointed out that the smooth texture had the hallmarks of industrial chocolate,[19] and the packaging had no ingredients list – usually a point of pride for 'bean-to-bar' chocolatiers.[20]

Eventually the truth came to light. In the beginning, the Mast brothers had been re-melting a commercial chocolate called Valrhona.[21] They had built a successful business based on what some considered to be a fraud. Brother Rick had even told *Vanity Fair*, 'I can affirm that we make the best chocolate in the world.'[22]

That this scandal emerged years after they had switched to a genuine bean-to-bar process didn't diminish its impact. Some retailers reported that Christmas sales figure were down 66 per cent in 2015.[23]

The uproar had little to do with whether the product tasted good or not – the obvious way to judge a chocolate bar. What customers ultimately cared about was whether the brand image matched the brand reality.

Case study: Beats by Dre

In just four years, headphone and speaker brand Beats by Dre captured 64 per cent of their target market in the US,[24] and were bought by Apple for $3 billion.[25] A phenomenal achievement.

Their success came from creating unparalleled sign value – a brand image that reflected the target customer's aspirations and identity. Dr Dre, basketball legend LeBron James, tennis star Serena Williams and a host of other popular-culture icons all wore the distinctive headphones, with their fans following suit. But will their success last? Despite their premium price point, Beats seem to be developing an equal reputation for poor quality.

Apple's website describes the urBeats in-ear headphones as: 'Grid-iron tough. Whether you keep urBeats pristine or throw them in and out of your bag, you don't have to worry about them breaking or fraying anytime soon.'[26]

At the time of writing there are fifteen customer reviews on the same page, with twelve giving the product one star. The headphones are described as 'garbage . . . trash . . . terrible quality . . . disposable' and 'not worth the money'.[27] Clearly the brand image and the brand reality are out of alignment. People expect better quality for the price.

The appeal of any brand is strengthened when it is expressed consistently.[28] A large part of establishing this consistency comes from managing the brand, proposition and customer experience so that they reinforce rather than undermine each other. The brand reality must fit the image. To end this section on a positive note, here's an example of getting the whole lot right.

Case study: Patagonia

I am a fan of outdoors brand Patagonia. Their ethics, their environmental stance and their quality products all appeal to me. I bought my first wetsuit there, and was happy to pay a premium price for it – not just to support the brand, but because the product was well designed and constructed. Durable, comfortable, warm and backed by an ironclad guarantee – there were clear reasons to choose it.

After four years of abuse the suit had developed a couple of holes and I had ripped the lining from the cuff on one leg, so I took it to my local Patagonia store to have it repaired.

A cheery assistant gave me a short address form to complete and said they'd handle the rest. She thanked me for bringing it in and said she was glad that the product was getting used. The repair could take up to thirty days but might be a little quicker. It would be free of charge.

Two weeks later, a box turned up at home. Inside was my wetsuit (looking brand new) and a free copy of the *Surfer's Journal* (a magazine that costs $16.95) to say thank you. I was impressed and delighted.

In this example, you can see Patagonia's proposition, customer experience and brand image all reinforcing each other.

Part of their mission statement is to 'Build the best product – *quality clothing and gear that lasts you for years*' and to 'Cause no unnecessary harm – *reduce the adverse social and environmental impacts of our products.*'[29] Both the wetsuit and the repair service support this mission – the former by being a quality product with a long lifespan; the latter because repairing something causes less environmental harm than replacing it. The brand and proposition fit together.

To encourage us to repair rather than replace the product, they've made that proposition a no-brainer: it's free, quick and you feel good about doing your bit for the planet – all solid rationales.

The assistant carefully managed my expectations to make the experience delightful. I was happy when the repaired wetsuit arrived earlier than expected; and the free magazine was an unexpected delight when I unboxed it at home. I couldn't resist telling my friends (especially the surfers) about the service I'd received. Guess where they'll be buying their next wetsuits? This is a business whose brand image fits perfectly with the brand reality that customers experience, the final topic of this chapter.

Customer Experience

In 1996, psychologist Daniel Kahneman and his colleague Don Redelmeier made a discovery that should have permanently changed how we think about customer experience, but hasn't (as yet).

Their experiment was simple. During a colonoscopy, patients were asked to indicate every minute the level of pain they were experiencing, on a scale from 0 to 10. When the procedure finished, patients were then asked to rate the total pain they had felt.

The psychologists expected those final assessments to reflect the length of the procedure and the sum of the patient's preceding ratings. Instead, they found the total rating reflected the average of the highest pain intensity the patient had experienced – *the peak* – and the intensity at the final moment of the procedure – *the end*. This phenomenon, known as the *peak–end rule*, has been demonstrated by other experiments countless times since.[30]

Kahneman explains this phenomenon by distinguishing between our *experiencing self* and our *remembering self*.[31] Whilst the *experiencing self* answered the questions throughout the procedure, the *remembering self* gave the final assessment based on their memory of it, which is influenced by the peak–end rule.

This has profound implications for every business, since it reveals that customer satisfaction doesn't accurately reflect what customers experience. It reflects *what they remember of the experience*, which isn't the same thing.

If you want satisfaction to go up, you need to create a better memory of the experience. But what makes an interaction memorable?

Memory and the zone of tolerance

Marketing professor Leonard Berry and his colleagues found that we have two levels of expectation for all our interactions as customers: the *adequate*, the service we would find acceptable, and the *desirable*, the service we hope to receive. Between these points is a grey area known as the *zone of tolerance*, where events are satisfactory, yet unremarkable.[32]

Interactions within the zone of tolerance have little impact on our perceptions because they aren't memorable. Interactions outside these boundaries, however – below adequate or above desired – lodge in the memory because they are unexpected. It is these interactions that most determine our satisfaction.

If you want to alter the customer's perception of the experience, you need only to consider what was below adequate or above what was expected. Fiddling with interactions in the zone of tolerance (even if you improve them slightly) won't make a noticeable difference.

Last year I spoke at a conference at a luxury hotel. The room was nice, the staff were polite, the gym well equipped – all within the zone of tolerance given their reputation. However, when checking out two things happened. First, I found my bags left unattended outside the entrance. Then I was left to lug them into the taxi whilst the staff joked around inside. These below-adequate interactions – I had expected much better – cast a shadow over everything else, especially because they happened at the end. They dominate my memory of the stay. We're often told how important it is to create a great first impression, but in reality, the last impression can be more important.

The implications are frightening, but in fact there is a tremendous opportunity here. Most organisations seeking to improve customer experiences end up redesigning entire customer journeys as if *every interaction carries equal weight*. This typically costs a fortune, takes months or years to deliver and has little impact on satisfaction because it doesn't actually end up creating a better memory of the experience. Furthermore, in the time it takes to launch these improvements, customer expectations have risen, leaving the organisation right back where it started.

It's also possible to think you've improved a customer experience on paper, but then discover that satisfaction has *gone down* because all the interactions have been homogenised in the zone of tolerance – there's nothing to remember about the experience at all.

What is therefore essential is not so much to engineer satisfaction into every experience, but – in typically less time and at less cost – to concentrate on the key interactions.

First, you must make sure the *final part* of any journey ends on a high – a positive peak beyond what was desired, since this has a disproportionate impact. Any interaction that concludes a process is ripe with opportunity.

Next, you need to eliminate any troughs – interactions that are below adequate. This stops the customer from having any negative memories of their experience.

Finally, you should create the occasional positive peak by including a couple of interactions that are better than the customer might usually expect, leaving them with nothing but positive memories. You can even create a set of 'memory-makers' – interactions that you can use semi-randomly to inject delight or reinforce a brand message during the experience.

To apply this approach in practice, begin by mapping the full scope of your interactions with your customers, identifying what you think they would consider *adequate* and *desired* service for each stage of the experience. There are various ways you can do this: through interviews with customers; by watching how they use your products or services; from direct feedback (complaints and reviews); and by comparing how your service stacks up against the norms of your particular sector. Most of the time, simply asking the right question – What would you consider adequate? What would be ideal? – will give you all you need to know.

Next, you should map your current performance onto a chart that allows you to see at a glance precisely where you fall short, exceed expectations or operate within the zone of tolerance. A five-stage journey might look like this:

	STAGE 1	STAGE 2	STAGE 3	STAGE 4	STAGE 5
MEMORABLE (GOOD)					
	Desired Service	Desired Service	Desired Service	Desired Service	Desired Service
FORGETTABLE INTERACTIONS	Zone of Tolerance	Zone of Tolerance ●	Zone of Tolerance ●	Zone of Tolerance ●	Zone of Tolerance
	Adequate Service	Adequate Service	Adequate Service	Adequate Service	Adequate Service
MEMORABLE (BAD)	●				●

Figure 10 Overlaying customer interactions on a journey's stages. There are two troughs – stages 1 and 5. The other interactions are within the zone of tolerance so are easily forgotten.

In this particular example, the first and last stage are both below adequate, while less impactful middle ones lie within the zone of tolerance. The obvious first step, therefore, is to turn stage 5 into a positive peak. Next, stage 1 needs to be bumped up into the zone of tolerance, so that the customer is left with no memories that are negative. It might also be worth engineering a positive memorable peak somewhere in the middle, say at stage 3.

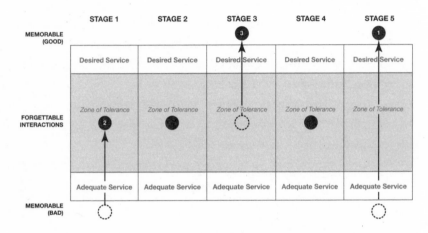

Figure 11 Creating a positive peak at the end (1) is the logical starting point for improving the customer's experience. Next, stage 1 is moved up into the zone of tolerance (2). Finally, a positive peak is created in stage 3 (3). Although much of the customer's overall experience may be in the zone of tolerance, their overall impression will be positive.

Once you've decided which interactions require your attention, you need to decide how to improve them.

Setting expectations

The most cost-effective solution is to set the right expectations in the first place. Where an interaction can be improved through better communication, you should seize it. Most disappointments are caused by a business saying one thing and doing another.

Pulling the right levers

If expectation management is not sufficient, the next step is to consider which of the factors I discussed at the beginning of the Deep Dive are at work: does the functionality simply not achieve what the customer wants? Does it require too much effort? Is it stressful? Are you making the customer feel unimportant? Identify which two or three factors could be used to transform that interaction.

Note that the factors you use to improve a customer experience don't have to be the same as your product rationales. Even though people may buy your product because it's accurate or durable, you can still improve the ordering process by making it effortless, or by employing staff who are delightful to deal with. Here are three examples of this approach in action.

Example one – a sweet ending

My wife and I saw a movie at a local cinema recently. The facilities were what you'd expect – a comfortable seat, a big screen and decent sound. The surprise came at the end as we left and came across a staff member giving out sweets to say thank you for coming. This unexpected interaction (well placed at the end of our experience) probably had a greater impact on customer satisfaction than any costly upgrade of the cinema's facilities would have done.

Example two – an unexpected thank-you

A week or so after speaking at an event, I usually send a small token of appreciation to the organiser or client – perhaps just a postcard, thanking them. This simple gesture is always unexpected (until now, at least) and creates a peak right where it is most powerful – at the end. You'd be surprised how often such a small thing can result in rebookings, referrals and ongoing opportunities, simply because they remember you.

Example three – serious fun

Air New Zealand took a dull stage of the air-travel experience, the safety video, and turned it into an unexpected delight, creating their unusual 'Bare Essentials' safety video in 2009 –the first of a series of viral sensations that have racked up more than 83 million views online.[33]

These amusing videos stick in the memory, not only improving engagement with the important safety message, but influencing customer satisfaction. When we think back on the flying experience – most of which is sleeping or watching movies – the safety video leaps out as memorable and expressing the brand's personality. Air New Zealand have won AirlineRating's Airline of the Year for the last four years (2014–17).[34]

Let's conclude this section with an example that brings together everything I've covered so far.

Case study: Domino's Pizza

Domino's proposition combines two rationales: *effort* – customers want a takeaway or delivery, rather than to make their own meal – and *sensory* – pizza is supposed to taste good.

Back in 2009 the business was not in good shape. Employees had posted a video online of them abusing the food, and their flavourless pizza was driving customers away.[35] The proposition was clear in theory, but the reality was way off with the brand suffering as a result. How did new CEO J. Patrick Doyle turn things around?

First, Domino's improved their recipes until they started winning taste tests against direct rivals Papa John's and Pizza Hut.[36] This strengthened a key rationale. Next, they got to work bolstering their other selling point: effortlessness. They already had a reputation for fast delivery, so they turned their attention to another stage: the ordering process.

This focus culminated in their 'AnyWare' strategy, allowing customers to order pizza in a variety of effortless ways. You can order by texting Domino's the pizza-slice emoji; you can use a 'zero click' app that places an order automatically after ten seconds; or you can voice order through 'Dom', a virtual assistant within their mobile app.[37] Another innovation, their Pizza Tracker, both sets and then meets customers' expectations by allowing them to follow the progress of their pizza through preparation, cooking, quality-checking and delivery, and reduces the stress of uncertainty whilst waiting for an order to arrive.[38] When it was introduced, it generated a lot of buzz because it surpassed customer expectations for that stage of the experience – the dead spot between finalising their order and the food arriving. To be clear: there's nothing inherently interesting about hearing that a pizza is in an oven. It became a peak because the tracking was unexpected.

The results speak for themselves. Domino's have recently enjoyed eight consecutive quarters of double-digit sales growth, and now sell one in five pizzas in America. Since 2010, their share price has gone up 1,200 per cent.[39]

It's perhaps worth comparing this briefly with a poor customer experience I recently had. I had come across a wooden ornament online and decided to order it as a gift for someone. However, when I'd completed my purchase and checked for an order-confirmation email, there wasn't one. A few minutes later, still no email. The email never arrived, leaving me wondering if the order had gone through.

The product did arrive, but when I opened the box I found it full of foam packing peanuts, one of my pet peeves: they have a tendency to spill all over the floor while you grope around for the gift and invoice; then you need to scoop them into a bag before you bin them. These ones couldn't be recycled either.

Three forces made this a negative shopping experience:

- *Stress* – uncertainty over whether my order had gone through and whether it would arrive.
- *Effort* – clearing up the mess from the packaging.
- *Emotion* – non-recyclable packaging made me feel guilty.

This may seem a trivial example, but it demonstrates how the same basic sources of value are at work regardless of whether what's on offer is a luxury hotel, a pizza, an airline, or a wooden ornament.

Key Questions

Proposition

- What aspects of existing alternatives can you improve upon, and will the target customer care?
- Is your combination of rationales sufficiently distinctive from those of your rivals?
- Where can you surpass industry norms? Where can you out-perform alternatives?

Brand appeal

- What associations do you want people to have with your brand? What associations have they formed independently?
- Do you express your brand values consistently?
- Where are the gaps between your brand image and brand reality?

Customer experience

- Do your customers' journeys end on a high?
- How might setting better expectations improve customer satisfaction?
- If your customers were in charge for a day, what one thing would they change?

	desirability	**profitability**	longevity
customer	**WANTS & NEEDS** ◯ values & beliefs ◯ goals ◯ barriers	**REVENUES** ● revenue model ● price ● volume (qty & freq.)	**CUSTOMER BASE** ◯ awareness ◯ acquisition ◯ retention
market	**RIVALRY** ◯ category ◯ territory ◯ alternatives & substitutes	**BARGAINING POWER** ◯ with customers ◯ with suppliers ◯ rules & regulations	**IMITABILITY** ◯ legal protection ◯ durable advantages ◯ competitor lag
organisation	**OFFERINGS** ◯ proposition ◯ brand appeal ◯ customer experience	**COSTS** ◯ fixed costs ◯ variable costs ◯ capital expenditure	**ADAPTABILITY** ◯ cash position ◯ scalability or capacity ◯ complexity & rigidity

Deep Dive Four: Revenues

Every business must eventually make a profit to survive. To generate that profit, revenues must exceed costs. I'm unlikely to win a Nobel Prize for those insights, but the surprising truth is that revenues – half of that profit equation – are often mismanaged. Many fail to maximise sources of revenue, or make decisions that grow revenues but shrink profits.

Many businesses – even multinationals – also have no recognisable pricing strategy at all. Not only that, they admit to guessing what their prices should be or make them up based on their costs, and never experiment to see if they're leaving money on the table. Most have no idea how dramatic an effect even a small price change can have on profitability.

When it comes to increasing sales volumes, most businesses either spend more on advertising or just slash their prices, without really considering whether another approach might be more effective. But there are other avenues to consider that may well yield more dramatic improvements.

Revenue Model

If I asked you to rattle off a list of visionary entrepreneurs, chances are hip-hop group the Wu-Tang Clan wouldn't make the list. They should, though, because their recent revenue-model experiment was ingenious.

Instead of getting a pittance from streaming royalties, they made just one copy of their new album *Once Upon a Time in Shaolin* and auctioned it, generating no shortage of buzz and controversy in the process. The single copy was finally sold for $2 million to controversial biotech CEO Martin Shkreli.[1] As this example shows, changing your revenue model can transform your earning potential.

A revenue model has two components. One is the *revenue stream* – the source of the income. The other is the *revenue mechanism* – the way people are charged: a fixed price, or by the hour, for example.

Identifying your revenue streams shouldn't be hard by this stage: they flow from the customers whose wants and needs were considered in the first box of the grid. When it comes to the *revenue mechanism*, several options are common.

Auction

An auction can be beneficial to both buyer and seller – it gives the buyer more control over what they are willing to spend, and rewards the seller if they own something scarce and desirable. The flip side is the inherent uncertainty, inconsistent supply and demand and potentially more effortful experience for all involved.

Fixed price

Fixed prices – like an all-you-can-eat buffet or unlimited mobile data usage – give customers clarity. The challenge for the business is to execute such a scheme profitably and implement safeguards to prevent abuse.

Pay as you go

Paying for the amount you use seems logical to most people, and suits a broad range of scenarios from buying cheese by the kilogram to data by the gigabyte. It even works for jet engines.

Rolls-Royce introduced 'Power-by-the-Hour' in 1962, charging customers a fixed rate per flying hour for engines and maintenance.[2] This benefits the customer massively, giving them predictable expenses and lowering the up-front cost of the equipment, whilst incentivising the manufacturer to build the most reliable product they can.

Cloud computing services like Amazon Web Services or Salesforce also have the pay-as-you-go model at heart, allowing customers to easily scale up or down based on their demand, without having to own any physical hardware – a major selling point.

Licensing

Businesses who sell intellectual property are often remunerated through royalty payments. This is common with writers, musicians and artists but has also been used brilliantly in unconventional ways.

ARM, for example, designs but does not manufacture computer chips, earning a royalty on every chip sold that makes use of its blueprints. Its designs are used in more than 90 per cent of all smartphones and tablets.[3]

Performance-based

No business has been more successful with performance-based pay than Google, whose pay-per-click revenue model was a stroke of genius. Unlike traditional advertising mediums where you pay whether people pay attention or not, Google charges their AdWords advertisers only when a visitor clicks through to their site. Another example is the 'no win no fee' model used by personal injury lawyers.

Razor and blade

In this model, a key piece of the product is either given away or sold at low cost (the razor handle), and the profit comes instead from costly consumables (the blades). A common example is inkjet printers, where the money is made selling high-priced ink cartridges, not from the actual printer; an approach pioneered by Hewlett-Packard in 1984.[4]

Subscription

Subscription models have flourished in the last few years. Customers benefit from both the predictable service and the minimal effort required to complete transactions, while providers have an ongoing revenue stream. Examples of successful subscription businesses include Dollar Shave Club, Dropbox and Netflix.

Revenue models and offerings

Whilst any species can, within reason, adapt to its environment, none can overcome its genetic makeup or basic morphology. A rhinoceros cannot fly. A goat cannot breathe under water. Similarly, because the revenue model becomes part of the genetic makeup of a business, it dictates many of its fundamental characteristics (especially when it comes to the offering) and is very hard to change.

Auctions are typically more stressful, but might result in a bargain or windfall. Subscriptions require little effort but customers might end up paying for things they never use. Flat fees make customer costs predictable, but might give them less control over their usage. In all these cases, the revenue model determines fundamental features of the customer experience and proposition, and can also affect the brand.

The recent history of Burberry offers a compelling example. In the eighties and nineties, many fashion brands saw licensing as a win-win. By licensing their brands to foreign operators, they could expand their territory quickly without having to build distribution and local knowledge. The downside was that licensees were often free to create whatever products they felt suited their local market, whether or not they fitted with the brand.

When Angela Ahrendts took over as Burberry's CEO in 2006 she quickly realised that the company's licensing policies had damaged its brand. Burberry had gone into partnership with twenty-three licensees internationally, allowing them to make everything from kilts to dog leashes. It had little control over what they made and almost none over the prices they charged. The iconic Burberry trench coat sold at wildly different prices in different markets. Overall, the brand had been decimated by overexposure and a product range that was out of control.[5]

Ahrendts concluded that the root of Burberry's problem was their revenue model, so in a courageous move, she bought back all twenty-three licences. 'I feel like I spent my first few years here buying back the company – not the most pleasant or creative task, but we had to do it,' she said.[6]

With control over the brand and the product range now centralised under her 'brand czar' Christopher Bailey (now the CEO), she refocused the business on its core heritage products. In the six years that followed, Burberry's annual sales and share price more than doubled.[7]

There are two key lessons to be learned from this story. First, that we must choose our revenue model based on what will make our offering most desirable, rather than starting with whatever model we have and retrofitting offerings onto it.

Second, that every model has a finite amount of value it can generate. As wants, needs and technologies change, the revenue models best suited to monetising those opportunities may well change too.

This explains why the revenue models used by many current high-growth businesses – Airbnb, ARM and Spotify spring to mind – are different from their more established rivals. In each case, the revenue model is not only a fundamental part of what makes their propositions desirable, it distinguishes them from the incumbent alternatives.

Revenue models and imitability

Your revenue model forms the nucleus around which the organisation is built. Once it's in place, it's hard to change. There is thus a strong connection between your choice of revenue model and how easily others can imitate you.

If a business must change its revenue model to remain competitive, management will have to bleach their brains of how the world used to work and the consequence will be no end of dilly-dallying, uproar and expense. Firms therefore change their revenue models extremely reluctantly, if at all, meaning that if you're a smart new upstart you can get a free ride in the meantime (see Deep Dive Eight: Imitability, p. 225).

Unfortunately, this sword cuts both ways. One day your own revenue model may become a limitation, and like everyone else, you'll find it challenging to change. The key is actively to question whether your revenue model is constraining your offerings, and if so, to summon the courage to change it. It's better to jump into a new model of your own volition than be pushed by a rival.

Price

Once you've established your revenue model, it's time to turn your attention to pricing. Setting the right price for a product or service is the single most effective way to maximise profitability, and relatively minor changes often have a dramatic impact. A McKinsey study of the S&P Global 1200 companies found that – assuming demand remained the same – a 1 per cent price increase would give an *11 per cent increase in profit*.[8]

To explain why pricing has such a powerful effect on profitability, here's a simplified example.

Imagine you're in the business of selling scented candles. Each candle sells for $10 and costs $8 to make. This gives you a *contribution margin* of $2 on each candle. If you sell a million candles a year this gives you $2 million of profit.

Now let's see what happens to that profit if you change either the price or the volume by 4 per cent. As the table opposite shows, a 4 per cent price increase (just 40 cents per candle) yields a $400,000 increase in profit, but a 4 per cent volume increase gives much less: $80,000.

	as is	+ 4% price	+ 4% volume
Price (per candle)	$10.00	$10.40	$10.00
Cost (per candle)	$8.00	$8.00	$8.00
Contribution margin	$2.00	$2.40	$2.00
Volume (units)	1,000,000	1,000,000	1,040,000
Total profit	$2,000,000	**$2,400,000**	$2,080,000

The reason for the difference is straightforward. When you increase volume, you incur the cost of making a candle for every extra unit you sell. When you increase price, your costs remain the same. Increasing the price is more effective because it has a disproportionate effect on *the margin each candle makes.*

This example is simplified, of course. Apart from anything else, a price change may well affect the quantity you end up selling. But the fundamental points remain the same: first, pricing has huge leverage on your profits; second, small differences can have massive impacts; and third, the amount of profit you leave on the table by slightly underpricing your product can be seismic.

See's Candies have raised their prices around 5 per cent each year since they were bought by Berkshire Hathaway in 1972. Taking cost increases into account, this means their profit margins have increased steadily by a single percentage point each year.

These small gains have added up. In 1972, pre-tax profits were $4 million. Thirty-five years later they were $82 million, without much of an increase in volume. Berkshire Hathaway reaped $1.35 billion in profit over that time period for their $25 million investment.[9]

With results like these, you'd think pricing would be an obsession in most businesses. Incredibly, though, this is not the case. Cost control and demands for extra market share typically receive more attention.

Pricing is a huge opportunity for those willing to put some energy into getting it right, and this section will help you get started down that road. You won't be a pricing guru by the end – the subject is too broad and too deep for that – but there are some basic principles that every business should understand.

Value-based pricing

All pricing luminaries agree that the price must reflect a product's value to the customer – it must reflect what they are willing to pay. However, many businesses instead set prices based on their costs, typically by applying a fixed markup or percentage margin.

This doesn't make sense for one simple reason: customers typically don't know or care what your costs are – they care what represents value to them. A 'cost plus' approach can lead you to overprice if you have high costs (as we saw with the wheelchair in Chapter Two) or to underprice if your costs are low, all the while ignoring what customers are willing to pay.[10] However you look at it, short of a lucky guess this approach leaves money on the table, either as lost volume or lost margin.

The opposite approach is far better. When launching a new business or product, you should start with the price you think customers will pay, then work backwards to the costs you can incur to generate a profit.[11]

This is a crucial point: pricing should be considered right from the very beginning of product development, not as an afterthought once you've built your product or service. By then it's often too late to fix what may well prove to be a fundamental problem.

Price setting

How do you identify what that price should be? There is a bewildering array of research techniques and methods that pricing professionals use, none of which is perfect in isolation, and we can never know exactly how customers will respond to a price. There are, however, a handful of perspectives that you can consider, each of which can help you towards the optimum price.

Start with the next best option

In Deep Dive Two: Rivalry (see pp. 85–99), I showed how to plot competitors onto a market map. Such a map reveals the price points of neighbouring rivals, and so gives you a rough price range to work within (see pp. 95–6). The next step is to choose a specific alternative – the customer's next best option – to use as a reference point to guide you towards the optimum price.[12]

If your product is demonstrably superior or your brand carries a premium, you can factor this into your pricing decision – and charge more than the alternative. If your product is superior but you don't have the brand cachet, you could sell at a similar price to a mid-market player, thus making what you have to offer a no-brainer for the customer. If your product is effectively the same in all ways as the competition, you'd be foolish to think you can charge more, especially if direct comparison between the two is straightforward.

Where there are clear alternatives, one approach to setting the price is adopting what pricing guru Hermann Simon calls the 'magic of the middle'.[13] It's based on research that suggests that in situations where customers have straightforward requirements and a large range to choose from, they tend to pick something from the middle.

Gauge price sensitivity

Price sensitivity is the extent to which price affects customer buying behaviour. As a general rule, one can expect customers to become more sensitive to the price the greater the proportion of their budget or costs it represents. That's why people negotiate hard when buying a house, but not when buying a marker pen. Customers also become more price sensitive the easier it is to compare options.

By contrast, buyers become less price sensitive the more import-ant the product or service is to them; if prices are strongly associated with quality; or if direct comparison with alternatives is difficult to make. They are also less price sensitive if they face high switching costs to move to an alternative supplier, since they'd typically rather lump a small increase in price than go through the pain of switching.[14]

There are many more elaborate and powerful techniques for establishing price sensitivity, such as *conjoint analysis* – a means of understanding relationships between willingness to pay and combin-ations of product attributes – and the Van Westendorp Price Sensitivity Meter, an analysis that helps gauge customer willingness to pay for a particular product.

Set the right expectations

A foam roller is a dense, cylindrical piece of foam used to work the knots out of muscles – a product with which I became familiar when I injured my knees.

Dièry Prudent, a personal trainer from Brooklyn, had the insight that foam rollers are, as a rule, pretty ugly, so he decided to create one that could take pride of place in the finest residences. The result was the RolPal, a handmade creation that looks like a rolling pin covered in silicon blobs.

Initially, he set the price at $189 instead of the usual $30, but nobody would take it seriously. Following his wife's advice, he upped the price to $365 and the crowd went wild: celebrities and exclusive gyms bought them; customers gushed about the product's brilliance, claiming 'nothing gets as deep'.[15]

As the RolPal demonstrates, a price is not just a number – it can carry symbolic significance, and plays a part in expressing the customer's beliefs, values and self-image. Some customers find products more appealing the more expensive they are. After all, nobody ever shouts, 'Waiter – fetch me a glass of your second-finest champagne!'

The price also sets an expectation. Products that are noticeably cheaper than alternatives will tend to be treated with suspicion. Those that are more expensive are generally assumed to be of better quality. Think of the price as an envoy for the product – what should it say about it?

Be prepared to experiment

With so many factors to consider, and no dead-certain way of knowing how customers will react, try experimenting a little to find the optimum price for your offering. This process isn't as risky as it sounds.

Customers often don't remember what they paid for things previously, making direct comparison with a previous benchmark difficult. Experiments needn't be expensive either – the Internet is an excellent environment for A/B testing different options, as prices can be changed at little or no cost.

Some degree of experimentation is no bad thing, and customer research is a must – hopefully the potential gains will incentivise you to give it a go. Remember that businesses are more inclined to underprice their products than to overprice them – you might be leaving money on the table unnecessarily.[16]

Price changes

At some point you will need to raise or lower prices to reflect changes in the environment. Setting prices is like brushing your teeth – you don't just do it once then forget about it. The golden rule is to work out how a price change will affect your margins, costs and overall profitability *before you do it.*

To illustrate the impact of price changes, let's work out how many more candles you'd need to sell to make your current $2 million profit if you lowered the price by 4 per cent. As the table overleaf shows, at the usual $10 price, the contribution margin is $2, but if you reduce the price to $9.60, it drops quite drastically to $1.60 – a 20 per cent drop.

	as is	- 4% price
Price (per candle)	$10.00	**$9.60**
Cost (per candle)	$8.00	$8.00
Contribution margin	$2.00	**$1.60**

To calculate how many candles you would need to sell to make the same profit at this lower price, you divide your current profit figure ($2 million) by the new margin ($1.60):

$2,000,000 profit ÷ $1.60 contribution margin = 1,250,000 candles

With just a 4 per cent price drop, you need to sell an additional 250,000 candles – a 25 per cent increase – to make exactly the same profit as before. As mentioned before, the reason for this massive change is simple – a small change in price has a disproportionate effect on the margin. The slimmer your margins are to begin with, the greater the effect of a price change.

Sales and price reductions are commonplace in business, but as this example illustrates, the extra volumes you need to sell to make up the profit shortfall can be far greater than you might expect. Not only that, discounting has several other downsides.

Price promotions don't always *increase* demand, they can just bring purchases forward, often causing sales to crater at a later date. The classic case study is GM's insane decision in 2005 to offer their cars to customers at the same prices they sold them to employees in a bid to increase market share. Their plan worked, in that they succeeded in driving up volume, but sales tanked immediately afterwards, residual values were demolished, and GM posted a loss of $10.5 billion.[17] Four years later they filed for bankruptcy.[18]

Regular discounting trains your customers to buy or stockpile goods when the price is low. They can also permanently devalue a product, making it difficult to raise the price later, and only boost appeal in the short term until your rivals match the new price. In a downturn, it is usually far more prudent to maintain prices and sacrifice volume.

The following approaches can help you avoid falling into the trap of giving profit-sapping discounts.

Communicate your value clearly

To protect yourself against the perils of discounting, the first step is to make sure you are communicating the value of your offering in a clear, concise and compelling way. An excellent example comes from furniture brand Vitsœ, who in the run-up to Black Friday published an article on their website entitled 'The True Meaning of Value'. Here is an extract:

> At Vitsœ there will never be a sale because our prices are always fair . . . Our prices honestly reflect the cost of people, suppliers and materials, plus a modest profit that allows us to continue investing in the long-term good of all concerned.
>
> Our approach negates the need to jostle or queue, and our commitment to quality, longevity and service gives you the assurance to make a considered investment when the time is right.
>
> Our New York shop will be closed on Black Friday, 25 November 2016, but if you need to contact our planners, they will be available behind the scenes to offer you advice on our chairs and tables, or plan a shelving system that is exactly right for you – this service is free of charge.[19]

Understanding your product and how it stacks up against alternatives gives you the confidence to stick to your price and earns you the respect of customers. Caving in and lowering prices can set an expectation in the customer's mind that they will always get a discount – something that can be all but impossible to change later.

Incentivise for profit, not revenue

To avoid profit-sapping discounts you should ensure that sales staff are incentivised correctly. In organisations where the sales force is remunerated based on the revenue they bring in, they will often win orders by offering deep discounts, without considering the impact on profits. In these situations, it's better to reward profitability than revenue.

Don't obsess over market share

Market share is often an obsession in business. A greater share of the market is taken as evidence that you are beating your rivals, and since many successful, highly profitable businesses happen to have the biggest market share, it's easy to equate it with success. A large market share is not the cause of superior performance, though, it is a by-product.

Measuring market share is a valuable exercise that can reveal changes to the competitive landscape, but obsessing over your share can lead to suicidal strategies that annihilate profits. When more than one player is determined to have the greatest market share, the heat of competition can evaporate profits for all.

With the exception of markets dominated by network effects (where the more customers we have the more valuable our product becomes), it is better to focus on creating the most desirable, profitable products you can and to allow market share to take care of itself.

Volume

The final piece of the revenue equation is volume: how often customers buy, and in what quantities. Most of this section is devoted to ways you can grow your business, if you want to. But before I go into those, it's worth considering how your brand might limit your volumes.

Your sales volumes should reflect your brand and your positioning. A low-cost player is expected to sell in high volumes, but as you make your way upmarket, increasing volume can become undesirable, especially if the appeal of your product is its exclusive nature.

For those at the top of the market, one proven way to increase volume without diluting appeal is releasing special or limited editions, which often command an even higher price.[20] The golden rule here is never to exceed the maximum number of units you advertise. If it's a limited run of five, don't whatever you do make a sixth; make a different edition and sell five of that instead.

Increasing volume using the grid

Assuming that you're not proposing to adjust prices or enter new categories, identifying ways to increase volume is a three-step process:

- First, you should select which aspect of the volume equation you want to adjust – purchase frequency or quantity.
- Second, you should decide whether that growth will be fuelled by new customers or existing ones.
- Third, you should identify which other elements of the grid can best help you achieve that goal.

For example, an online retailer could sell *more units* (quantity) to *new customers* by improving the *customer experience* – converting more prospects into sales.

Whilst in reality most businesses will pursue many approaches simultaneously, there is always a combination of those three factors behind each one: a part of the volume equation (frequency or quantity), an element of the customer base (new or existing), and a leverage point from the rest of the grid. The rest of the Deep Dive focuses on that last part – elements of the grid that can be put to work to drive up volume.

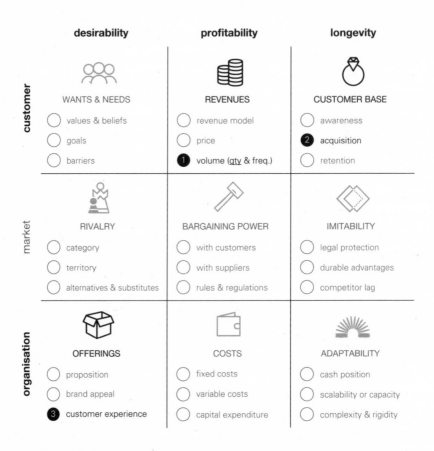

	desirability	profitability	longevity
customer	**WANTS & NEEDS** ◯ values & beliefs ◯ goals ◯ barriers	**REVENUES** ◯ revenue model ◯ price **①** volume (qty & freq.)	**CUSTOMER BASE** ◯ awareness **②** acquisition ◯ retention
market	**RIVALRY** ◯ category ◯ territory ◯ alternatives & substitutes	**BARGAINING POWER** ◯ with customers ◯ with suppliers ◯ rules & regulations	**IMITABILITY** ◯ legal protection ◯ durable advantages ◯ competitor lag
organisation	**OFFERINGS** ◯ proposition ◯ brand appeal **③** customer experience	**COSTS** ◯ fixed costs ◯ variable costs ◯ capital expenditure	**ADAPTABILITY** ◯ cash position ◯ scalability or capacity ◯ complexity & rigidity

Figure 12 An online retailer could sell more units (1) to new customers (2) by improving the customer experience (3)

Territory expansion

A common way to increase volume is to expand your territory. Workout phenomenon SoulCycle opened their first studio in 2006 in New York; their second a year later in the Hamptons. Ten years later there were more than sixty studios dotted around the USA.[21] Service businesses tend to follow the same pattern, opening offices in major cities one after the other.

Versioning your proposition

However astutely you set your basic price, there will always be potential customers who are willing to pay more, and those who will only pay less. You can increase volumes by offering different versions of your proposition at different price points.

A simple rule of thumb when versioning is *good, better* and *best*. Pricing strategist Rafi Mohammed suggests a stripped-down version for price-sensitive customers who would prefer a lower price for fewer features; a premium version with all the bells and whistles; and versions in between catering to distinctive customer needs. You can also offer custom configurations, bundles or add-ons like extended warranties.[22]

Musician Trent Reznor of Nine Inch Nails executed a brilliant versioning strategy when self-releasing the album *Ghosts I–IV*. Reznor offered *Ghosts I* as a free download in exchange for an email address; the full album *Ghosts I–IV* as a digital download for $5; a CD for $10; and a deluxe edition for $75. There was also an ultra-deluxe version for $300 – a bundle of four LPs and three hardcover books, limited to 2,500 signed and numbered copies. These sold out in less than two days, and in the first week total sales topped $1.6 million.[23]

Proposition improvements

A new and improved product can entice existing customers to upgrade, or new customers to buy. This is common with products where the underlying technology has ample room for improvement.

Some organisations have a strategy of 'planned obsolescence', deliberately releasing new versions of products that make older models unusable, or designing products that have a short shelf life so they must be periodically upgraded. Common techniques include discontinuing spare parts, making repairs impossible or prohibitively expensive, or foisting incompatibility on the old product by upgrading everything around it.

Aside from the dubious ethics of such a strategy, other downsides are the environmental cost and the risk of resentment if customers feel they are being forced into a new product they don't want or need.

Many brands are capitalising on this sentiment, making anti-obsolescence a key part of their appeal. RED Digital Cinema (see p. 95) have trademarked *'Obsolescence Obsolete'* – making a sales point of their modular design that allows individual components to be upgraded.[24]

Customer experience

Improving the customer experience can increase sales volumes by making it easier for customers to find the products they want and complete their transaction. The improvements can be substantial.

While testing an e-commerce site, experience design consultant Jared Spool and his colleagues discovered that customers were put off by an intrusive requirement to create an account during checkout. Repeat customers who had an account were often challenged by the form too, having forgotten their login details. As a fix, Jared's team replaced the 'register' button with a 'continue' button and let customers know that they didn't need to create an account to complete a transaction.

The volume of customers making a purchase went up by 45 per cent, creating $15 million in additional revenue in the first month, and an extra $300 million over the course of the first year. All by changing a button.[25]

Customer-experience improvements can increase sales volumes via both acquisition and retention. An exceptional experience not only encourages customers to complete transactions, it can increase positive word of mouth, advocacy, referrals and the likelihood of repeat purchases. I discuss retention strategy further in Deep Dive Seven: Customer Base (see pp. 191–208).

Awareness

People cannot buy a product if they don't know it exists. If you are confident that you have a valuable offering, but volumes are low, it might be that there is not enough awareness of the product, or that your brand doesn't spring to mind when the need arises.

This has always been my personal Achilles heel. Bashful Brit that I am, I was raised by my parents to believe that self-promotion (or promotion full stop) is distasteful, and that the work should do the talking. Whilst I love meeting new people, the thought of schmoozing and networking makes me cringe. I've learned the hard way, though: nothing succeeds without promotion, a topic I discuss at length in Deep Dive Seven: Customer Base (see pp. 191–208).

Finding the right approach for you

With so many possible options to increase sales volumes, it can be a challenge to know which will yield the best results. Imagine wasting a fortune on advertising when changing a button on your website could increase sales by millions of dollars. The question is, how do you decide where to focus?

A logical approach is to compare a broad range of metrics, then follow a process of elimination. Consider, for example, the table below, where each column shows a different combination of results across some common metrics.

	SCENARIO A	SCENARIO B	SCENARIO C
Awareness	**HIGH**	LOW	**HIGH**
Leads	LOW	LOW	**HIGH**
Conversion	LOW	LOW	**HIGH**
Sales/Active Users	LOW	LOW	**HIGH**
Satisfaction	LOW	**HIGH**	LOW
Problem Area	**Proposition**	**Awareness/ Expectations**	**Customer Experience**

Figure 13 A table showing how combinations of metrics highlight different opportunities to increase volume.

Scenario A

In the first scenario there is strong awareness of the product, but poor leads, conversion, sales and satisfaction; in other words, your product is a turkey. People don't want what you're selling. You've either misunderstood their wants and needs or there is a superior rival. You need to go back to the drawing board.

Scenario B

Here the service has high satisfaction, but low awareness, leads, conversion and sales. This suggests problems in two areas. First, low awareness – people don't know about you. Second, you might be mismanaging customer expectations. If people are delighted with a product and keep using it but sales are low, it could be that you aren't communicating its benefits well enough through your marketing. You might be underpromising, which is why satisfaction is so high.

Scenario C

In the final scenario, everything is going well until a prospect becomes a customer, at which point they become dissatisfied. This suggests a customer-experience problem. They must like the idea of the product or they'd never buy it, but the reality doesn't match their expectations.

In an ideal world, you'd improve the experience to meet that expectation, since your promises are generating a lot of interest and sales. Were you to lower expectations, you might not get the same interest.

The point of these deliberately simplified scenarios is to show that looking at any one metric in isolation can lead to ineffective knee-jerk decisions. Many spend a fortune on customer-experience improvements that yield few results because the problem is elsewhere. Others spend on advertising, which drives customers to a broken experience, generating little return for their investment.

Most businesses constantly attack all angles simultaneously – spending on advertising, customer-experience improvements and expansion into new territories. These may well be the right things to do – increasing volume isn't an either/or decision, and it often makes sense to pursue multiple approaches. But it's also important to consider what impact each strategy might have so that you make decisions in a targeted way rather than wasting time and money by blindly throwing everything you have at the challenge.

Key Questions

Revenue model

- Which revenue model is best suited to monetising your offering?
- What restrictions does your current revenue model put on your offering?
- How might your revenue model be limiting the desirability of your products or services?

Price

- Are you selling your product or service at the optimum price? How do you know?
- Do you manage prices on an ongoing basis, or set them and forget about them?
- How might discounting be impacting your profitability?

Volume

- Do your volume targets reflect your brand position?
- Which elements of the grid offer the greatest potential to increase your volumes?
- Do you have a broad enough range of metrics to identify the real opportunity areas?

	desirability	profitability	longevity
customer	**WANTS & NEEDS**	**REVENUES**	**CUSTOMER BASE**
	○ values & beliefs	○ revenue model	○ awareness
	○ goals	○ price	○ acquisition
	○ barriers	○ volume (qty & freq.)	○ retention
market	**RIVALRY**	**BARGAINING POWER**	**IMITABILITY**
	○ category	● with customers	○ legal protection
	○ territory	● with suppliers	○ durable advantages
	○ alternatives & substitutes	● rules & regulations	○ competitor lag
organisation	**OFFERINGS**	**COSTS**	**ADAPTABILITY**
	○ proposition	○ fixed costs	○ cash position
	○ brand appeal	○ variable costs	○ scalability or capacity
	○ customer experience	○ capital expenditure	○ complexity & rigidity

Deep Dive Five: Bargaining Power

The most valuable currency in business isn't money, it's power.

It's obvious when you stop to think about it. Those in positions of power find wealth and profit easy to come by, since they can influence events in their favour. The reality is, you don't start with profits and build a power base. You start with a power base and build profits, then let the two feed on each other.

This may sound distasteful or amoral, but it's not. Until you understand the nature of power – where it comes from, who has it and how it shapes events – you will be incapable of acting in your own interests. You will unwittingly expose yourself to exploitation and will be constantly outmanoeuvred by others.

For those in elevated positions, this understanding is even more important since those who wield their power with a brutish clumsiness soon precipitate their own downfall. Gaining power is only half the problem; learning how and when to use it is as much of a challenge.

Through the course of this chapter you will start to see the world in a different light that can aid your decision-making. Once you appreciate the power you have, you can use it effectively, rather than 'giving it away for free, and having it sold back to you', as a friend so elegantly put it.[1]

The secret is learning when to compete and when to cooperate. We instinctively think of these as opposites, but the reality is more nuanced. As Galinsky and Schweitzer explain in *Friend and Foe*, 'Our most important relationships are neither cooperative nor competitive. Instead, they are both . . . we need to understand that cooperation and competition often occur simultaneously and we must nimbly shift between the two.'[2]

Your relationships with customers and suppliers are fundamentally cooperative, yet each party is ultimately serving their own interests, bringing a competitive tension to proceedings. Understanding this dynamic, and how it can guide your decision-making, is the opening theme of this chapter.

Customer and Supplier Power

Michael Porter, a professor at Harvard Business School, rose to prominence in the eighties with the release of a magisterial tome, *Competitive Strategy*. His central theory was that the profitability of a firm depends on the structure of their industry, and that this in turn is determined by the interplay of five forces.[3] Three are concerned with aspects of rivalry: the threat of substitution, the threat of new entrants and the intensity of competition (see Deep Dive Two: Rivalry, pp. 85–99). The final two are concerned with the exercise of power, by both the supplier and the customer.

The basic theory is simple. Every business is sandwiched between its suppliers and its customers. Naturally, everyone wants the best deal for themselves. Suppliers would be happier if they could charge you more for less, since they'd be more profitable. Customers naturally seek the best deal for themselves too – financially or otherwise. Whoever has the most bargaining power in the arrangement – your suppliers, your customers or you – gets to profit the most from the arrangement.

The delicate ecology of this balance is well exemplified by what has recently happened in the West Village in New York City. On the one hand, it has never been more affluent. On the other, local businesses are going under at a frightening rate.[4] This might seem paradoxical: if there's more money sloshing around than ever, shouldn't companies in the area be doing fine? The explanation becomes clear, however, when one considers the shift that has taken place in the bargaining power of the key players.

Landlords have become more powerful, because the surge in demand for property has enabled them to increase commercial rents. At the same time, customers are not always willing to pay the tenants – the small businesses – more in order to offset their higher costs. As the bargaining power swings to the landlords, the rent goes up. The local businesses can't make a profit and they go under.

When the bargaining power in an industry changes, the impact is often seismic. The future seems unpredictable as each player jostles for position in the new order. Nobody seems sure of how the chips will fall.

Since the nature of the relationship between a supplier and your business and between your business and your customer is essentially the same – one is buying from the other – the factors that underpin both supplier power and buyer power are basically the same, allowing them to be explored at the same time. The complex interplay of these relationships is essentially governed by five principles.[5]

1. The more you buy, the more power you have

A customer who contributes a significant part of a company's revenue inevitably has more negotiating power than one who contributes a small amount, since the business will lose more if the big customer walks away.

When it comes to your suppliers, the implications are simple: if you want more bargaining power, you need to place bigger orders. Small medical practitioners and hospitals have done this by forming group purchasing organisations where they pool their resources. Individually they have little negotiating power, but add together a few thousand small practices and suddenly it's a different conversation. By placing one large order with suppliers instead of many small ones they can gain sizeable discounts.

When selecting suppliers, you should consider how important

your business is to them. The more of their sales you account for, the stronger your bargaining position. There is, however, a trade-off to be made. If a supplier fails it can threaten your own survival. Many firms are therefore careful that a supplier doesn't become too dependent *on them*. It's something that start-ups targeting big firms often experience to their cost – the fledgling firm isn't big enough to meet their target customer's criteria for supplier selection, which can mandate that their relationship only accounts for a certain percentage of their supplier's turnover.

When it comes to your customers, the same rules apply. The more customers you have, and the more evenly they contribute to your revenues, the less power they have over you. You should be wary of a single customer accounting for too much of your business because they can drive down your prices. In extreme cases, an all-powerful customer can drive such a hard bargain it bankrupts a supplier.

Basecamp, a project-management software business, is one example of a firm that understands the risk. As co-founder Jason Fried wrote in an article for *Inc.*, 'Large enterprise customers can be enticing – but they can upend your product, your staff, and the stability of your business.' He went on to explain: 'At Basecamp we believe there's strength in numbers. Not large numbers of dollars, but large numbers of customers . . . A diverse customer base helps insulate you; a few large accounts can leave you vulnerable to their whims.'[6]

2. The harder it is for you to switch, the less power you have

If you can swap suppliers at the drop of a hat without incurring penalties, you have a powerful negotiating position – you can just threaten to leave if you don't get your way. If, however, you face high switching costs, your bargaining power is weaker.

Forgetting about these switching costs is a classic mistake. Seduced by a low sticker price, customers eagerly adopt a supplier's offering, unwittingly making it central to a key aspect of their business. The pain comes later when they require some modification to the service or product, only to find the cost of doing so is outrageous. They have given their power away to the supplier, who then sells it back to them, holding crucial parts of the business to ransom.

When it comes to buying any kind of product or service, you must consider your switching costs. By the same token, the ease with which your customers can leave you will affect your bargaining power with them.

3. The more important your product, the more power you have

When a product or service is crucially important – life-saving surgery, or business-critical infrastructure – customers naturally have less negotiating power. Driving a hard bargain is too risky. There is more to be gained by cooperating than competing.

The simplest way to maintain or increase your bargaining power is therefore to pay constant attention to how customer wants and needs are changing, and stay focused on solving their most important problems.

Similarly, when a supplier is critical to the success of *your* business you should be wary of being 'penny wise and pound foolish'. I am often surprised by how poorly some businesses treat their contractors – throwing their weight around with exploitative payment terms and penny-pinching with day rates – not realising that these people are crucial to their own success. If suppliers are distracted by trying to get paid, the quality of their work will suffer, or they may refuse to continue working, delaying projects by weeks or months.

4. The more rivals you have, the less power you have

When I left university, I enjoyed some success as a freelance photographer, a field that was fiercely competitive. With so many keen to work for them, the art directors at the big magazines knew they had the strongest bargaining position and weren't shy of making it clear. With two hundred people willing to step into my shoes at a moment's notice, I was powerless to negotiate favourable terms.

The volume and diversity of options available to the customer determines their bargaining power. If all of their choices are essentially the same, you can't expect them to choose on anything other than price, driving down margins. If you don't maintain a distinctive, desirable offering, customers will walk all over you.

The same dynamic governs our relationships with suppliers. If demand for their products or services increases, or the number of alternatives dwindles, their bargaining power will increase, and with it their prices.

This explains why some firms actively encourage new suppliers into a market – to prevent a dominant provider from gaining too much power over them. In some cases, dividing a workload between two or more suppliers puts their competitive focus on each other, whilst making them more cooperative with you.

5. The more easily they could do your job, the less power you have

If I can do the job of my supplier, what do I need them for? If customers can do my job themselves, what do they need *me* for?

Where customers can easily bring the work you do in-house – a threat known as *backward integration* – it limits your bargaining power. Attempt to charge too much and they'll find someone else or just do it themselves. By the same token, if a supplier could easily do your job – *forward integration* – it limits your negotiating power too.

Over time Dell outsourced more and more of their operations to a Taiwanese supplier called Asus, starting with some basic circuitry, then motherboards and eventually their entire assembly and design. At each step the decision looked great since profits went up, until Asus integrated forwards and launched their own computer brand using the expertise they had accumulated – a situation management guru Clayton Christensen called 'a Greek tragedy'.[7]

Case study: buyer power and supplier power

Several years ago, a web-based retailer contacted me about outsourcing the design of their website. They'd met with a few agencies who were enthusiastic, and they wanted an independent consultant's opinion.

To their surprise I suggested this was a risky idea. Their website *is* their business – the only channel their customers interact with. Surrendering control of such a crucial part of their operation would give their new supplier immense power.

Over time, the supplier would take control of information and expertise that was critical to running the business, and as the creative and intellectual epicentre of the business drifted outside the office, so would the bargaining power.

As the businesses became bound together, switching costs would naturally go up – it would be difficult and expensive for the firm to manage a transition if they wanted to change partners. Losing the capacity to do work in-house would further increase the supplier's negotiating power. Costs would likely mushroom.

I suggested that a better route forward might be a few strategic hires and an investment in training. They could improve their capabilities, keep the work in-house at reasonable cost, and avoid the risk of their business being held to ransom.

As is so often the case, they had only thought about the up-front costs, and hadn't considered the longer-term implications. They shelved the plan, hired some key people and have succeeded with their in-house approach for a few years now.

Rules and Regulations

A regulation sets out the rules of the game a business must follow. It is the primary lever authorities use to control market conditions and organisational conduct. When regulations change, the implications are therefore often far-reaching, even though some may not be immediately obvious (either to the regulator or to industry participants).

The grid is a valuable tool for assessing these changes, since any regulation will affect one or more boxes. Let's look at their leverage points one box at a time.

Wants and needs

Regulators can directly affect customers' wants and needs, mostly by changing beliefs and erecting or dismantling barriers. When it comes to customer beliefs, for example, advertising is monitored to make sure products or services are described accurately.

A recent case concerns the use of the 'Made in the USA' label by America's largest watch brand, Shinola. The Federal Trade Commission requires 'all or virtually all' of a product carrying this label to be made in America, so when Shinola's watches were found to contain Swiss movements, the FTC took action. Shinola were required to update marketing copy and advertising, redesign the case backs of their watches and drop their slogan, '*Where American is made*'.[8]

Regulators can also erect a variety of barriers to discourage purchasing – none more obvious than making something illegal. By the same token, decriminalising a product can open up new markets – marijuana was recently legalised in Colorado, for example[9] – as can lowering regulatory requirements to own or operate a product.

In 2016, for instance, the Federal Aviation Authority changed the rules controlling the use of commercial drones. Instead of needing a pilot's licence to fly them, anyone over the age of sixteen who passes a background check and an aeronautical knowledge test can operate one. This has had the effect of significantly lowering barriers to purchasing and using a drone for commercial purposes, and so has opened up the market to new customers: real-estate advertisers, for example, who can now take aerial photographs of properties on their books.[10]

Rivalry

Providing subsidies or tax breaks for new entrants and putting laws in place to prevent anti-competitive behaviour are typical means of controlling rivalry. Large mergers and acquisitions generally require government approval to prevent deals that would lessen competition, and penalties for anti-competitive behaviour are common.

The European Commission have not shied away from handing out fines when they have felt that organisations have overstepped the mark. One notable case is Microsoft, who were fined $731 million for failing to offer Windows users a choice of web browser.[11] Another is Intel, whose $1.4 billion fine for anti-competitive behaviour set a new record at the time.[12]

Offerings

Regulators can directly determine the parameters of an offering, whether it be the brand, the proposition or the customer experience.

The Lanham Act, for example, states that US trademarks cannot 'disparage . . . persons, living or dead . . . or bring them into contempt, or disrepute'.[13] In 2015 a judge invoked this regulation and cancelled the Washington Redskins' trademark because it was deemed offensive to Native Americans.

Whilst the regulation relates to trademark law, the issue is fundamentally one of brand appeal. The NFL team's lawyers, who opposed the ruling, claimed the brand was worth $214 million and that the ruling diminished its value.[14]

When it comes to propositions, most products or services are subject to basic regulations, but some categories have been dramatically affected by specific rulings. The British government reduced the number of single-use plastic bags by 85 per cent in less than a year, just by mandating a 5p charge for them at the counter. That's a reduction of six and a half billion bags.[15]

In Australia, the government's Pharmaceutical Benefits Scheme subsidises only the medicines that present the most compelling value proposition. They compare each new drug to existing alternatives – in terms of effectiveness and patient safety – then negotiate a price with suppliers.[16]

Regulators will often mandate that businesses meet a minimum standard of customer service, too. OFCOM, the UK's telecoms regulator, recently handed Vodafone a £4,625,000 fine for 'serious and sustained' breaches of consumer-protection rules, specifically mis-selling, inaccurate billing and poor complaints handling.[17]

Revenues

Authorities frequently intervene directly to control revenues. In India, regulators recently capped the price of some medicines commonly used to treat cancer, heart disease and diabetes to make them more accessible.[18]

Anti-gouging laws also prevent businesses from exploiting situations that distort demand. Take the case of John Shepperson. After Hurricane Katrina, he bought nineteen generators, hired a truck and drove down to Mississippi, hoping to double his money. Instead he was arrested for price gouging, the generators were confiscated and he spent four days in jail.[19]

Costs

Tax regulations, unsurprisingly, are interesting to profit-seeking organisations. Some go to considerable lengths to minimise their bills, using techniques like the 'Dutch Sandwich' or 'Double Irish' to funnel profits into offshore subsidiaries. As I write this, Apple are appealing a €13 billion fine over a 'sweetheart' tax deal with the Irish government that was judged to have violated European state aid rules.[20]

Another major consideration is the cost of complying with regulation itself, which can run to millions of dollars a year for some firms, who dedicate entire departments to compliance. This can have a knock-on impact on rivalry, limiting competition to the firms who can afford to jump through the necessary hoops.

Customer base

Legislation can directly impact a firm's ability to attract and retain customers, often by specifically reducing switching costs. This has been common practice in the UK where regulators are systematically making switching easier in financial services, energy and telecoms to encourage providers to be more customer-centric.

Imitability

Authorities grant the patents, trademarks and copyrights that protect intellectual property – the legal means of preventing imitation – as well as provide the forums for addressing violations. When launching a new business, you must not only consider whether you can protect your idea (see Deep Dive Eight: Imitability pp. 211–34) but whether you are infringing on someone else's intellectual property.

A key part of intellectual property strategy is to determine whether you have sufficient rights to enter a category and to understand the likely cost of obtaining them if you don't. In a complex scenario, there may be thousands of patents standing between you and a marketable product – the rights to which must be licensed to avoid litigation.

Adaptability

A common criticism of regulation is the complexity and bureaucracy it brings, which can diminish a firm's responsiveness. It can take more than a decade for pharmaceutical brands to bring a new product to market – but, of course, much can change in those ten years.

That said, governments have also intervened when organisations have been unable to respond to change, even if it's their own fault. There may never be a better example than the $700 billion bailout fund the US government put together in the wake of 2008's financial crisis to help cash-strapped businesses continue operating.[21]

Conclusions

The key message of this section is that regulatory changes have far-reaching implications beyond the most common considerations – cost and competitiveness. They can affect any and every element of the grid.

It is no surprise, then, that many organisations lobby governments to influence regulations affecting their industries. Lobbying is a multibillion-dollar industry in the US alone, where it is not uncommon for a single large company to have more than a hundred lobbyists representing their interests.

The practical implications of regulation are straightforward. If you are starting a new business you must consider the regulatory environment through the lens of each box. For those already in business, when regulations change you must consider how certain elements will be affected, since one new regulation can impact many boxes simultaneously.

Perhaps a more philosophical conclusion is to acknowledge the role that organisations themselves play in bringing about unfavourable regulatory changes. The Sarbanes–Oxley Act – a set of stringent regulations imposed on public companies – was the direct result of the epic frauds committed by WorldCom, Enron and others.[22]

The Diverted Profits Tax, or Google Tax as it is known, reflects the aggressive practices of global corporations to minimise their tax bills, regardless of how such activities are perceived by the public.[23] The European ban on roaming charges was a clear response to excessive profiteering by mobile carriers.

The truth is, regulation is often simply the by-product of businesses abusing their power – an ever-present risk for those in positions of influence, and a subject worth expanding upon.

The Power Paradox – a Word of Warning

Mohamed Bouazizi made ends meet by selling fruit at the roadside in a small Tunisian town, where he faced constant harassment from authorities he could not afford to bribe.

One day, after a female police officer slapped him and confiscated his weighing scales, he marched down to a local municipal building to complain and was told nobody was available to meet with him. Overwhelmed by years of abuse and humiliation, he doused himself with gasoline and set himself on fire outside the governor's office.

Within hours, protests supporting Bouazizi began in the town, soon spreading to other cities. Efforts by the police to contain the unrest only made things worse. As years of simmering resentment came to a head, rage and violence overtook Tunisia. President Ben Ali's twenty-three-year reign was brought to an end as he fled the country.[24] Similar protests soon erupted in nearby countries, creating a wave of uprisings known as the Arab Spring. Hosni Mubarak was forced from power in Egypt, as was Muammar Gaddafi in Libya.[25] One man's resentment had permanently altered the course of world history.

Situations like this arise because of two fundamentally incompatible human traits. On the one hand, we have an innate sense of fairness that provokes strong emotional reactions when violated. On the other, power has an intoxicating effect that blinds us to the perspectives of others. The result is that those in positions of power routinely accrue dangerous levels of resentment, with dramatic consequences.

Fairness is not just a virtue, it is a universal instinct. Once our ancestors realised the merits of teamwork – whether hunting together or using specialist skills for the benefit of all – we evolved an innate sense of fairness that encouraged cooperation and reciprocation. To seal the deal, we developed equally strong emotional reactions to unfair behaviour by others: vengeance, revenge and rage amongst them, as the people of Tunisia demonstrated.[26]

A keen sense of fairness also evolved for another reason – to help safeguard our reputation. In early societies, we would frequently cross paths with other members of our tribe. If we gained a reputation for antisocial behaviour, we'd soon find ourselves ostracised and fighting for survival.

The question is, if people react with such aggression to unfairness, if it is detrimental to our reputation and if trust is so crucial in business, why would anyone attempt to exploit their customers, suppliers or workforce? The answer is simple. Once we are in a position of power we don't see the world in the same way.

One of the words most frequently used to describe the effects of power is 'intoxicating', and for good reason: power has a similar psychological impact to drunkenness. We feel invincible, becoming overconfident and reckless. We become arrogant, reacting aggressively if challenged, and most dangerously of all, we lose sight of the consequences of our actions. The laundry list of toxic side effects also includes: diminished morality and empathy, overconfidence in the support of others, increased hypocrisy, selfishness and willingness to cheat.[27]

It also results in what Dacher Keltner calls 'narratives of exceptionalism' – the belief that our own unethical actions are acceptable because we are extraordinary, whilst the same actions by others are deplorable and should be punished.[28] The result is Keltner's power paradox: in gaining power we lose touch with reality, setting in motion events that cause us to lose that power.

Few people will remember the Storm – BlackBerry's first attempt at a touchscreen smartphone – but Verizon do. After AT&T secured exclusive rights to the iPhone, Verizon needed a competitive product and greeted the prototype Storm as a knight in shining armour.

Unfortunately, after being rushed to production in just nine months, quality and design issues rendered the device all but unusable. At a meeting with BlackBerry's CEO Jim Balsillie, Verizon made their feelings on the matter clear. Almost all of the first million Storms had to be replaced, and they expected BlackBerry to pay. It was, after all, their fault. The figure they had in mind was $500 million.

Despite Verizon being their biggest customer, Balsillie refused. He knew they'd signed up to a deal that meant they were stuck with the units and had no choice in the matter, and he held them to it, even after they warned him it would damage the relationship.[29]

Soon, however, Android arrived on the scene, the new alternative shifting the balance of power in Verizon's favour. Incensed by Black-Berry's unwillingness to play fair, and armed with a superior alternative, Verizon shifted their massive marketing budgets to back Android, just as BlackBerry would face their most challenging rivals yet.

Within two years, Verizon went from buying 95 per cent of their smartphones from BlackBerry to just 5 per cent. Balsillie's distorted view of reality had conspired against him just when he needed the support of his customers the most.[30]

It is extremely difficult to use the power you have over people to enrich yourself at their expense without accruing resentment that ultimately precipitates your downfall. It has a wonderfully karmic quality to it.

Whilst Porter's work on the connection between buyer power, supplier power and profit is lucid and compelling, his analysis does not explicitly consider the long-term consequences of the power paradox, namely that the experience of having and using power can result in us losing more than we bargained for.

Exerting power over suppliers or buyers is counterproductive if it generates too much resentment. This isn't a moral argument, it's a commercial one. Resentment directly encourages new alternatives into the market; customers leave in protest as soon as they can; and it can goad governments into creating restrictive regulations that neuter your power permanently. A near-perfect case study fell into my lap as I was drafting this chapter.

In 2007, pharmaceuticals firm Mylan bought the rights to market the EpiPen – an emergency treatment for life-threatening allergic reactions – from the German giant Merck. Between then and the time of writing, sales have shot up from $200 million a year to more than $1 billion.[31]

How did a product developed in the seventies, whose ingredient has been around for a hundred years, become such a massive money-spinner? The answer is bargaining power. Let's examine the pieces of the puzzle, starting with the impact of regulation.

First, in 2008 a regulatory change allowed the product to be marketed to people who were *at risk* of an anaphylactic reaction, instead of just those who had a proven history. Next, two years later, FDA guidelines were changed to state that patients who typically received a 0.3 mg dosage should receive two 0.3 mg doses. From that point on, EpiPens only came in twin packs.[32]

Then in 2013, the Obama administration signed the School Access to Emergency Epinephrine Act, which required elementary and secondary schools to maintain a supply of epinephrine (the medicine in the EpiPen) in case a student had a severe allergic reaction on site.[33]

The net result of these regulatory changes was impressive growth to the company's customer base: over a seven-year period patient numbers increased by 67 per cent.[34] Earlier in the chapter I explained how the more customers you have, and the more evenly they contribute to your revenues, the more bargaining power you have. Mylan's growth had already made them a more powerful player, but there was more to be gained.

To further increase sales volumes, Mylan funded public-awareness campaigns encouraging patients to have an EpiPen wherever they were – in the car, at home and at work. One such campaign called 'Anaphylaxis for Reel' featured Sarah Jessica Parker talking about her son's life-threatening allergy to peanuts and imploring viewers to have an epinephrine injector with them at all times.[35]

Whilst the market had grown substantially, unusually rivalry *decreased*. In 2015, the EpiPen's only real rival, Auvi-Q, was withdrawn after some devices were found to inject insufficient dosages.[36] Another potential alternative from rival drug company Teva failed to win regulatory approval, leaving the EpiPen as the only player with a substantial presence in the market.[37]

Earlier I suggested that the more important your product is to the customer, the more bargaining power you have. I also pointed out that – all other things being equal – your power increases if there are fewer alternatives.

One can also hardly imagine a product more important than a life-saving drug, and with one rival being withdrawn from the market and the other failing to pass regulatory approval, customers had little choice but to buy from Mylan. With all that bargaining power, guess what happened to their prices – they went up.

Mylan had been steadily increasing their prices since the beginning. At first these increases were 10 per cent, twice a year, then 15 per cent increments.[38] By 2014 these raises had increased margins to 55 per cent (from 9 per cent six years earlier), but Mylan's bargaining power was still growing.[39]

A 2015 *Bloomberg* article mentioned a price increase of 32 per cent in the previous year, with commentators warning of a possible backlash if increases continued.[40] One story told of a customer reduced to tears because they could no longer afford the medicine. Others bought their EpiPens from Canada, where the cost was much lower owing to a different regulatory environment.

By 2016 any pretence at fairness – so crucial in relationships with customers – had completely evaporated. In 2007, an EpiPen cost about $57. Nine years later the price topped $600.[41] As kids headed back to school many parents found they could no longer afford the product. Mylan had taken things too far, and resentment boiled over.

A petition started by an angry New Yorker quickly gained momentum through social media, resulting in 121,000 letters being sent to Congress within seven weeks. Parents began sharing photos of receipts online, including one parent in Arizona who had paid $1,698.28 for six pens. The mainstream media soon picked up the story and both Democratic presidential candidates called for the price to come down.[42]

Reflecting the moral outrage the public were feeling, lawmakers started attacking Mylan. Senator Amy Klobuchar, whose daughter carries an EpiPen, called for a Judiciary Committee inquiry and a Federal Trade Commission investigation.[43] Another group wrote to the Food and Drug Administration enquiring about the approval process for a market alternative, ramping up pressure to bring competition to the market.[44]

Committee members also called for an investigation into whether Mylan had overcharged the government's low-income health-care programme for the treatment. This led to a $465 million settlement with the US Department of Justice after the product was found to have been wrongly classified as a generic drug.[45]

Earlier I showed how those in positions of power are prone to narratives of exceptionalism. During a televised interview with CNBC, Mylan's CEO Heather Bresch was asked whether she understood the outrage at the price increases. 'No one's more frustrated than me,' she replied.[46]

But while many of her customers were unable to afford the life-saving drug, Ms Bresch's pay packet had skyrocketed. In 2015 she received more than $18 million – a 671 per cent increase since 2007.[47] It's difficult to see how she could be more frustrated than a parent who could no longer afford life-saving medicine for their child.

Under attack from angry patients, the public, the mainstream media and the government, Mylan's share price dropped 19 per cent in the second half of August.[48] Their first attempt at damage limitation was to offer a $300 coupon to customers without health coverage or with a high-deductible policy, but this did little to quell the outrage. Within days Mylan announced that they would release an identical generic alternative to the branded EpiPen at a list price of $300 – a more than 50 per cent price reduction.[49]

It's too early to say what the long-term consequences will be for Mylan, its CEO, the EpiPen or the pharmaceuticals industry more broadly, but it's safe to say that Mylan would have preferred to avoid the brand damage, the congressional scrutiny, the likely increase to competitiveness in the market, the cost of regulatory investigations, and being forced to release an alternative product at half the list price.

Mylan's business will remain lucrative, but one must wonder whether exercising a little restraint would have been in their better interest. As usual, firms in positions of power struggle to keep it from going to their heads.

How do you reap the benefits of a strong bargaining position without stockpiling toxic levels of resentment? The following guidelines can help you find a balance.

Remember the true source of your power

Keltner's twenty years of research into the dynamics of power has led to some surprising conclusions. We often think of power as something that comes from manipulation and coercion, but his research reveals quite the opposite: power is both gained and maintained by focusing on other people. Power is granted to us when we improve the lives of others and contribute to the greater good. This makes perfect sense. The true source of any business's power is the value of their product to the customer.

Keltner suggests that the path to enduring power is simply to stay focused on others: to prioritise your customers' needs as much as your own; to maintain an empathic connection with the customer base; and to treat them with respect and gratitude.[50] In other words, treat the customer as you would like to be treated, and create the most desirable offerings you can.

Think of your reputation

Your reputation is like a battery. It stores the power that you can use to influence others. If you want to maintain a position of power, you must always keep your reputation charged.

In June 2015, Apple announced a music streaming service to rival Spotify, Tidal and Pandora, called Apple Music. To entice customers they offered a three-month free trial. What they weren't as vocal about was the fact that the artists and musicians weren't going to get royalties during these three months.

In response, Taylor Swift – one of the world's most successful recording artists – penned an open letter to Apple explaining that her latest album would not be released on the service as a protest against the way musicians were being treated. 'We don't ask you for free iPhones,' she said. 'Please don't ask us to provide you with our music for no compensation.'[51]

Apple's response was interesting. As one of the biggest companies in the world, they have incredible bargaining power and typically are not shy of using it.[52] They could have ignored Ms Swift and gone about their business.

Instead, by capitulating and changing their policy at the last minute, they reduced the risk of brand damage, avoided accruing any unnecessary resentment from the incident and made a powerful ally in the pop world.[53]

The first step when making decisions that involve exerting leverage over buyers or suppliers is to consider how it might impact your reputation. If you wouldn't want people to find out, it might be best not to do it. Pausing to consider how you want to be remembered can be a sobering tonic.

Enter arrangements with a cooperative spirit

Relationships with customers and suppliers are not a zero-sum game. The essence of trade is benefit for all. You are better off finding suppliers and customers where the dynamic is cooperative and mutually beneficial than strong-arming them into acting in your interest. If your buyers or suppliers are too powerful for you, you must look elsewhere, or improve your offerings to level the playing field.

Consider the long term

Creating resentment amongst customers has a compounding effect. First, it creates opportunities for rivals, who can capitalise on any ill will that might be felt towards you. Second, when these rival products make it to market, customers will eagerly support them as an act of revenge.

The problem with resentment is that it's both cumulative and, to begin with, largely invisible. Those in power do not see its effects until it is too late. They frequently short-change their future for a short-term benefit. When making decisions where there is a risk of accruing resentment, you must carefully ponder both short- and long-term consequences. Years can pass between cause and effect.

If you continue to create the most desirable offerings you can, and are judicious with the customers you serve and the suppliers you partner with, you can succeed without needing to gouge or frack your way to a better bottom line.

Resentment is highly destructive and its exact flashpoint is unpredictable. That the balance of power will one day shift away from you is also inevitable – it happens to every business eventually. Who will have your back when you hit troubled times? Are the short-term gains worth the long-term pains? Consider these things before turning the screw, not afterwards.

Key Questions

Buyer and supplier power

- Do you choose suppliers with bargaining power in mind?
- What factors are affecting your customers' bargaining power?
- How might changing rivalry affect your bargaining power?

Rules and regulations

- How does the regulatory landscape impact each of the nine boxes of your grid?
- Are there any upcoming regulatory changes?
- How might they affect each of the boxes on the grid?

The power paradox

- Might your decisions be creating resentment amongst your buyers or suppliers?
- What might the long-term consequences be?
- Is the risk worth the reward?

	desirability	**profitability**	longevity
customer	**WANTS & NEEDS** ◯ values & beliefs ◯ goals ◯ barriers	**REVENUES** ◯ revenue model ◯ price ◯ volume (qty & freq.)	**CUSTOMER BASE** ◯ awareness ◯ acquisition ◯ retention
market	**RIVALRY** ◯ category ◯ territory ◯ alternatives & substitutes	**BARGAINING POWER** ◯ with customers ◯ with suppliers ◯ rules & regulations	**IMITABILITY** ◯ legal protection ◯ durable advantages ◯ competitor lag
organisation	**OFFERINGS** ◯ proposition ◯ brand appeal ◯ customer experience	**COSTS** ● fixed costs ● variable costs ● capital expenditure	**ADAPTABILITY** ◯ cash position ◯ scalability or capacity ◯ complexity & rigidity

Deep Dive Six: Costs

In April 2016, Dropbox employees arrived at their office to find a chrome statue of a panda – the company's mascot – standing in the foyer. The statue, rumoured to have cost $100,000, had a note attached to it that read:

> Pandas have meant many things to Dropboxers over the years, and the idea here was to commemorate the original . . . It wasn't the right call . . . When it comes to building a healthy and sustainable business, every dollar counts. And while it's okay for us to have nice things, it's important to remember to ask ourselves, 'would I spend my own money this way?'[1]

Despite entering a phase of tightened cost control, they decided to keep 'Austerity Panda' as a reminder to be thoughtful about spending.[2]

Speaking at the Bloomberg Technology Conference, Dropbox's CEO Drew Houston shared some valuable insights. 'Costs can get away from you one day at a time; expenses that start small turn big,' he said. 'In these boom times, you get really disconnected from the fundamentals . . . You don't win by managing costs, but it's an important step for any business.'[3]

To reduce their costs, Dropbox are targeting an estimated $38 million of employee perks, which have included a Michelin-star chef on-site, an open bar and a laundry service. Dropbox have yet to generate a profit.[4]

Frugality is an admirable trait, regardless of a firm's success, and cost management an essential part of running a business. This is true for start-ups and existing firms alike – the entire lean movement is about getting to a viable product in less time and for less cost, and if you need funding, lower costs mean giving away less equity, or taking on less debt.

It is also easier to control costs than revenues. You cannot know for certain how a customer or rival will react to a price change, but you can choose what you spend money on and who you spend it with. Even though costs can be difficult to estimate or predict, you ultimately have control over your spending.

It's important to understand, though, that costs are not some single entity that needs to be addressed. They are incurred in different ways, and appreciating their source and nature makes it easier to control them.

Fixed Costs

Fixed costs – often referred to as *overheads* – are those costs that don't change with sales volume, like employees' salaries or the cost of an Internet connection. Even if you sell nothing you still have to pay them.

Whilst in reality no cost is truly independent of sales volumes – scaling a business past a certain point might require hiring additional staff, for example – treating fixed costs as a specific category is helpful because they affect the volumes you need to sell to reach or maintain profitability.

The most common source of fixed costs for most organisations is the workforce. When it comes to cost management, these people costs warrant particular attention for four reasons. First, they are usually much higher than generally imagined once associated costs beyond the salary (equipment, benefits, insurance, etc.) are taken into account; second, they cannot easily be reduced at will (laying people off is never an easy option, for both emotional and procedural reasons); third, salaries tend to go up over time; and finally, headcount tends to increase exponentially if left unchecked. Hire a manager and they'll hire a team beneath them; each of that team will want their own underlings. Soon the costs will have mushroomed.[5]

Doomed tech start-up Powa Technologies offers a fascinating and cautionary example. After raising close to $200 million in funding, the company all but abandoned cost control. Sales staff received a £2,000 bonus just for a signed letter of intent from a potential customer. The firm took up residence in the prestigious Heron Tower in London (at a cost of £6 million over three years), with additional offices in Hong Kong, New York and Europe. Then there were the parties in Mayfair with fine wines and strippers. But where they really blew the money was headcount.

In 2012 staff costs were around £660,000. Three years later they'd reached £25 million, for a start-up that was 'pre-revenue', in CEO Dan Wagner's words. In February 2016, the firm went into administration after running out of cash, an outcome the CEO described as 'one of those things which sometimes happens which is completely random'.[6]

Always consider whether a new hire is really necessary, and make sure any case for increasing headcount is thoroughly justified. If people leave the business, question whether they really need replacing or whether you could continue without them.

Variable Costs

Variable costs are ones that vary with output. You don't incur the cost of the raw materials to make a product unless you are making one, or shipping charges until you send your product out. Variable costs are hugely important because they affect the *contribution margin* – the amount of money that each sale contributes to covering fixed costs and eventually generating profit (see Deep Dive Four: Revenues, pp. 123–43). The lower you can keep your variable costs, the higher the contribution each sale makes towards profitability. A couple of simple techniques can help keep your variable costs under control: target costing and minimising waste.

Target costing

Target costing – setting maximum production costs with a level of profitability in mind – can help you keep costs down from day one. It also helps because decisions made at the design or development stage often determine the subsequent profitability of the product or service.

One business where target costing is widely used is SpaceX, the rocket and space-exploration business, whose low-price proposition relies on keeping costs down. Before starting the company, Elon Musk spent months studying the various elements that go into creating a rocket and then compiled a spreadsheet of cost estimates for building and launching it. Industry veterans then helped him refine his calculations and work towards a viable proposition.[7]

Once the business got started, Musk personally signed off any expense over $10,000, and set tough target costs. These included a $10,000 target (which they very nearly achieved) for building a rocket's computing systems, which would typically cost more than $10 million; and a $5,000 target for making a part to steer the upper stage of the rocket. That part ended up costing $3,900 – one supplier had quoted them $120,000.[8]

It is not only start-ups that benefit from target costing. Key to Lego's transformation from near-bankruptcy in 2004 to the most valuable toy company in the world was a renewed focus on cost control, including the reinstatement of strict target costing.

Product development teams were given strict full manufacturing cost (FMC) targets, including raw materials, mouldings, packaging and depreciation charges on equipment. The ability to meet these targets became part of the designers' annual review to ensure they were taken seriously.[9]

SpaceX and Lego also demonstrate another key point about target costing, and cost reduction in general. The secret to success is often simply persistence and individual accountability, as veteran cost manager Andrew Wileman explains. 'For tough cost management you have to have single primary accountability,' he says. 'Once the people in your organization believe that you'll keep on asking until you get a good answer, they'll come up with the goods. But you have to earn that belief with tenacity and single-mindedness.'[10]

In Tesla's early days under CEO Martin Eberhard, an operations expert sent in by an investor found that production costs had soared out of control. The cost of producing each car could apparently reach $200,000 – more than double the sales price. After the CEO was dismissed by the board, an intense cost-reduction programme was put in place.

At 7 a.m. every Thursday, employees gave a bill of materials update, presenting the current cost of every part with a plan for getting it down. These costs were tracked every month, and if people failed to reach their targets there were severe consequences.[11]

If an organisation expects its employees to save money, the leadership must set the tone themselves. There may be no better example of this than Ingvar Kamprad, the billionaire founder of IKEA, who realised that leaders must act as role models if they expect employees to pay attention to costs. He flies economy, wears second-hand clothes, and even tries to get his hair cut when visiting developing countries to save money.[12]

In his 'IKEA Bible' *The Testament of a Furniture Dealer*, Kamprad details his philosophy. 'Time after time we have proved that we can get good results with small means or very limited resources ... Wasting resources is a mortal sin at IKEA,' he writes. 'Expensive solutions to any kind of problem are usually the work of mediocrity.'[13]

Jørgen Knudstorp took a similar approach when he was tasked with turning around Lego. He believed that 'breaking the back of the culture' was crucial to achieving the necessary cost reductions to avoid bankruptcy.

He closed offices, moving people into smaller facilities in the belief that large spaces gave people a feeling of abundance. He also sold the head office, moving the leadership team into a packing plant to reinforce a sense of scarcity, and shunned executive transport in favour of a modest Citroën.[14]

Eliminate waste

No discussion of cost management would be complete without mention of the Toyota Production System (TPS), a revolutionary approach to manufacturing that allowed Toyota to set new standards for quality at a greatly reduced cost.

A central TPS theme is the continuous drive to eliminate waste: any operation that does not add value to the final product or service.[15] Four sources of waste are common:

- *Overproduction* – the cost of manufacturing and storing excess inventory is wasteful.
- *Waiting* – paying staff to be inactive is wasteful.
- *Overprocessing or incorrect processing* – inefficient processes soak up time, poor processes result in defective products, and products of higher quality than necessary waste resources.
- *Defects* – the production of defective parts can be highly disruptive and time-consuming.

The last of those – defects – is the one I have noticed most clearly in my work life. As projects progress, mistakes become ever more expensive to correct. A faulty component discovered during assembly may slow production, but that's still cheaper than shipping a customer a faulty product. An inherent design flaw may require complete recalls, or even cost lives if it makes it all the way through to the finished product.

A simple way to reduce costs, then, is to address potential issues as early as possible. For a manufacturer, this means inspecting the quality of raw materials when they arrive at the facility, not just when the finished product comes off the line.

Extending this idea beyond the realm of production, product development teams should also use basic checklists to eliminate weak ideas, and create low-cost prototypes or pilot programmes to test new ideas as soon as is practical. These simple steps can help avoid the biggest waste of all – creating products that aren't desirable.

Cost Structures

The main reason the grid distinguishes between fixed and variable costs is because it is crucial to understand the interplay between them when making business decisions. To explain why, let's start by looking at the break-even equation – a vital calculation to establish the viability of any offering:

$$\text{break-even volume} = \frac{\text{fixed costs}}{\text{price} - \text{variable costs}} = \frac{\$50,000}{\$10 - \$8} = 25,000 \text{ units}$$

You break even when you make enough from your sales to cover your fixed costs. In the example above the *contribution margin* is $2 on each unit (the $10 price minus $8 variable cost), which means that 25,000 units will have to be sold to cover the $50,000 fixed costs. After that the venture will be making a profit.

As this calculation shows, price and cost changes have a huge impact on profitability because they move the break-even point. In the example above, a price increase of just 50 cents would mean breaking even 5,000 units earlier.

However, the calculation also shows how a change in the *proportion* of fixed and variable costs affects profitability. A firm with low fixed costs but high variable costs will break even sooner, but will have lower margins past that point. A firm with higher fixed costs but lower variable costs will take longer to break even, but past that point will make larger profits, relatively speaking.

The proportion of fixed and variable costs your business incurs – its *cost structure* – matters enormously because it has a powerful influence on what products you can make profitably, who you can compete against and at what price points, and your ability to adapt. To illustrate, let's imagine two businesses making the same amount of profit in totally different ways.

Matt's Candles buys the wax, wicks and packaging pre-made from three different suppliers. This means his business has low fixed costs – it doesn't need the facilities or staff to make those things. However, because each supplier has those overheads and must make a profit themselves, he pays more for each component than if he made the parts himself.

Louise's Candles has a different approach. They make everything themselves from scratch. This means they have higher fixed costs – they own the machines and employ the staff who make wicks, wax and packaging – but have lower variable costs, since they aren't paying suppliers as much for those things.

This difference between these two cost structures, or the *operational leverage* as it's called, has a deep impact on the product and pricing strategies the two firms can follow, and on how price changes will affect them.

Since Matt's business must pay his suppliers more for every candle, his *contribution margin* – the amount from each sale available to cover his fixed costs – is smaller than Louise's. With each sale making a smaller margin, if prices fall he will need to sell a lot more candles to make the same profit as before.

By contrast, Louise's business has a much higher contribution margin. Whilst neither business would want prices to fall, should competition become price-based, Louise's business should find it easier to sustain itself.

If prices stay the same but demand drops dramatically, Matt's Candles will be in a better position, since he doesn't have the same level of fixed costs to cover through his sales. He is also in a better position if he must change direction suddenly, since he can just stop buying candle parts, and start buying something else.

This brief foray into the world of cost structures explains why businesses that compete on price (or a combination of low price and high quality) and sell in high volumes tend to be *vertically integrated* – doing things themselves rather than buying things in from suppliers.

An example of this logic in action is Harry's – a business that set out to offer high-quality men's shaving products at a low price. To deliver this combination of quality and price, they made two crucial make/buy decisions.

The first was to sell their products direct through their website rather than paying retailers to stock them, which cut variable costs per sale. The second was to buy a factory in Germany that had been making razors since 1920.[16]

By making their own razors, Harry's have gained complete control over product quality and a cost structure where fixed costs are higher (since they own a factory) but variable costs are lower (since they aren't paying a supplier for a finished product). This gives them a higher contribution margin on each sale whilst eliminating the possibility of their razor supplier driving up prices or becoming a rival – launching their own products onto the market themselves.

The key point bears repeating. Your cost structure has a powerful influence on what products you can make profitably, who you can compete against and at what price points, and your ability to adapt. Fortunately, you can – to an extent – decide what your cost structure looks like, since it depends on whether you do things yourself or pay suppliers to do them for you.

Suppose you are starting a consultancy business. Demand at the beginning may be uncertain – you might have periods of intense activity followed by lulls. In this situation, you want your costs to be variable if possible, so they can go up or down with demand.

You could start by using a network of associates – independent consultants keen to work on ad hoc projects. This makes your labour cost variable since you only pay them when they are working, but your profit margin will be relatively low.

Once you've grown or demand has stabilised, you might hire full-time employees at a lower rate than independent contractors. This makes the cost fixed, since you must pay them whether there is work to do or not, but when they are on assignment your margins will be much larger.

Not all make or buy decisions will have a profound impact on your cost structure, and even if they do you must consider your decision from a multitude of perspectives, something the grid can help you with. Here are the key elements to consider.

Total cost of ownership and economies of scale

A supplier may be able to perform an activity at a much lower cost than you could ever achieve. Their size might give them economies of scale that you could never match, or they might operate in a geography with lower costs. It might be that you simply can't afford to bring things in-house because of the investment required.

To compare options, when considering outsourcing you must calculate the total cost of ownership (TCO) rather than just looking at the headline figures. What will happen to your variable costs? Will they go up or down? What will happen to your fixed costs and capital expenditure? Bear in mind that unless people are laid off or existing machinery is sold, there may be no cost reduction through outsourcing in the real world.

Bargaining power

A change in bargaining power is a longer-term risk of outsourcing. If you lose your ability to perform an activity, the supplier could increase their prices once you're dependent on them. They might gain experience from working with you that allows them to become a direct rival in the future. High switching costs might lock you in even if the arrangement is unfavourable. These are crucial factors to consider before you decide to outsource.

Imitability

Before outsourcing an operation you should consider whether it contributes to your inimitability. If what is being produced is straightforward or predictable, there's little risk in outsourcing it to a low-cost provider. If, however, it plays a crucial part in distinguishing you from your rivals then outsourcing could weaken your competitive position. If all the players in the market end up outsourcing their operations to the same suppliers, there is no long-term advantage at all – cost or otherwise.

Offerings

Saving the most important until last, you must consider how outsourcing might have an impact on your offerings. If the supplier goes out of business, will it leave you unable to provide your service? If their service level or product quality suffers, will it damage your own proposition or customer experience? If the decision to outsource messes with your offering, it might be a false economy.

Cost Reduction

Businesses can easily lose control of their costs. When the money is rolling in, it's natural to be a little more indulgent. When the emphasis is on growth, cost management often takes a back seat. If a business makes expensive, premium products it's tempting for it subconsciously to apply that premium mentality to its own expenses, needlessly spending more than it should.[17]

It may also find that 'what goes up can't come down'. Once a particular budget or perk becomes a matter of habit, it becomes an expectation rather than a privilege, making it hard to cut back.

The emphasis in a well-run organisation should be on careful day-to-day cost management, rather than periods of excess followed by deep cuts. It's much harder to reduce an expense that's already been incurred than to prevent it from happening in the first place. If you find yourself in a position where costs are starting to spiral out of control, or sense that there may be an opportunity to reduce them, the following guidelines may prove useful.

Good data is crucial

One theme underpinned the cost issues at both Tesla and Lego that I explored earlier in the chapter – poor data and reporting. In Tesla's case people didn't like the software that tracked costs so some didn't use it, whilst others just guesstimated their costs.

When CFO Jesper Ovesen took the reins at Lego in 2003, he discovered an organisation in financial disarray. With no robust accounting system, the organisation had no idea where they made or lost money. They didn't know the cost of making individual products or whether sets were profitable or not. At the time, they were running a $160 million negative cash flow and were on the verge of defaulting on $800 million in debt.[18] What gets measured gets managed. You can't control costs without knowing what they are.

Prioritise

Once you've identified your opportunities for reducing cost, you need to prioritise them. Andrew Wileman recommends a simple approach in his book *Driving Down Cost*. He suggests plotting opportunities in a two-by-two matrix, as shown opposite.

The top left are the obvious priorities, since they provide the greatest returns and are easiest to do, followed by the top right, which are also straightforward to implement. Next is the bottom left, where the gains may be worth the effort to implement them, then finally the bottom right, since they offer the least reward for the most effort.[19]

Consider the rest of the grid

It's crucial that cost-cutting doesn't compromise other elements of the business. A classic cautionary tale comes from the world of contact centres, where the trend for moving them offshore to low-cost countries led to declining levels of satisfaction among customers; as a result, having a domestic contact centre has become a selling point. It's also important to make sure that over-zealous cost reductions

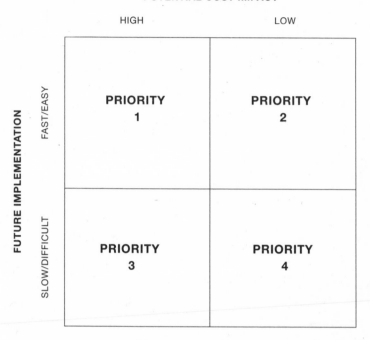

Figure 14 A simple approach to prioritising cost reduction opportunities.

don't mean you underinvest in the future. As ever, the lesson from the grid is to take a balanced view that considers the business as a whole.

Capital Expenditure

So far I've been looking at operating expenses. Now let's turn to capital expenditures. First, what's the difference?

Operating expenses are those incurred to keep the business going day to day, such as rent, insurance or raw materials. These operating expenses are subtracted from a firm's revenues to yield a figure for that year's profit.

Capital expenditures are longer-term investments, like machinery, computer equipment or buying a factory. They don't show up on the profit and loss statement in the same way, since the cost is spread over many accounting periods.

Instead, capital expenditures are shown as assets on another statement – the balance sheet – and only their *depreciation* (the amount those assets go down in value over the year) is shown as a cost on the profit and loss statement.

For example, if I spend $20,000 on a computer system, I show that as an asset on my balance sheet. If it's reckoned that that system is worth $18,000 a year later, I put a $2,000 depreciation cost on my profit and loss account for the year and decrease the asset value on my balance sheet by the same amount.

How can you tell if a purchase is an operating expense or capital expenditure? The answer is, it depends. Some class capital expenditures as items that are expected to generate revenues for more than a year. Other companies classify anything over a certain amount as a capital expenditure. It's not always black and white, so it's no surprise that some tasty accounting scandals have involved capitalising operating expenses.

WorldCom fraudulently reclassified line costs – fees paid to phone companies – as capital expenditures rather than operating costs to disguise their declining profits and bolster their share price. When their internal audit team discovered that their superiors had deliberately misreported $3.8 billion of operating expenses it created one of the biggest accounting scandals in history.[20] The company filed for bankruptcy,[21] CEO Bernard Ebbers went to prison for a twenty-five-year stretch,[22] and an unamused Congress passed the Sarbanes–Oxley Act to try to stop such a thing happening again.

Whether it's an operating expense or a capital expenditure, the reality is you are still spending cash, and cash is what really matters. Spreading that cost over future accounting periods doesn't make it go away, so it's important when making capital expenditures that you carefully consider the returns they are likely to generate.

There are many ways to evaluate a capital expenditure. None are perfect, all of them rely on assumptions and estimates, and not all of them are strictly financial. Some expenditures that look great on paper can be pointless. Others that defy straightforward quantification can be of obvious value.

My aim here is to introduce a generic approach to constructing a robust business case. There are already plenty of brilliant resources online to help with the numbers, and several excellent books on the subject already written, so I'll focus on the logic behind the formulas, rather than the calculations themselves.

If you have an idea for a capital expenditure, I suggest the following approach to building the business case:

1. Consider the constraints.
2. Estimate the total cost.
3. Estimate the benefits.
4. Calculate the return on investment.

1. Consider the constraints

Imagine you run an airport and your goal is to get arriving passengers through to their waiting families as quickly as possible. The process involves border control, collecting baggage from the carousel, then passing through customs. Where should you invest your money for the best results?

The logical answer is to identify where the bottleneck is and tackle that first. There's no point speeding up border control if it causes an enormous backlog at the baggage carousel. There's no point speeding up the baggage carousel if the bags arrive there half an hour before the passengers – that just creates a pile-up of luggage at the belts.

This line of thinking is – in a nutshell – Goldratt's theory of constraints and it has direct application when prioritising capital expenditures.

Just as the weakest link determines the strength of the whole chain, the constraint on a system limits its entire performance. If you have a factory that uses five machines and one of them can only produce half the number of parts a day as the others, that machine limits the productivity of the entire factory. Improving things that don't impact the constraint is an inefficient use of money, since those improvements or cost savings will exist only on paper and not in the real world.

Identifying constraints helps you prioritise capital expenditure. After all, if you have capacity that massively outstrips demand, any investment in expanding capacity is clearly a waste of money. Conversely, if you have far too many orders coming in, ramping up advertising spending is equally pointless: you don't have capacity to deliver those orders promptly and it will just further degrade the customer experience.

Whilst a thorough exploration of the theory of constraints is beyond the scope of this chapter, you don't need to be a guru to apply the essence of the idea.[23] Thinking about constraints leads to better investment proposals, can nip wasteful ideas in the bud, and can encourage people to see themselves as part of a bigger whole – all positive outcomes.

2. Estimate the total cost

Once you've passed the constraint test, the next step is to estimate the *total* cash outlay required. Be sure to include any ongoing costs for the useful lifetime of the investment: maintenance, installation, training, staff time, so on and so forth.

Be as thorough as you can with estimating both the useful life of the equipment and the total cost of ownership. Consider getting help from someone who has made a similar purchase before.

3. Estimate the benefits

This is the most difficult step, since the future is inherently uncertain and benefits can be difficult to quantify. Some investments that help you comply with regulations or avoid unacceptable risks are necessary, even if they produce a negative return on paper. The grid helps because it allows you to think through the impact of an investment on every element of the business.

Let's say you're a bank, considering whether to overhaul your systems to make applying for a mortgage easier. You could start by estimating the impact on converting prospects into customers. You could then consider how it might affect awareness if your improvements generate positive word of mouth. Next, you could estimate how these increases might impact overall sales volumes. Then you could turn your attention to costs. Could your investment save you money through moving more customers to a lower-cost channel? Working around the grid box by box can help you identify the benefits of your proposal.

4. Calculate the return on investment

Once you know your costs and benefits, the final step is to calculate the return on investment. The most popular approaches are the *payback* and *net present value* (NPV) methods.[24] Even if you never perform these calculations it is useful to understand them since it offers a glimpse behind the curtain at how finance teams decide which projects are approved.

The payback method
This is the quickest but least useful approach. You take the total cash outlay and divide it by the extra cash it generates each year to calculate when the investment will have paid for itself. For example, if I invest $3 million in a new machine that saves me $1 million a year in cash, the payback period is three years.

The payback method gives a quick sense check to see if an investment will pay for itself in a sensible timeframe and can also be useful for comparing proposals. But it doesn't tell you the actual returns you'll generate or whether they are acceptable to the business.

The net present value method
What makes the net present value method more useful is that it provides an actual return on investment figure and tells you whether it exceeds the company's *hurdle rate* or not.

The hurdle rate is the minimum return that investments must generate to be approved by a company's finance department. It's based on the returns the business needs to generate to keep the people who supply the funds happy, such as shareholders who expect a return for their money or lenders who receive interest payments on the money they've loaned the business. A company may set different hurdle rates depending on how risky the request is – it could be 12 per cent or 20 per cent depending on how bonkers your proposal is.

The method is called 'net present value' because it takes the cash you think your investment will generate over the coming years and translates it into how much money it would be worth if you had it today.

If the result of a net present value calculation is a positive number, the project is forecast to generate a return that exceeds the hurdle rate and stands a good chance of being approved. If it's zero, or a negative number, the forecast returns don't exceed the hurdle rate and the business would be better off investing the money in something else.

If, for example, your finance team calculate the NPV for your proposed investment as $50,000, this tells you that your investment exceeds the minimum return required by your hurdle rate by $50,000. Understandably, the formula to perform this calculation is quite complex, which is why Excel has an NPV function and there are financial calculation apps both online and for smartphones, so you don't have to do the calculations yourself.

Evidently this approach, as with any other, is not without its downsides. First of all, if garbage goes in, garbage comes out. A precise return figure isn't necessarily accurate because the equation still relies on assumptions and estimates. Being conservative with your estimates and testing different assumption sets – higher costs and lower benefits – will help you see if your investment still looks favourable.

Second, the figures can be massaged and manipulated to make the sums work. As the chief financial officer at a friend's previous company would ask: 'Do you want the spreadsheet black or red?'

By messing with the hurdle rate, the estimated cash flow and the initial outlay, it's not too hard to make a project look appealing. The only solution is for finance to interrogate the proposal rigorously and question the assumptions with sceptical hats on.

Finally, as with the theory of constraints, just because the sums make sense on paper doesn't mean they'll translate into returns in the real world. If your projections apply to a piece of equipment that sits behind a bottleneck there may be no benefit at all. Something to bear in mind.

Key Questions

Fixed costs

- What are the biggest fixed costs within the business and could they be reduced?
- Are headcount costs under strict control?

Variable costs

- Do you hold people accountable for cost reductions?
- Where could you eliminate waste from your operations?

Cost structures

- What is the optimum cost structure for your business, considering your offerings, price point and volumes? How might that change over time?
- How does your cost structure impact the other elements of the grid, like rivalry, imitability or adaptability?
- How might your current cost structure be limiting your strategic options?

Cost reduction

- Are your management accounts good enough for you to make informed decisions about costs?
- How might a decision to reduce costs impact the rest of the grid?

Capital expenditure

- What is the key constraint in your business? How would your investment impact it?
- What is the benefit of the expenditure? How does this translate into cash over the lifetime of the investment?
- What would the return on investment be?

	desirability	profitability	**longevity**
customer	**WANTS & NEEDS** ◯ values & beliefs ◯ goals ◯ barriers	**REVENUES** ◯ revenue model ◯ price ◯ volume (qty & freq.)	**CUSTOMER BASE** ● awareness ● acquisition ● retention
market	**RIVALRY** ◯ category ◯ territory ◯ alternatives & substitutes	**BARGAINING POWER** ◯ with customers ◯ with suppliers ◯ rules & regulations	**IMITABILITY** ◯ legal protection ◯ durable advantages ◯ competitor lag
organisation	**OFFERINGS** ◯ proposition ◯ brand appeal ◯ customer experience	**COSTS** ◯ fixed costs ◯ variable costs ◯ capital expenditure	**ADAPTABILITY** ◯ cash position ◯ scalability or capacity ◯ complexity & rigidity

Deep Dive Seven: Customer Base

Businesses fail either because they leave their customers or their customers leave them. That's the conclusion business historian Richard Tedlow came to, and it's hard to argue against.[1] A healthy customer base is key to any business's longevity. But how do you build one in practice? There are three moving parts to consider.

First, customers can't buy something they don't know exists, and even if they've bought before they can easily forget about you. Building and maintaining **awareness** of your brand is therefore a vital activity.

Second, that awareness should lead to **acquisition** – new customers joining your business. Without acquisition there's no customer base to begin with, and if you don't continue to win new customers, your growth opportunities are limited.

Finally, your customer base won't grow if existing customers leave at the same rate as new ones join. **Retention** – keeping hold of the customers you've worked hard to win – is, consequently, also an important consideration.

Awareness

In 2004, two firms launched wearable cameras for recording action sports: GoPro and Contour. Nick Woodman, GoPro's founder, became a billionaire.[2] Contour went out of business. What accounts for the difference?

'We spent our money on great product and distribution, leaving nothing left to compete against GoPro in the marketing arms race,' explained Contour's founder, Marc Barros. 'I learned a very hard lesson . . . The best product doesn't always win, the product everyone knows about does.'[3]

People cannot buy a product they don't know exists, and we instinctively prefer the familiar. It's entirely possible, as GoPro demonstrated, for customers to prefer one product to another simply because they're more aware of it.

If you're already spending money on raising awareness but sales are still low, you might conclude that people just don't want the product. Before jumping to that conclusion, though, make sure your advertising is effective. These simple guidelines can help.

Have a clear objective and measurable success criteria

Effective communication begins with a clear purpose: to inform, persuade or encourage an action. Before undertaking any communications work you must be clear as to what you're trying to achieve, and how you'll measure your success.

This sense of purpose is often absent, even from multimillion-dollar campaigns and website redesign projects. Yet the fact remains that without these guide rails you'll haemorrhage cash on directionless work, with no idea whether you're succeeding or not.

Have a clear audience in mind

In the early nineties the microprocessor was a computer component few knew existed. One brand saw this as an opportunity and decided to focus their marketing efforts on consumers themselves, rather than just on computer manufacturers.

That brand was Intel and the results of their 'Intel Inside' campaign make it one of the most successful in history. Within a few years both Intel and Pentium (their key product line) were household names. Buyers clamoured for machines with the Intel sticker on the box, whether or not they knew a semiconductor from a lightning conductor – a clear result of Intel's determined focus on that audience.

Create distinctive assets

A distinctive appearance helps customers notice your product in the first place and recognise it again in the future. A distinctive asset can be anything that makes you stand out, like your logo, colour choice or name.

Ideally, you want to create what Laura Ries calls a 'visual hammer' to nail the brand into the customer's mind. EasyJet's orange, McDonald's golden arches and the chrome finish on Airstream trailers are all great examples.[4]

A brand director I know has a simple approach to this, called the logo swap test. The idea is to take your packaging, advertising or website and see what happens if you put a rival's logo in place of your own. If it doesn't look obviously wrong, confusing or out of place, your appearance isn't distinctive enough.[5]

Remind them of you

I recently arrived home to a strange advert hanging over the handle of our front door. It featured a large photo of a baby wearing a chef's outfit and sitting in a cooking pot, surrounded by fresh vegetables. Above it a headline read: 'What's cooking with home values in your neighbourhood?'

Nothing about this advert makes you think of property sales. Instead you think of babies, cooking, or cooking a baby, none of which is helpful. This is a surprisingly common mistake. Ensure your communications remind the customer of you: your category, your product and your brand – not something else. I only gave it a second glance because I'm constantly on the lookout for fresh case studies!

Manage expectations

A customer's satisfaction is shaped by their expectations, and these in turn are largely created by the product or organisation with which they are dealing. A mismatch between what is promised and what is actually experienced can prove disastrous.

I know of one firm, for example, that ran a campaign informing customers that their service engineers arrived on-site within four hours on average. Customers fixated on the 'four hours' part of the message, ignoring that this was just the average response time, and so were disappointed with anything slower, which happened half the time.

The firm would have been much better off had they promised visits within, say, six hours – and then met their target consistently. It's always as well to examine the expectations your communications set and consider whether you're meeting them.

Craft a simple message

It's a tragic waste to craft a compelling proposition but then fail to communicate it effectively. All too often, especially on social media, adverts don't even tell potential customers what the product on offer actually is or does. Only very familiar brands can afford to take this kind of risk.

It's also important, when communicating a proposition, to focus on the key selling points, not list every one that comes to mind. The more rationales promoted, the fewer are remembered. As a friend of mine put it: 'If you throw me one orange at a time I can catch them. If you throw me ten at once I won't catch any.'[6]

Apple, who usually excel at product marketing, fell into this trap when releasing the Apple Watch. It was marketed simultaneously as a fitness tracking device, a status symbol, a fashion accessory, a new way to communicate, a notification tool and a timepiece. Prices ranged from $349 to $17,000.[7]

The problems here were twofold. First, the message was confusing.

If I was looking for a fitness tracker, was I buying a status symbol by accident? If notifications were the key rationale, why was the product so expensive? Each message conflicted with the other.

Second, different rationales call to mind different alternatives against which the proposition is judged. Those in the market for a fitness tracker might consider a Fitbit – an alternative with strong rationales: a discreet wrist presence, better battery life, water resistance and a lower cost. Those wanting a status symbol might consider Cartier or Rolex, which have heritage and longevity on their side. By promoting so many rationales, the Apple Watch wasn't the *obvious, easy choice* for many situations.

Contrast this with Marine Layer clothing ('Absurdly soft shirts'[8]), Headspace ('Meditation made simple'[9]) or even the original iPod ('A thousand songs in your pocket'[10]) and the challenge for the Apple Watch becomes clear: the compelling pitch wasn't there yet. Ideally, we want to be able to express our proposition in one or two crisp sentences.

Apple have clearly become aware of the problem. The marketing for the Apple Watch Series 2 offers a much tighter rationale, focused on health and fitness and including a partnership with Nike.

There is still a luxury element on offer – a partnership with Hermès, and a ceramic case edition – but the uppermost price is currently $1,499, not $17,000.[11] Apple's message is far simpler and I suspect the product will be more appealing as a result.

Identify your triggers

People might find your offering appealing in principle, but still fail to think of it when the need arises. This is especially common when adopting your product would require customers to change ingrained habits. In these situations, you must discover the cues that cause customers to act, and raise awareness as close to these times and places as possible.[12]

Simplehuman, who make kitchen and bathroom accessories, have a mobile app that enables users to reorder liners for their trash cans. Rather than emailing or sending mailshots about it, they place advertisements for the app within the free bag of liners that comes with the bin. Customers are thus reminded of the app at the perfect moment: when they're just about to replace a liner.

Appeal to the emotions

Numbers and performance figures are too abstract to be engaging. Facts and product details might pique our interest, but they don't get us moving. If you want people to do something, you need to provoke an emotional response.

Social-change activist Kristen Grimm provides a simple guideline to achieve this: evoke feelings that empower – hope, anger, pride, admiration or joy – rather than those that deflate – guilt, fear or shame.[13]

Insurance companies have often relied on fear of loss and dull statistics to sell their services, neither of which is particularly effective. GEICO, however, have taken a different approach, communicating their sales message via funny adverts that have often captured the public's attention.[14] Since adopting this approach in 1994, they have gone from the eighth- to the second-largest car insurer in the U.S.[15]

TransferWise, a service for sending money abroad, have capitalised on another powerful emotion that compels us to act – anger. By raising awareness of the hidden fees that banks charge, they have made themselves seem the obvious alternative. To date they have handled more than £3 billion in foreign transfers.[16]

Maintain a consistent, continuous presence

Finally, you cannot hope to establish your brand in people's minds if you are inconsistent: if you're constantly changing your message, style, appearance or tone, or making a big show one moment and then disappearing from view, you won't get noticed. High-performance brands are consistent, finding creative new ways to tell the same old story.[17] It is only through repetition that brand associations become deeply engraved in the customer's mind.

Acquisition

In *How Brands Grow: What Marketers Don't Know*, Byron Sharp explains why, in his view, acquiring customers offers most brands a greater opportunity than retaining them. Imagine, he says, that you are a car manufacturer who maintains a steady 2 per cent market share even though half your customers change brands when they're choosing a new model.

You might understandably elect to improve your market position by focusing your efforts on retention. And if you did, and you managed to stop all your old customers leaving, you would, of course, build your customer base by 50 per cent. That would be a great result. And yet, Sharp points out, that only amounts to 1 per cent growth in market share (from 2 per cent to 3 per cent). Even if you retain everyone, that's the best you will do.

Now consider acquisition. If half of all new car buyers in your category switch brands each time they buy a new vehicle, that means that 50 per cent of the entire market is up for grabs. Acquiring new customers is therefore self-evidently a much larger growth opportunity than simply retaining what you already have. In this simple example, it's *fifty times* bigger.[18]

'In market after market the potential gains from acquisition dwarf the potential gains from reducing defection,' Sharp says.[19] Citing research from a cross-section of industries, he concludes that in almost every case 'It was good customer acquisition that led to growth, and poor acquisition that caused decline.'[20]

He also points out that new customers can drive word of mouth more powerfully than existing ones. Because the brand or product is new to them, they are more likely to talk about it than an existing customer for whom it's old news.[21]

I can bear personal testimony to the truth of this. Recently, I bought some Bose noise-cancelling headphones before a flight and was astonished at how good they were. The usual background noise of the plane disappeared almost completely. Raving about the headphones to a friend, I was met with a whimsical smirk – they'd had a pair for years but hadn't thought to mention them.

Sharp's research has several implications for marketers.

First, that acquiring new customers is essential not only to maintaining the brand, but to growing it. There will always be some existing customers who leave for reasons beyond your control, and campaigns that explicitly aim to attract new customers are – according to Sharp's research – far more likely to improve key metrics like sales and profits.[22]

Second, that you should try to reach people who are infrequent or light buyers because they generally constitute a very large sector of any given market. To remind them that you exist, you will need to advertise extensively.[23]

Finally, marketing to already loyal customers is pointless because their behaviour is unlikely to change much as a result. 'Overinvesting in already highly loyal customers, while neglecting to reach new buyers [is a commonplace mistake],' he says.[24]

It might be that a renewed focus on acquisition could be the key to growing your business. If you've geared your awareness efforts towards acquisition; if you're confident your communications are clear and compelling; and if, even then, you're still not attracting new customers, the chances are that there is a problem with your basic proposition and you need to revisit the desirability column of the grid to root out where that problem lies.

Retention

Acquiring new customers is only half the battle. Once you've got them you want to keep them, and many, unlike Sharp, argue for a skewed focus towards retention. Three supporting arguments are particularly common.

First, the cost of selling to an existing customer is usually lower than acquiring a new one; second, existing customers often spend more when they do shop; and third, if you'd like your customers to be loyal to you, you should be loyal to them in return.

The concepts of 'loyalty' and 'retention' are joined at the hip, and a passionate, committed customer base is the holy grail for many marketers. In reality, though, loyalty to a brand is not the same as loyalty to a husband, wife or sports team. Nobody should expect customers to be monogamous. When it comes to brands, loyalty is more about inclination than devotion – a slight preference, rather than outright rejection of alternatives.

Most customers are also slightly loyal by default, since we are creatures of habit, and generally risk- and effort-averse. I've used the same pet insurer for years but not because I'm devoted to the brand. The renewal is automatic every year, the price seems fair, and I can't be bothered to shop around. It's a marriage of convenience, not a genuine romance.

As this example shows, customers don't have to be obsessive loyalists to be retained. You just need to keep giving them reasons to stay, whilst minimising reasons to leave, both of which can be designed into your offerings. The following approaches can help.

Retention/loyalty schemes

A popular approach to increasing loyalty is to implement some form of rewards programme. Such schemes typically involve offering points (like frequent flyer miles), discounts on future purchases (buy nine coffees and get the tenth free), or access to privileges (VIP events, a higher level of service, or advanced previews).[25]

Advocates point to two key benefits. First, if you reward your customers they will buy more or show a marginal preference for your brand over another. Second, the insights you can glean from buyer data can help you target promotions, identify new product opportunities and enhance your decision-making.[26]

Cosmetics brand Sephora's loyalty programme Beauty Insider is a good example. They use a points-based currency, encouraging customers to spend their way up to VIB Rouge status in exchange for exclusive privileges – granted to those spending over $1,000 a year. They also use the data from the scheme to enhance the customer experience by recommending relevant products. According to Bridget Dolan, the VP of Interactive Media at Sephora, 80 per cent of all their transactions run through the Beauty Insider programme.[27]

Loyalty schemes are not, however, without their downsides. Some argue that they don't actually increase loyalty at all – people just have loyalty cards for all the brands they frequently shop with. They can be difficult to turn off once started, and the ongoing cost of managing them is typically underestimated.[28] Moreover, research by Capgemini found that 89 per cent of social media sentiment on loyalty programmes was negative, typically because the rewards were not relevant to the customer or the customer experience was poor. However well intended, businesses seem to struggle with the execution.[29]

Critics rightly argue that reward schemes can sap potential profits from customers who would have paid the full price anyway, and it is no surprise that Byron Sharp, whom I mentioned earlier, is a vocal opponent. His reasoning is logical enough.

He points out that the most loyal buyers are the ones who are most likely to notice the loyalty programme in the first place. Typically, only customers who already buy the brand see the benefits of joining, which limits their ability to generate real growth.

Furthermore, the economic rationale for joining a loyalty scheme is strongest for the heaviest buyer, who is rewarded for doing what they already do. If the customer is truly loyal, they would keep buying anyway. By implementing a loyalty scheme, Sharp argues that companies needlessly decrease the profitability of repeat customers.[30]

Insights from Joe LaCugna, the director of analytics and business intelligence at Starbucks, suggests these advantages and disadvantages can be reconciled. Speaking at a big data conference in 2013, he explained that Starbucks uses the data from their loyalty programme to reward customers they think might not come back, rather than their most loyal customers. On the topic of rewarding ultra-loyal customers devoted to Starbucks, he quipped: 'Why would we give them a discount?'[31]

Contractual terms

Loyalty programmes aren't the only way to stop customers leaving. You can – depending on the offering – mandate it with contractual terms that penalise customers for switching. Cancellation fees, minimum contract periods, lower rates for longer-term arrangements – these are all strategies that businesses use to stop their customers defecting.

However, these measures risk degrading the customer experience, can create resentment and lead to negative word of mouth. If you're dependent on fine print and hoodwinking customers with terms and conditions, it could be that your offering needs a rethink.

Personalisation

The more a customer invests in tailoring a product to their specific needs, the less likely they are to abandon it. An obvious reason why a customer can be reluctant to change banks is because they have all their direct debits set up with their existing account details. Similarly, I'm discouraged from leaving Spotify because I'd need to rebuild my existing playlists in the new alternative. By encouraging customers to configure your service to best suit their needs, you can discourage them from leaving.

Cross- and upsell

A simple way to sell more to existing customers is to introduce complementary products or to expand your range into adjacent categories, especially if your product is an infrequent purchase. Makita make great drills, renowned for their quality and longevity. If they are going to retain customers it won't be by making them buy a new drill every year – planned obsolescence is the opposite of what their brand stands for.

Their best bet is to create complementary or additional products that customers might buy to go with the drill – like a rotary saw or a demolition hammer – which is exactly what they do. Creating cross-selling opportunities is a straightforward way to sell more to existing customers for many kinds of business.

Ecosystems and reduced inter-operability

Taking cross-selling a step further, if you can combine your products into an ecosystem where all the parts fit together, the customer's switching costs rise and the likelihood of them leaving goes down. This is one reason why bundling products is such a common phenomenon, especially if the individual products are relatively undifferentiated.

A related technique is to reduce the interoperability of complementary products. Canon lenses won't work on a Nikon camera. Some devices use proprietary cable or socket designs or require specialised tools to work on them. Some computer games are only available on certain platforms.

These are all techniques used to increase switching costs for the customer. You just need to be careful that the benefits outweigh the potential frustration from customers who may find the intentional lock-in distasteful.

Habit-forming

Products that are habit-forming will benefit from high repeat usage, with the added benefit that customers don't require constant prompting to keep them coming back. Ethical concerns are front and centre on this particular point. Is it right to design a product to be addictive? Is it right to systematically engineer the 'bliss point' of a foodstuff to make us crave it – regardless of the health implications? Managers, regulators and consumers are all stakeholders in this important discussion.

That said, habits and automatic behaviour are an intrinsic part of what it means to be human, and evidently not all of such behaviour is 'bad'. There is no reason why certain habits can't help people improve their health, save money, perform random acts of kindness, or any other positive outcome.

Increase satisfaction, or is it desirability?

Last but not least, there is a largely unquestioned relationship between satisfaction and loyalty. If you want customers to be loyal, you just need to increase their satisfaction, or so the thinking goes. As I have written a book on customer experience you'd think I'd agree whole-heartedly, but I don't.

Yes, a deeply satisfying experience means I'm more likely to come back or stick around than with a dissatisfying one, so if retention is sliding, taking a look at satisfaction scores and how you might improve the customer experience can be a good place to start. But there is a risk here of oversimplifying a complex issue.

I was satisfied with my Motorola Razr until I got my first iPhone. I was satisfied with my Shure earphones until I bought my Bose head-phones. I was satisfied with Flickr until Instagram came along. Being very satisfied with one product doesn't mean I wouldn't be more sat-isfied with another.

I'm not alone in thinking this way. Ray Kordupleski arrived at a similar conclusion when working at AT&T as far back as the late 1980s. One year they ran 60,000 surveys a month with 95 per cent of customers saying they were satisfied, only to lose six points of market share (worth $3.6 billion) that year.[32]

On further scrutiny of their data he gained two key insights. First, that willingness to repurchase tails off dramatically for satisfaction scores that are below excellent. He found that only customers who rated AT&T as truly outstanding were likely to show something approaching true loyalty. In other words, a marginal increase in satisfaction may not be enough.[33]

Second, that what counts isn't whether your satisfaction scores are going up or down, it's how they compare to the alternatives.[34] It's entirely possible for your ratings to go up while you are losing customers to a rival.

The risk with an exclusive focus on satisfaction is that it may blind you to other issues. Sometimes doing the same but better simply isn't enough. You are on far safer ground if you focus on increasing the overall desirability of the offering. You must always question where you should focus your attention to get the best results.

Acquisition and Retention Metrics

High acquisition rates suggest strong awareness, effective communication and a compelling proposition. Low retention can suggest low satisfaction, a poor customer experience, changing wants and needs or a more appealing rival.

What should your priorities be? To find out you must first make sure you're measuring the right things, then compare and contrast these metrics to understand the dynamics of your customer base. There are a slew of popular metrics that can help.

Customers (or active users)

This metric is simply the number of customers or active users the business has during a given time period. Knowing whether your customer numbers are going up or down is an obvious indicator of whether your efforts to acquire and retain customers are working.

The biggest challenge is agreeing on what constitutes 'a customer' and applying that definition consistently. Measuring households, account holders or policies, for example, might give you different perceptions on the data, which may skew your results.[35]

Retention (and churn) rate

Your retention rate is the percentage of customers who stay with you when they could choose to leave. For example, if 10,000 people get to the end of their mobile phone contract in June and 7,000 stay, the retention rate is 70 per cent. The churn rate is the proportion who leave – in this case 30 per cent.[36]

The retention rate can help you determine whether your existing customers are satisfied, whether the customer experience you offer is good enough, and whether your proposition is still competitive.

Customer profitability

Understanding which of your customers are profitable and which are not is immensely useful, since it helps you determine which kinds of customers you want to acquire and retain.

If it's costing you more to serve a customer than you make from them, you may be better off letting them go. Conversely, if you find one group of customers significantly more profitable than others you should set out to acquire more customers of the same profile. Understanding customer profitability can also help shape your loyalty programme to make sure you don't needlessly compromise margins.

Customer lifetime value

The aim of customer lifetime value (CLV) is to calculate the financial value of a customer over the entire duration of the relationship. Knowing the typical lifetime value of a customer can help determine how much it's worth spending both to acquire and to retain them.

CLV is not without its limitations, though. Lifetime values can vary dramatically between individual customers, and as with any forecasting approach, the figures are an estimate, not a fact.[37]

Acquisition and retention costs

These equations – the cost of acquisition and the cost of retention – are simple. You take how much you spent on acquiring new customers and divide it by how many new customers you got, then do the same for retention.[38]

The figures can reveal how effective your campaigns and loyalty programmes are, and can suggest changing market conditions. If the cost of acquisition is rising, for example, it may be a sign of increased rivalry or that your category is reaching saturation.

The difficulty is knowing how much you spend on each – acquisition and retention – and whether they are truly distinct. As with many things data-related, it sounds easy in theory, but it can be difficult in practice.

A word of warning: the cost of acquiring new customers should be of crucial concern to start-ups. All too many do not include it in their initial cost calculations, the result being that when they do later come to factor it in they realise either that it is impossible to generate a profit or that the company will run out of funds before a sufficient number of customers has been acquired.

You should try to estimate acquisition costs up-front, basing your calculations on the likely cost of advertising and on possible conversion rates, and include these in your break-even calculations so that you avoid any nasty surprises down the line.

Net Promoter Score and the Word of Mouth Index

The Net Promoter Score (NPS) is a popular means to assess customer loyalty, advocacy and satisfaction, in part because of its simplicity. To implement it, the business asks its customers a single question: *How likely is it that you would recommend our brand/product/service to a friend or colleague?* (Scored on a scale of 1 to 10.)

Anyone who responds with a 9 or 10 is classified as a *promoter* – likely to make positive referrals to other potential customers. Those who score 7 or 8 are *passive*, while those with 6 or below are classed as *detractors* – likely to spread negative word of mouth. To arrive at your NPS, you subtract the percentage of detractors from the percentage of promoters and you have a single number.[39] Even better, Bain – the creators of the metric – claim a link between NPS scores and organic growth.[40]

It's easy to see why this approach has been so popular. It is not, however, without its shortfalls. Consultant Larry Freed, whose findings are based on millions of customer satisfaction surveys, concludes that 'as a management tool, NPS just does not work.'[41] His investigation found that the simplification of respondents into three buckets masked significant differences between scores. Those who rated themselves as a 10 were 57 per cent more likely to purchase than those who gave a 9, though both were labelled simply 'promoters'.[42] Freed also found that results often overstated true detractors by 260 to 270 per cent.[43]

To counter the problems he believes to be inherent in NPS, Freed suggested a new metric called the Word of Mouth Index (WoMI). This supplements the classic Net Promoter question with another: *How likely are you to discourage others from doing business with this company?* By including this additional question, he claimed we can better understand customers' true word of mouth behaviour by identifying the genuine detractors.

Calculating the WoMI score is simple. You subtract the percentage who gave a 9 or 10 on their likelihood to discourage from the percentage who gave a 9 or 10 on their likelihood to recommend.[44]

This keeps the appealing simplicity of the original Net Promoter Score, whilst enhancing its value to the business. Freed has been quick to point out, however, that even the Word of Mouth Index is still just one number, and he rightly advocates drawing on a variety of sources to monitor customer behaviour and make informed decisions. This bears repeating – it's only by tracking multiple metrics that you gain an accurate picture of where to focus your efforts, and the true health of your customer base.[45]

Key Questions

Awareness

- Would you pass the logo swap test? Is your product easy to recognise?
- Can you clearly explain your product in a couple of sentences?
- Does your communication reinforce your rationales?
- Do your communications have an emotional appeal?

Acquisition

- Should acquiring new customers be a stronger priority for you?
- What proportion of your sales comes from light or infrequent buyers?

Retention

- What techniques will have the greatest impact on retention?
- Can you improve satisfaction enough to create true loyalty?

Acquisition and retention metrics

- Are you measuring the right things?
- What are the metrics telling you?
- Where do the greatest opportunities lie for your business?

	desirability	profitability	**longevity**
customer	**WANTS & NEEDS** ○ values & beliefs ○ goals ○ barriers	**REVENUES** ○ revenue model ○ price ○ volume (qty & freq.)	**CUSTOMER BASE** ○ awareness ○ acquisition ○ retention
market	**RIVALRY** ○ category ○ territory ○ alternatives & substitutes	**BARGAINING POWER** ○ with customers ○ with suppliers ○ rules & regulations	**IMITABILITY** ● legal protection ● durable advantages ● competitor lag
organisation	**OFFERINGS** ○ proposition ○ brand appeal ○ customer experience	**COSTS** ○ fixed costs ○ variable costs ○ capital expenditure	**ADAPTABILITY** ○ cash position ○ scalability or capacity ○ complexity & rigidity

Deep Dive Eight: Imitability

If customers want what we're selling, competitors will want a piece of the action. When this happens, our future depends on how easily rivals can copy us, as Meerkat, a social media start-up, discovered.

Investors were excited by their live-streaming mobile app, but there was a wrinkle in the plan: streaming your videos is pointless without anyone to watch them. To overcome this barrier, Meerkat registered users with their Twitter accounts. *Voilà!* A ready-made audience. But whose customers were they really – Meerkat's or Twitter's?

On the same day Meerkat announced that they'd raised $14 million of funding, Twitter made their own announcement. They had acquired a similar service called Periscope.[1] Soon after, Meerkat was blocked from piggybacking on the Twitter network.

By the following Sunday, Periscope was charting in the top-thirty apps. Meerkat had tumbled out of the top 500.[2] A few months later Meerkat had thrown in the towel, unable to compete not just with Twitter but with Facebook, who had launched a similar offering.[3]

As this story demonstrates, it's an obvious truth that it is easier to survive if our ideas stay out of our rivals' reach. The harder we are to imitate, the better. If our whole product is just a new feature to a competitor, we're not going to last long. However, imitability is often not an active consideration when product ideas are being formulated.

A three-pronged approach helps keep imitators at bay. We can seek **legal protection** – patents, trademarks and copyrights. We can build **durable advantages** – such as a unique cost structure or product ecosystem. Finally, we can create **competitor lag** – constantly moving forward so rivals must aim at a moving target.

Legal Protection

A friend introduced me to the AeroPress coffee machine a few years ago and I've used one every day since. It works a bit like a large syringe. After mixing the coffee grounds and water, you squeeze the brew through a filter into the cup below.

This design has several benefits: the coffee tastes great, it takes only a minute to make a cup, and the little puck of grounds left behind can be disposed of without causing a mess. More than a million Aero-Presses have been sold to date.[4]

The design is protected by a patent, and for good reason – imagine what would happen if anyone could copy it. Once it proved popular, other manufacturers could pile in with their own model and whoever had the biggest brand or distribution network would capture the market. As the AeroPress demonstrates, if we can exercise a legal right to prevent others from copying our intellectual property (IP), we should strongly consider it.

Intellectual property rights fall into four broad categories: patents, trade secrets, copyright and trademarks. These are worth a whopping amount of money – around 40 per cent of the total asset value of all corporations – so understanding a little about each is essential, not only because such knowledge can inform decision-making at a very fundamental level, but because it can reveal opportunities we might otherwise never have considered.[5]

Patents

A patent excludes others from making, selling or using an invention (without permission) for a number of years. Patents can be used as a shield or a sword – to deter rivals from copying us, or to attack those who infringe our rights. We can also license our patents for use by other businesses.

Patents are granted for inventions – typically machines, processes or manufacturing techniques – but usually exclude abstract ideas like mathematical models or business methods.[6] To qualify, an invention must be new, non-obvious, and must also have been kept a secret.

Acquiring a patent is expensive and time-consuming. Experts are required to draft the documentation and there are filing fees to pay. In total, obtaining a patent can cost anything from $10,000 to millions of dollars. But this is small change compared to the cost of taking legal action to defend one. A typical case costs $3 million to $10 million[7] and defendants only win a dismal 26 per cent of the time.[8]

When people do win, however, the payouts can be extraordinary, often running into the billions. These enormous windfalls have led to the business of 'patent trolling', where a non-practising entity (NPE) buys patents just to seek out potential infringers and sue them.

Having a patent is also no guarantee people won't copy you, especially if they think you can't afford to litigate. Andreas Pavel, inventor of the portable cassette player, found this out the hard way. He patented his design in 1977, two years before the first Walkman was released, but Sony only paid out the millions that rightfully belonged to Pavel after a twenty-year legal battle, by which point Sony founder Akio Morita had passed away.[9] James Dyson struggled to get anyone interested in manufacturing his bagless vacuum cleaner so decided to go it alone. But once his product became a hit, his challenge became stopping rivals like Hoover from infringing his patents.[10]

Part of the problem is that anyone can see a patent after its publication. This can help rivals design a copycat product around the specific wording of the patent, or can expose the idea to rivals in countries where the patent isn't registered. Rather than protecting an invention, it can actually make one easier to imitate.

With this in mind, patents are best used when an invention is highly valuable, visible, straightforward to imitate or likely to be discovered by another inventor. They are not the only option, though. Making a design difficult to reverse engineer is one alternative. Another is to keep it a secret.

Trade secrets

A trade secret is confidential information that gives a business an advantage.[11] To prevent a trade secret from leaking out, it will need to be protected by either physical or technological security measures and by non-disclosure agreements that carry penalties if broken. When in 2007 a Ferrari engineer shared a secret dossier with arch-rival McLaren, for example, court cases followed in Italy and Britain. In addition, McLaren were fined $100 million by Formula One's governing body, the FIA.[12]

Should you patent something or keep it a secret? Many grapple with this difficult decision. Patents are expensive, visible to all and eventually expire. Keeping something a secret often costs less and can last indefinitely. However, if somebody discovers your invention independently, you've no legal protection if you don't have a patent. You can't prevent them from copying you. They might even patent the idea themselves.

Copyright

Art, music, film, writing and other creative works are protected by copyright, which grants the owner exclusive rights to reproduce, distribute, perform or display them. Once a work exists in a concrete form the copyright is automatically granted to the creator at no cost.

Deciding what constitutes an original work is not always straightforward, as Vanilla Ice found when his hit 'Ice Ice Baby' was deemed to infringe on Queen and David Bowie's 'Under Pressure'.[13] But the more immediate practical problem is that copyright can be difficult to enforce, particularly now that digital technologies have enabled piracy on such an unprecedented scale.

In many instances of copyright infringement, strict enforcement may simply not be realistic: it can, for example, be very difficult or time-consuming to force a website to take down copyrighted material, particularly if that website operates from another country. Large organisations will often have no choice but to resort to court action, but individuals sometimes find ingenious ways of bowing to the inevitable: some musicians, for example, accept that their music will be pirated and capitalise on this by regarding it as a form of advertising for live concerts.

Attitudes to intellectual property also vary from country to country. Some Chinese car brands, for example, have cloned the designs of their European rivals, who are powerless to stop them. Jaguar Land Rover's Ralf Speth was understandably upset at the launch of the LandWind X7, which looks almost identical to the Range Rover Evoque but is a fraction of the price.[14]

Trademarks

The most valuable asset for many businesses is their brand. The iconic Coca-Cola bottle, Intel's catchy jingle and McDonald's' golden arches are worth a lot to their owners because they help their products stand out, help customers recognise them and are emblematic of the qualities, reputation and appeal of the business.

Trademarks prevent rivals from duping customers into buying a product that isn't the real deal, and reduce the risk of confusion about who makes a particular product. Microsoft, for example, agreed to change the name of their cloud-based storage service, SkyDrive, after a British court ruled that it infringed the trademark of broadcaster BSkyB, whose channels have names like Sky Sports and Sky Movies.[15]

Trademarks typically cover names and logos, but can also include other distinctive features like a colour, shape or sound. The better known and more distinctive a brand, the stronger their case is likely to be in court.[16]

A trademark costs money to register, but typically far less than a patent. As with other forms of intellectual property, the bigger cost is enforcement. Luxury goods, fashion, pharmaceuticals and even food are commonly counterfeited, in clear violation of intellectual property rights. Counterfeit goods are thought to make up 5–7 per cent of world trade, a figure that has grown as the Internet has made distribution easier and production has moved to countries with weak protection.[17]

For many brands the cost of enforcement is prohibitively expensive. I can only imagine how much Oakley, Rolex or Louis Vuitton might have to spend to stop even a small fraction of the knock-offs of their goods finding their way to market. Some indication of the scale of the problem in just one sector is provided by the Federation of the Swiss Watch Industry, which reports that one million counterfeit Swiss watches were seized in 2016 alone, along with the removal of an equal number of online adverts selling them.[18]

Businesses are finding they must pursue multiple avenues: educating their customer base about the differences between genuine and counterfeit products; making sure their goods aren't escaping through the back door of the factory; and pressuring law enforcement to stop the inflow of fakes at the border.

Managing intellectual property

If you don't carefully manage your IP, you can put your business at risk or miss opportunities.

The first step is to get organised, cataloguing your assets and confirming who actually owns the rights to them. Many businesses assume that they own the rights to something when they might not. For example, in the absence of an explicit arrangement, a contractor can own the rights to an invention even if they are being paid to work on it by the client.[19]

You should also have clear policies and procedures to protect your IP. Employees and suppliers need to understand what they are signing up for when they do business with you. It's one thing filling contracts with legalese, it's another making sure that people within a business understand what it means – often they do not.

A lot of freelancers and contractors squiggle their lives away on a piece of paper without realising what they've agreed to. If you're an independent expert with any intellectual property of your own, make sure you aren't signing it away to your clients!

Finally, you should carefully consider your attitude to your own IP, and how it can best be put to work. As John Palfrey explains in his book *Intellectual Property Strategy*, you have three options when it comes to managing your assets: full exclusion, partial exclusion and open access.[20]

Full exclusion

The most obvious approach is to zealously protect your assets. Bose offer an example of a brand pursuing such a strategy. They have not shied away from asserting their rights in both trademark and patent litigation.

In a recent filing against Beats for infringing their noise-cancellation patents they made their strategy clear: 'Because Bose invests heavily in research and development, and because Bose has built its reputation on producing superior products through innovative technology, Bose's continued success depends in substantial part on its ability to establish, maintain, and protect its proprietary technology through enforcement of its patent rights.'[21]

A full exclusion strategy can stop competitors from copying you, or at least force them to cough up if they do, but there are downsides. Not only does it cost a lot, it can make you lazy – with money rolling in from patent litigation, why build anything new?

The Wright brothers are a case in point. After patenting their solution to controlling a flying machine, they defended it ferociously, suing anyone who attempted to make an aeroplane. Unfortunately, they were so focused on defending their precious patents that they neglected to put them to good use and the US aviation industry fell far behind Europe's until the government stepped in to break the legal logjam.[22]

At the same time, an overly zealous approach to full exclusion can cause resentment and brand damage. To the layman, for example, it seems absurd that Warner/Chappell would exploit their copyright to

'Happy Birthday to You', but they did – charging thousands for the rights to use it in a movie scene, for example. This continued until early 2016 when a judge ruled the copyright claim invalid. Warner/ Chappell paid $14 million to settle the suit against them.[23]

Partial exclusion

Partial exclusion, by contrast, gives a select group access to your intellectual property, usually through licensing deals. Licensing can be hugely lucrative if you own valuable patents or trademarks, not least because it tends to generate cash at little marginal cost.

Executives at 20th Century Fox were surprised when George Lucas passed up a $500,000 directing fee in exchange for keeping the merchandising rights to *Star Wars*, but it was a stroke of genius on his part. In 1978 alone, more than forty million *Star Wars* figures were sold.[24] Merchandise sales from *The Force Awakens* are expected to top $5 billion in 2016 – more than the combined ticket sales of the entire franchise.[25]

Another example of partial exclusion is patent pooling. In this scenario, member firms share their patents with one another for mutual benefit, and to avoid expensive litigation. The first example of a patent pool in the US was the 'Sewing Machine Combination', formed in 1856. At the time the intellectual property necessary to make a sewing machine was mostly in the hands of four businesses and one individual, who were stuck in the 'patent thicket' – a legal spaghetti of overlapping infringement claims – with everyone's products and profits suffering as a result. By combining their intellectual property into a trust, these manufacturers could pursue mass production at far lower costs and the market took off.[26]

Since then, patent pools have become especially popular for complex technology products, where overlapping claims would make it near impossible for anyone to create a desirable product, and where an established standard is therefore to everyone's benefit. The appeal of the pool is lower product-development costs and less time and money wasted on litigation. It can, however, be complex and time-consuming to form – often requiring the bargaining power of an industry leader to get the ball rolling.

Open access

This approach allows anyone to make use of your intellectual property, which can make sense in some cases. In a market dominated by network effects, establishing your technology as the industry standard might work best in the long run, and sharing ideas for free might raise awareness of your brand.

If you are trying to encourage other players to enter your category to help it grow and gain credibility, removing the threat of IP litigation lowers barriers for potential entrants. That's why Tesla switched to an open-access model for their electric-vehicle technology.

'Tesla Motors was created to accelerate the advent of sustainable transport,' reads a blog post on their website. 'If we clear a path to the creation of compelling electric vehicles, but then lay intellectual property land mines behind us to inhibit others, we are acting in a manner contrary to that goal. Tesla will not initiate patent lawsuits against anyone who, in good faith, wants to use our technology.'[27]

Which approach works best? The sword and shield, licensing or open access? There are no easy answers – it depends entirely on the situation. The key is to maintain a flexible approach, always asking how the intellectual property you own can best advance the goals of the business.

Durable Advantages

The term *competitive advantage* has been a fixture of boardroom chat since Michael Porter's 1985 book of the same name. Since then, as with all business jargon, the spotlight has bleached its meaning, so let's start with a definition.

A competitive advantage is any benefit that allows a business to outperform its rivals. Two tests can determine whether you have one. First, you should be more profitable than your strongest competitor.

It would be hard to claim a competitive advantage if you make less money than rivals, and comparing yourself to the weakest in the pack is cheating. Second, your relative market share should be stable (or growing) over time. If new rivals are pouring into the market or you are losing share to competitors, it's hard to support the idea that you have an advantageous position.[28]

Applying these tests, one conclusion should be apparent. Most who claim to have a competitive advantage – especially a durable one – are kidding themselves. There are, however, some firms with genuine advantages over rivals, and understanding where these advantages came from helps us replicate them.

Chain-linked activities

How has furniture giant IKEA managed to stay dominant for so long? The answer, according to strategist Richard Rumelt, is *chain-link logic*.[29]

What makes IKEA special isn't the catalogue or website, or the self-assembly furniture, or the enormous warehouse-style stores, or the appealing design of the products – it's the combination of all of them. To outperform IKEA you can't just copy one of these things, you need to do them all. Mastering the necessary skills – product design, cost control, logistics, e-commerce – then linking them together is all but impossible for a new entrant.

One way to build a competitive advantage, then, is to create a proposition that requires a unique combination of skills or activities to deliver, where all are necessary to succeed.

Lower costs and economies of scale

If a litmus test for a competitive advantage is higher profits than your rivals, lowering costs is one approach. This is difficult in practice because most cost-cutting measures are easy to replicate. Whether you outsource, insource, move production to countries where labour is cheap or adopt clever processes and systems, it's hard to stay ahead indefinitely. It is also very difficult to reduce costs beyond a certain point without messing up the offering.

Some firms do manage it by fanatically paring back costs wherever they find them. Jim Sinegal, co-founder of Costco, famously changed the packaging of their cashew nuts from a round to a square container to fit more onto a pallet, saving 400 truck journeys a year.[30] Supermarkets Aldi and Lidl have barcodes on all sides of their products to make them quicker and easier to scan at the checkout.[31] The cumulative effect of many such decisions can result in a competitive advantage.

A more effective route to a cost advantage is often a fundamental rethink of the product and how it is sold and distributed. Here, the advantage stems from a different cost structure, not just operating more efficiently.

American Giant can sell high-quality clothing at affordable prices because they take the money most clothing brands spend on marketing and distribution and put it into making a quality product. They can provide quality at lower cost because they don't spend money on paid advertising and glitzy stores.[32]

Mattress brand Casper have a cost advantage over traditional mattress retailers because they offer only one model (less inventory), vacuum-packed into small boxes (lower storage and shipping costs) and sold direct to customers online, rather than through huge showrooms (lower distribution costs). Casper sold $20 million of mattresses in their first ten months – an incredible achievement.[33] Whether they have a durable advantage over similar online rivals is a different matter.

Economies of scale can also provide a durable advantage, the source of which is twofold. With fixed costs spread over a much larger number of customers, the average cost of serving each goes down. And larger firms have much greater bargaining power with their suppliers, getting greater discounts than smaller rivals.

You cannot, however, assume that operating at a larger scale automatically brings economies of scale, or a cost advantage. You need to make sure that the average cost of serving customers is actually declining as you grow.

Retention

If your customers can't or won't leave you, that means you may have a durable advantage over your competitors. As Deep Dive Seven: Customer Base demonstrates (see pp. 191–208), four factors may be in play here:

Switching costs
These are contractual or operational difficulties in moving from one brand to another, like penalty fees, effort, training costs or the risk of a bodged transition.

Habits
These are ingrained patterns of learned behaviour that have built up over time, like constantly checking social media feeds for updates, or buying everything from Amazon on autopilot.

Loyalty schemes
These involve building up points leading to future discounts or special offers with one brand that deter us from using another.

Ecosystems
These are a set of products that work together, making it hard to switch one without switching them all.

Location, location, location

Despite broken appliances and ancient air conditioning (which matters when summer temperatures top 40 °C), I rent the cabin I'm now writing in because of one thing – the view.

The cabin is nestled high in the Santa Monica mountains and looks out over a shimmering lake. The view from my desk is like a postcard – the perfect place to think and write undisturbed. The location is almost impossible to beat.

Similarly, a business occupying a uniquely desirable or convenient location has an advantage over its competitors because it is more likely to be chosen by potential customers or clients, often on account of being more visible. Location can also be an advantage for businesses that are near to suppliers or raw materials since their costs will be lower than those of rivals who are further away.[34]

Network effects

The value of some products depends on the number of people who use it, a phenomenon known as the *network effect*. A telephone is only valuable if there's someone to talk to on the other end. The more people you can connect with, the more valuable it becomes. The same is true for a software platform like the App Store. The more consumers you have, the more developers you attract. The more developers you have, the more apps become available to customers and the more valuable your platform becomes.

Network effects create markets that can lock in customers and raise entry barriers at the same time, making the potential returns enormous. This is a fascinating and much misunderstood topic, and whilst only relevant to a small number of businesses, when it matters it *really matters*. With that in mind, I've included more detail in a separate section at the end of the chapter (see pp. 229–33).

Government protection

Governments sometimes deliberately reduce or eliminate competition, bestowing a durable advantage on the chosen ones. Saudi Aramco, the world's largest exporter of crude oil, for example, is owned by the Kingdom of Saudi Arabia.[35]

In other cases, regulations inadvertently raise barriers to entry because new firms cannot bear the financial burden of getting into the market. For example, the cost of meeting FDA requirements gives existing pharmaceutical companies an advantage, especially if they operate on a large scale because they can spread that cost over a massive customer base.

Combinations

The durable advantages that I've just explored – chain-linked activities, lower costs, economies of scale, retention, location, network effects and government protection – become even more powerful when they are combined.

Apple combined high retention, network effects and economies of scale to create one of the most valuable companies in the world. Fashion brand Zara combine stores in great locations with a chain-linked, ultra-efficient supply chain. Their profits have exploded in recent years.[36] As these companies show, combining two or more sources of advantage might make the difference between a temporary and an enduring lead over rivals.

Competitor Lag

Patents expire. New technology becomes old-hat. Even the best ideas have a finite shelf life. In our dynamic world, no advantage endures for ever. The only way to keep imitators at bay is to keep moving. If you're already on to the next big thing by the time rivals catch up, imitability isn't such a worry. It's only when you rest on your laurels that you expose yourself to this danger.

This is hardly a new idea. Almost three decades have passed since Hamel and Prahalad stated that the aim of strategy is to 'create tomorrow's competitive advantages faster than competitors mimic the ones you possess today'.[37]

You gain a head start over rivals by exploiting their inertia and resistance to change. 'Big' and 'fast' are almost mutually exclusive in the business world, and the more successful a firm is with the status quo, the less likely they are to respond to change.[38] This gives nimble entrants the opportunity to get a foothold in the market.

The key is to force rivals to make a trade-off: between the familiarity of their current strategy and the uncertainty of a new one; between the safety of a mature market and the risk of an emerging one; or between protecting current revenue streams and cannibalising them with new offerings. These decisions are tough for any firm to make, so it's often easier to do nothing, giving new entrants a head start in the meantime. The following techniques are especially good for tying rivals up in knots.

Change the revenue model

If a business has to change their revenue model to stay competitive, you can bet they'll take their sweet time doing it. The risk, the cost of operational changes, the complexity they'll have to wade through and the inevitable political fallout will mire them in gloop for years, giving you a free ride in the meantime.

Blockbuster's revenue model depended heavily on charging customers if they returned videos late. Then Netflix arrived on the scene, offering a flat monthly rate, with no late fees. This put Blockbuster in a strategic bind – change the revenue model and lose profits or keep the revenue model and risk the lot? Blockbuster never fully committed to a new strategy,[39] and filed for bankruptcy in 2010.[40]

Change the basis of competition

Market leaders like to incrementally improve their products and services. Each new version is fundamentally the same, but a little better – a refinement of the status quo. They favour this approach because it plays to their strengths and follows the path of least resistance internally.

The danger, though, is overshooting – making a product that is too good for what the customer needs. This opens a window of opportunity for new businesses to launch products with fresh, distinctive benefits.

Faced with a competitor offering something radically different, established incumbents either wait until the market for the new product is big enough to meet their growth targets, by which point it's often too late, or don't commit to an opportunity that looks risky on paper because they are so successful elsewhere. Many once-great firms come unglued this way.

What can you learn from this? For new entrants, the trick is to avoid going up against market leaders with an incremental improvement on what they already do – they'll crush you in no time. Instead, try to establish where existing leaders underperform and bring to market a fundamentally different product that addresses this defect. This will almost guarantee that current market leaders will ignore you, at least until it's too late.

If you are a market leader, overshooting is a road to nowhere. As Clayton Christensen – whose research is most closely associated with this phenomenon – explains, 'A company that finds itself in a more-than-good-enough circumstance simply can't win: Either disruption will steal its markets, or commoditisation will steal its profits.'[41]

Bundling and unbundling

Jim Barksdale, who made his fortune as the CEO of Netscape, is renowned for his colourful proverbs, once announcing to a room of investment bankers: 'Gentlemen, there's only two ways I know of to make money: bundling and unbundling.'[42]

A bundle is a collection of products or services that are sold as one, like a McDonald's Happy Meal or Microsoft Office. Unbundling involves the opposite: taking one component of an offering and selling it by itself. Both can offer advantages to the customer and provider. The question is, which approach should you pursue?

As a general guideline, when markets are dominated by bundles the opportunity lies in unbundling them. When markets are unbundled, and incompatible offerings are strewn all over the place, you can do well by bundling them together.

Take, for example, the world of banking. Large retail banks offer bundles: savings, current accounts and loans, accessed through online banking, branches and telephone services. It doesn't make sense to attack a bank with another bundle unless you're already a bank. Instead, you should target one part of the bundle where you can outperform the established competition. Their structure, bureaucracy and mess of legacy systems will leave them unable to attack you. They probably won't want to either – in isolation your little slice may be too small to concern them.

This ignores the real problem, though. In *The Song of the Dodo*, author David Quammen compares a biological ecosystem to a Persian rug. If you cut the rug into small squares, you don't have many small rugs; you have bits that unravel until there is nothing left, a phenomenon known as *ecosystem decay*.[43]

The same kind of decay can apply in business. Once the bundle is sliced up, the business can start to unravel. It can't win every battle when it's being attacked on all sides. Eventually the bundler is forced either to find new categories to play in where their bundling strategy can work, or to retreat to a specialism themselves.

The cycle of bundling and unbundling is never-ending, and different opportunities present themselves at different times. If you are a bundler, you will eventually be unbundled. If you start life by taking a small slice of another offering, building your own bundle will be a tempting avenue to growth.

Unbundling is a current trend in several industries. The cable TV package is being unbundled: we have Netflix, HBO GO, Hulu, iTunes and Amazon Prime Video, which we can use interchangeably.

The traditional mobile phone bundle of minutes, texts and data is being undermined by WhatsApp, Snapchat, iMessage, Skype, FaceTime and others, all of which do one or two things of that bundle well. London research firm Ovum predict that mobile operators will lose $386 billion in revenue to these kinds of applications between 2012 and 2018.[44]

Some firms take the lead and unbundle themselves voluntarily. Graze started life as an online service, delivering boxes of four healthy snacks to customers each week. Once their brand was well known and they had the infrastructure to operate at high volumes, they pursued a strategic masterstroke. They broke apart their existing online offering, allowing supermarkets and other retailers to sell single snack portions at the checkout alongside the less healthy confectionery. Within six months they had sold an additional three million snacks.[45]

Other businesses are currently pursuing bundling strategies successfully. Evernote, for example, can be thought of as a bundle. Rather than making notes in different places – on the phone, computer or paper – you make them once and they are available on all devices. Slack is taking a similar approach to team communications, bundling notifications, files and messages into one place.

Solve the next problem

Every technology creates a new problem in place of the one it solves.[46] The combustion engine creates poisonous emissions; smartphones have made us perennially distracted; social media has eroded our privacy; plastic bags end up in the ocean.

Once the problems start to overshadow the brilliance of the solution, a new opportunity is born. Chemical pesticides have increased the appeal of organic food. Climate change is moving us towards sustainable transport and energy sources. As more of our life is digitised, cyber security and encryption have become opportunity areas.

Current solutions point the way to future problems, and fresh opportunities. By looking at the problems current solutions are creating (especially your own) you can identify opportunities for the future and get ahead of rivals.

Change the underlying technology

All technologies – the processes and devices we use to fulfil a goal – eventually reach their full potential. Each component in a system reaches its ultimate level of refinement, and in the pursuit of greater performance the overall system becomes bewilderingly complicated. Past a certain point, improvements become very costly, and you enter the realm of diminishing returns. Supersonic passenger jets never took off (pardon the pun) for this reason.

Once a technology has fully matured, an entirely new approach to the same problem is needed.[47] Light bulbs replaced candles, quartz largely replaced the mechanical watch, digital cameras replaced film. Electric cars are starting to replace combustion-engine vehicles. Soon they will be autonomous, replacing the need for a driver.

When this happens, industries built around the old technology endure a monstrous upheaval. In the two decades that followed the introduction of quartz, the Swiss watchmaking industry was almost obliterated. Kodak invented the digital camera but kept it under wraps, worried that it would cannibalise film sales. They filed for bankruptcy in 2012.[48]

Conclusions

Two clear themes emerge from any study of competitor lag. First, what worked today might not work tomorrow. More of the same can be a recipe for disaster. Often a fundamental change of direction is required.

Second, the inner, psychological game of business is often decisive. Success can lead to complacency, arrogance and laziness. Instead of imitating rivals, companies often ignore them until it's too late. Forcing rivals to make trade-offs creates an organisational paralysis that gives confident new players a lead that can never be clawed back.

Both themes point to the same conclusion. To stay in front – in fact, just to survive – you must never compromise your ability to change direction. The real key to longevity isn't just to be inimitable, it's to stay adaptable – the subject of the next and final chapter.

Coda: Network Effects

In some situations, the value of a product depends on the number of people who use it, a phenomenon known as the *network effect*. The more Airbnb hosts there are, the more guests the service attracts. The more guests there are, the more hosts it attracts. The two parties feed off each other and as both grow, the value of the service does too.

Social networks like Facebook and Twitter depend on network effects too: the more people who use a given network, the more valuable it becomes for all the other users.

I mentioned earlier in this chapter that the potential returns from network effects are enormous, because of the combination of customer lock-in and the entry barriers that they raise for competitors. There's a catch, though. In their early days, these ventures are not for the faint-hearted. When two similar rivals go head to head in a market driven by network effects it can be almost impossible to say who will win, as seemingly random events can tip the outcome one way or the other;[49] and whilst the strong get stronger, the weak can get weaker.[50]

A business that relies on network effects will usually find itself in a catch-22 situation early on. How can you appeal to hosts if you don't have guests? How can you appeal to guests if you don't have hosts? How can you launch a social network from scratch, if users are the most valuable part of the product? Many promising ideas fail for this reason. You need luck as well as judgement to get your venture off the ground. That said, the following guidelines might just make the difference if network effects come into play.

Make migration effortless

The more easily a customer can get started with your product, the more likely they are to try it. A fanatical approach to effort reduction during the early stages of the customer experience is a must. Whether it's installing an app, creating a profile, migrating content or any other hoop the customer must jump through, it has to be as effortless as possible or people won't bother.

Offer a quantum leap in value or performance

An incremental improvement on the status quo is often not enough to succeed in any market, but when network effects are involved it's almost impossible.[51] Your proposition should be utterly compelling, and obviously so.

Skype attracted customers in the early days because it offered a giant leap in value over long-distance calling. It was free, had video calling and chat – it was a no-brainer. If, as with Skype, the value is obvious, not only are you more likely to try it, you're more likely to convince others to try it too. A daughter backpacking through Asia could easily convince a Luddite parent back home to install Skype, since the value to both is apparent. This brings me on to the next point – you must use your existing customer base to grow.

Turn customers into active advocates

When network effects come into play, the quicker you can grow your user base the better. To do this, you should turn each customer into an active advocate who does your marketing for you. If every customer recruits two more, your growth will be exponential, and at far lower cost than using traditional advertising methods.

Member-get-member or *referral marketing* schemes are a common feature of businesses that rely on network effects to succeed. A starting point is a prominent 'invite' function, making it easy for your customers to tell their friends about the service. This often also extends to discounts or rewards for getting others to sign up.

Dropbox is a great example. Inspired by PayPal's $5 sign-up bonus, Dropbox moved away from an ineffective paid advertising model and turned their attention to rewarded advocacy, giving both parties extra storage for free. Once they had adopted this approach, they went from 100,000 to 4,000,000 users in fifteen months.[52]

Concentrate, then replicate

How do you light a fire? You don't toss a lit match under a giant log – it will never catch. Instead, you start with dry grass or firelighters that catch easily. Next, you add some kindling – twigs and small sticks that your tinder has the power to ignite. Once your kindling is burning away, there's enough heat to throw some logs on. Starting small, you work your way up to a raging inferno.

The same is true for building network effects. It's best to build your audience incrementally rather than try to convert everyone en masse overnight. By targeting one small community at a time, it's easier to raise initial awareness, easier for word of mouth to spread, and easier for customers to experience the benefits. Once a cluster of users is up and running, you move on to the next, replicating your success over and over again, until all the groups start to overlap and merge.

Facebook started at Harvard University, then spread to other Ivy League schools. Uber launched in San Francisco, then New York, then Seattle, Boston and Chicago. Dating app Tinder expanded by spreading from one college campus to another.[53] Twitter's break-through moment happened at the SXSW festival, where the density of users made it particularly valuable.[54] These offerings all followed the same pattern – concentrate, then replicate. None of these brands succeeded by spreading themselves thinly.

It's not only easier to ignite network effects in a small, bounded community – one office, campus or city at a time – you can also learn from each roll-out and improve. Trying to launch globally in one fell swoop isn't only unlikely to work; if you make a mistake you can't turn back the clock and try again.

Win the expectation war

When faced with competing options in network effect markets, cus-tomer expectations take on greater significance, as Carl Shapiro and Hal Varian explain in their book *Information Rules*: 'If consumers expect your product to become popular, a bandwagon will form, the virtuous cycle will begin, and consumers' expectations will prove correct. But if consumers expect your product to flop, your product will lack momen-tum, the vicious cycle will take over, and again consumers' expectations will prove correct.'[55] The grim reality is that the best product might not win. When expectations are a self-fulfilling prophecy, marketing efforts must radiate confidence, tackling every expectation issue and every uncertainty the customer has, before they even try the offering.

Build capacity

In markets where the network effect is two-sided – the growth of one group benefits another – like Uber (drivers and riders) or Airbnb (hosts and guests), you may have no choice but to pour cash into building capacity.

This was exactly what Uber did to get started in London: they paid drivers £25 an hour to be active on the platform whether they had bookings or not. Uber's first London employee, Richard Howard, was authorised to spend £50,000 a week on getting drivers to join so there'd always be a car available if a new customer gave the service a try.[56] The plan worked. Within six months Uber were able to swap to commission-based pay for drivers without them losing income – the network effect had kicked in and the word was spreading like wildfire.

To win in these markets takes deep pockets and nerves of steel. You can't predict whether explosive growth is around the corner or you'll just fizzle out, and you must keep throwing money at the problem until you find out.

Airbnb's growth was modest from 2007 to 2010 until the network effect kicked in. Over the next five years, the number of guests grew 353-fold to seventeen million.[57] Who could have predicted that? When it's not clear whether you're about to fail or enjoy unimaginable success, it takes courage, commitment and perhaps some insanity to stay the course.

Key Questions

Legal protection

- What intellectual property do you own?
- What policies or procedures protect your intellectual property? Do people follow them?
- Which IP strategy best serves your current goals? Full exclusion, licensing or open access?

Durable advantages

- Do you have a competitive advantage? If so, how durable is it?
- How might you combine the sources within the chapter to create a durable advantage over rivals?

Competitor lag

- How can you avoid going head to head with market leaders, so they will ignore you?
- Would bundling or unbundling make it harder for rivals to copy you?
- What problems are current popular products creating? How might you solve those?

Network effects

- Is the desirability of your offering impacted by network effects?
- How could existing customers help drive the growth of the business?
- Which communities should you target to generate early interest?

	desirability	profitability	**longevity**
customer	WANTS & NEEDS	REVENUES	CUSTOMER BASE
	○ values & beliefs	○ revenue model	○ awareness
	○ goals	○ price	○ acquisition
	○ barriers	○ volume (qty & freq.)	○ retention
market	RIVALRY	BARGAINING POWER	IMITABILITY
	○ category	○ with customers	○ legal protection
	○ territory	○ with suppliers	○ durable advantages
	○ alternatives & substitutes	○ rules & regulations	○ competitor lag
organisation	OFFERINGS	COSTS	ADAPTABILITY
	○ proposition	○ fixed costs	● cash position
	○ brand appeal	○ variable costs	● scalability or capacity
	○ customer experience	○ capital expenditure	● complexity & rigidity

Deep Dive Nine: Adaptability

I was bitten by the surf bug on my first visit to California, and have led a semi-aquatic life since. It's a good job I was hooked because progress did not come easily. It took weeks of perseverance to get close to riding a wave. A few years have passed and I'm still a beginner.

At first, just paddling out through the whitewash was exhausting. Until you learn how to duck beneath the incoming waves, time your entry to the water or find a calm channel to paddle out in, you're constantly pushed back to where you started.

Once past the breakers, you discover that timing is everything – a lesson you can only learn the hard way. Catch a wave too late and it will break on you, carrying you spluttering towards the beach. Too early and you'll slump off the back and go nowhere.

Another early lesson is to pay attention to your surroundings. The waves are infinitely more powerful than you and are coming whether you like it or not, so turning your back on the ocean is a bad idea. You must stay vigilant and think ahead. Watch a line-up of surfers and you'll notice everyone is staring out to sea. Nobody wants to get caught off guard by a big set coming in.

I was lying in the water one afternoon when it struck me that surfing and running a business have some remarkable similarities. In both, timing plays a decisive role. Courage must triumph over fear. You must persevere if you want to see results. But the similarities don't end there.

Waves are formed by storms interacting with the surface of the ocean far away from land, sending packets of energy through the water. When this swell enters shallow waters it forms rideable waves.[1]

To identify the most promising opportunities, surfers pore endlessly over weather forecasts, swell and tide charts. You've got to go where the waves are if you want to surf. Waiting for them to come to you or picking a beach at random don't work.

The same is true in business. Events beyond your immediate horizon send pulses of energy through the market. To succeed, you must anticipate where and when a wave of opportunity will appear, and get into position ahead of time.

Surfers love waves. They realise that there is no opportunity without them. No waves means no surfing. If the waves are in Fiji, that's where they want to be. If the ideal tide is at 5 a.m., that's when they're in the water. When a surfer sees a wave looming on the horizon they accept it as a fact of life and decide what to do – head out past it for the next one, or get into position to ride it. Staying still is not an option. They can't turn off the waves.

Whilst the same is true in business, few share the same gleeful sense of opportunity when change looms on the horizon. Rather than being seen as a cause for celebration, waves of change are typically met with futile resistance, denial or distress.

Whilst understandable, this attitude ignores the fundamental reality of economic life: every business rides a wave that will eventually dissipate, and relies on continued waves of change for growth in the future. Without change, there is *no opportunity*.

The key to long-term success, then, is to remain adaptable. If you find yourself rooted in place, you'll either be pummelled by incoming waves of change or stuck in a flat market, bereft of opportunity. Adaptability, however, seldom gets the consideration it deserves.

Given the choice between maintaining our ability to adapt and improving some other element of the grid – cutting costs or bumping up revenues in the short term – it's adaptability that usually gets sacrificed. And as with many things in life, you don't miss it until you suddenly need it.

With this in mind, the final deep dive explores the factors that improve or compromise your adaptive capacity. I'll start this journey with perhaps the most crucial element in the equation – cash in the bank.

Cash Position

When it comes to longevity, cash is king, for reasons that make intuitive sense. If you run out of cash you cannot continue to operate the business, and the more cash you have, the more options you can pursue. Cash also acts as a buffer that insulates you from change – buying you time to figure out what to do, or allowing you to wait for the right opportunities.

Cash vs profit

Doesn't this just mean that maintaining profitability is important? Aren't cash and profit the same? Not quite.

First of all, cash doesn't have to come from profits – it can come from selling shares in your business or from borrowing money. Second, and more importantly, your profit figure for the year and your cash position will not be the same.

One reason is timing. There is often a delay between delivering your services and getting paid, and you can run out of cash in the meantime. Many new ventures fail for this reason – they experience strong demand for their offering but run out of cash trying to meet it. I'll return to this topic in a moment.

Another reason is capital expenditures. As shown in Deep Dive Six: Costs (see pp. 169–88), the cost of long-term investments is customarily spread over the useful lifetime of the asset, only including depreciation when profits are being calculated. But the cash has still been spent.

In the second quarter of 2016, Netflix, for example, showed a net profit of $41 million, but a negative cash flow of -$254 million. The reason for this was that they had invested significant capital in new shows.[2] As counter-intuitive as it sounds, a business may be profitable on paper, and yet have far more cash going out than coming in.

So what matters is not just a company's profits on paper; it's how much cash they have after they've made necessary investments to keep the business going. Charlie Munger, the vice chairman of Berkshire Hathaway, put it this way:

> There are two kinds of businesses. The first earns twelve percent and you can take the profits out at the end of the year. The second earns twelve percent, but all the excess cash must be reinvested – there's never any cash . . . We hate that kind of business.[3]

With this in mind, it's important to keep an eye on *free cash flow* – a useful metric calculated by subtracting any capital expenditures from the cash generated by the business. This reveals how much cash the business has to explore other opportunities or to insulate it from change – both of which are vital to longevity.

Working capital

The amount of money tied up in your day-to-day operations – your *working capital* – impacts your cash position.

As I mentioned earlier, for many businesses there is a delay between delivering their services and getting paid. Cash can also be tied up in inventory, either as raw materials, work in progress or finished items waiting to be sold.

The more inventory you keep and the longer it takes to collect revenues, the more cash is tied up in working capital. On the flip side, the longer you take to pay suppliers, the longer the cash sits in your bank account rather than theirs.

Changing any one of these elements – customer and supplier payment terms, or inventory costs – can dramatically impact the cash position of the business. For those with a small cash cushion or high working capital requirements, how these factors are managed can be the difference between success and bankruptcy.

You may remember that during the deep dives on Revenues (see pp. 123–43) and Costs (see pp. 169–88) I hammered on about the importance of the *contribution margin* – the amount each sale contributes to covering your fixed costs. Another reason this is so important becomes apparent when cash is brought into the picture.

Imagine you attack your rivals in the candle market by slashing your prices. Demand explodes, but now you've got more orders than you can handle and razor-thin margins on each. To fulfil them, you must expand your operations *and* increase inventory to keep customers' shelves stocked. In other words, not only must you spend cash on a bigger factory with more equipment, the amount of cash tied up in working capital has also ballooned.

Where will the cash come from to fund this expansion? One answer is to get a loan from the bank, but the repayments will further increase your fixed costs. Now you've got to sell *even more* volume to make a profit. This is what's known as a working-capital trap.

A business in this situation needs constant injections of cash to stop it imploding. If interest rates go up or volumes drop, with such thin margins it could start making a loss. If funding dries up but the business is still growing, they could run out of cash trying to meet demand and go bankrupt. It's a scary position to be in.

As this example illustrates, your cash position is inseparable from other elements of the grid. Changes to your price, volumes and costs all have an obvious impact, but so do many other factors. Let's look at some other common scenarios.

Scenario A

To improve your cash position you renegotiate your payment terms with suppliers – maybe from thirty days to sixty. This improves your cash balance, but suppliers are unhappy. They might increase their prices in response, or reduce the quality of their service. Your offering and costs are both adversely affected.

Scenario B

Rivalry intensifies in your category, but rather than focusing on better understanding your customers' wants and needs, you panic. Taking a carpet-bomb approach, you launch as many new offerings as possible in the hope that some stick. As your product line proliferates, so too does the amount of cash tied up in inventory. With customers struggling to choose the right product, they turn to another brand. You now have less cash and less revenue. Lego experienced something similar in their dark days.

Scenario C

Demand for a product line declines, but your factory – which measures speed and efficiency – keeps churning out units, tying up more and more cash in inventory, instead of slowing production.

As these scenarios show, everyday decisions can unconsciously affect the cash position of the firm. The opposite is also true – decisions intended to improve your cash position can wreak havoc elsewhere. Some simple guidelines can help you avoid these sorts of problems. For start-ups, there are three in particular.

Estimate your cash-to-cash time

For almost every new venture, cash starts flowing out a long time before it starts coming in. It's entirely possible for years to pass and millions of dollars to be spent before any revenues come in. It is therefore useful to have an idea of the 'cash-to-cash' time between when you start spending money and when you think your first revenues will come in.

Businesses tend to be optimistic when estimating timelines. Thinking through multiple scenarios for our cash-to-cash time – the best, worst and most likely cases – can help you to plan appropriately, especially if you're in the position with your start-up that at some point you need to quit your day job and commit to the new business full-time.

Keep an eye on your cash burn rate and runway

For start-ups, traditional accounting formats may not be too valuable – you may have no revenue for years, or have no assets to list – but you will definitely be incurring costs, and if you run out of cash, it's game over.[4]

This is why well-run start-ups keep track of their *burn rate* – the amount of cash that is spent each month. They also keep an eye on their *runway* – the cash in the bank divided by the burn rate – which reveals how long they have before they will run out of money.[5]

Produce a cash-flow forecast

When approaching your launch, producing a simple cash-flow forecast will help you estimate how much cash will go in and out of the business each week for the first few months of your venture, so you can be sure you've enough cash to get up and running.

Once your business is away from the start line, two further guidelines can help.

Consider how decisions might impact your cash position

Smart decision-makers, regardless of their department or the size of the operation, consider the implications of their actions on the company's cash position.

All too many decision-makers, however, do not. The designers who dream up a customisable product may have no idea of the cash implications of stocking each part in ten different colours. A salesman who offers generous credit terms to win a deal may not realise how it affects the firm's working capital.

The more people within the business who understand cash flow and working capital, and consider these factors when making decisions, the better off the organisation will be. Consider whether some basic finance training for non-finance professionals would be a worthwhile investment.

Consider the rest of the grid when trying to improve your cash position

Whilst many make decisions without considering the cash implications, the opposite is also true – some seek to improve their company's cash position without considering the broader implications.

Cutting inventory may free up some cash, but it can reduce sales volumes or ruin the customer experience if products are consistently out of stock. Underinvesting in new opportunities to preserve your cash balance can leave you trailing in the wake of your rivals. As with all significant decisions, you must aim for the good of the whole, not just improve one aspect of the business at the expense of others.

Scalability or Capacity

The ease with which your business can scale in response to demand determines its ability to adapt to changing market conditions. Similarly, how you manage your existing capacity also affects your adaptability because there is always a trade-off between efficiency and flexibility.

Scalability

After a popular online magazine described American Giant's sweatshirt as 'the greatest hoodie ever made', demand for the garment exploded.[6] Within thirty-six hours, they had sold their entire inventory. Orders continued to pile in, however, creating a backlog that took them nearly six months to ship.

At the time, American Giant came in for a lot of media flak – one commentator called the situation a 'catastrophic success'.[7] Given that there was no way to predict such a massive spike in demand, I think this was unfair, and the company have successfully expanded their capacity since. But their experience shows how tricky scaling an operation can be, and how much damage can be created by an inability to meet demand.

If you're outlining plans for world domination, you should be mindful of how easily your operations can scale, and should consider whether your cash flow will cover expansion costs and how you will meet demand without compromising the customer experience.

Some businesses are inherently easier to scale than others, owing to how easily production can be standardised or automated and the ease with which potential employees with the right skill sets can be brought in if demand increases. There is no equivalent of Walmart in neurosurgery, for example.

Your ability to scale can also be directly connected to your revenue model. The CrossFit gym movement expanded rapidly in part because of its affiliate model. CrossFit certificate holders could apply to become affiliates and, if accepted, could be promoted by crossfit.com and be allowed to use the CrossFit brand at their training facilities, in exchange for a $3,000 annual fee. At the time of writing there are more than 13,000 affiliates worldwide.[8] Achieving such scale any other way would have been far more challenging.

Your brand appeal can also present a challenge to scalability. If customers are choosing your brand because you are a small, local firm or because they enjoy the personal attention of a particular individual, you may end up undermining your appeal and destroying your initial brand rationale if you expand your business into a faceless mega chain.

Finally, your make or buy decisions can affect the ease with which you can scale your operations. If you buy something from a supplier you can often just order larger quantities from them if demand increases – scalability becomes their problem not yours. However, if you make those things in-house, you may run into limits imposed by your equipment, the size of your facility or the staff you have available.

Capacity

Scalability describes the fundamental ease with which a business model can expand or contract in response to demand. Capacity is the amount of work that can be undertaken with current resources.

You might, for example, have a business model that is difficult to scale but has ample capacity to handle current demand; or have a business that can scale easily, but which seeks to do more with its current capacity to make the enterprise more profitable.

Your spare capacity fundamentally determines your adaptability because there is always a trade-off between efficiency and flexibility. Without slack in your operations it becomes impossible to change direction.[9] If you are 100 per cent busy, when do you plan for the future? If people are *doing* the whole time, when do they *think*?

I've worked with several clients who spend their entire days in meetings. They do most of their 'work' – mulling over decisions or preparing presentations – outside office hours, in the evenings or at weekends. It's hard to think that their capacity is being used effectively.

Businesses in the service sector – advertising agencies or consultancies – will often have strict utilisation targets that determine how many billable hours a week must be spent on client work. This in turn often leads to individuals working across multiple projects simultaneously.

The problem is that these employees experience a *task-switching penalty* – losing time as they get into the right headspace when they move from one project to the other. As a result, whilst on paper they've worked an hour on each client, in reality they've only managed ten minutes of productive work for each. It's a false economy. Stacking people on multiple projects makes them less efficient, not more.

Whilst a preoccupation with efficiency can yield cost improvements in the short term, it is disastrous in the long run. If you've reached the point where extreme efficiency is required to generate acceptable returns, it may be that the market is trying to tell you that a change of direction is what you need. As Jules Goddard and Tony Eccles write in *Uncommon Sense, Common Nonsense*, 'Strategy is the rare and precious skill of staying one step ahead of the need to be efficient.'[10]

Complexity and Rigidity

However successful a company is at any given moment, and however unassailable it may appear to be, there will come a point at which it faces the prospect of decline. Every great civilisation in history has eventually collapsed. No business has stayed number one for ever. Yours won't be the exception to the rule – it's the natural order of things.

There's a simple reason why. What may start life as an energetic, aggressive enterprise inevitably gains complexity and rigidity as it grows and therefore finds it difficult to adapt when conditions change. When these organisations decline, it is not generally because of an external force or lack of resources, but because their operational and psychological baggage prevents them from responding to change. 'Business success', wrote Andy Grove, 'contains the seeds of its own destruction.'[11]

This transformation from sprightly young upstart to unwieldy bureaucracy can be thought of as a cycle composed of distinct, recognisable phases.[12] Not all businesses pass through them. Some never take off in the first place, or never grow large enough. But for those that do, the phases are like a line of dominoes. If one moves past a certain point it topples into the next. It's therefore important to recognise the characteristics of each, and see how adaptive capacity is compromised along the way.

Stage one: the outburst

With a pioneering spirit and hunger for success, a new player enters the market. Lightweight and nimble, what they lack in resources they make up for with a daring attitude.[13] These founders are women and men of action who don't hesitate to get their hands dirty, and boast of building the plane while they're flying it.

Adaptability is crucial at this stage. They must experiment, or 'pivot', until they find the magic configuration of elements that results in a viable enterprise.[14] As the business gains traction it finds itself riding a tiger. The infrastructure cannot keep up with the pace of change, and organised chaos is the order of the day. New hires sit three to a desk. The entire thing is held together by pizza, Red Bull and contagious excitement.

Stage two: steady growth

Once the business makes it through the initial melee, the frenzied dash of the start gives way to a steady onward stride. The focus turns to staving off direct rivals and refining the offering.

Improvised processes and duct-taped solutions are no longer enough – the business needs a robust infrastructure to support its continued growth. The organisation starts to mature operationally, implementing its first formal procedures.

Every time the business reaches capacity, it expands to allow growth to continue. Departments grow subdepartments; computer systems become more elaborate. Through this process of 'structural deepening' the organisation gradually becomes more complex.[15]

Stage three: conservation

As the original market begins to mature, the organisation must find new opportunities to fuel the next wave of growth. Unfortunately, as management guru Clayton Christensen points out, the high-growth markets of the future are inherently small today, and as such may not be appealing to an established corporation with a whale-sized appetite.[16]

As a result, with current offerings still performing well, few already-successful businesses are prepared to take risks on new, unproven categories. Trapped in a golden cage, many systematically ignore opportunities that would allow them to succeed in the future. Instead, they devote themselves to fracking greater returns out of current offerings, and aggressively defending their share of existing markets.

Stage four: high noon

Years of continued success may have made the management dogmatic and complacent. They laugh off new rivals, whose early offerings lack the refinement and quality of their own. Information is distorted and delayed as it makes its way from the ground floor to the executive suite, leaving leaders disconnected from the realities of their environment.[17] Politics takes precedence over progress, and action is replaced with endless discussion.

By now, the infrastructure has become so complex that the business must work around it. Rather than starting with the customers' wants and needs and creating offerings to match, the business cobbles together whatever offerings they can easily produce, whether customers will find them desirable or not. With neither the inclination nor the ability to adapt, the stage is set for decline.

Stage five: decline

Having waited too long to enter new markets, the growth opportunities for the future are captured by the next wave of entrepreneurial firms, who attack the incumbent mercilessly. Stifled by its own inertia, the organisation is unable to respond. CEOs distract themselves with acquisitions and rebranding exercises, or embark on a ruthless cost-cutting regime in the hope of producing returns.[18] When these knee-jerk measures are shown to be ineffective, reorganisation in some form becomes inevitable.

Stage six: reorganisation

The potential for renewal begins by 'unseizing' every element of the grid, so they can be reconfigured to suit the present environment. This requires a thorough reorganisation, which typically plays out in two ways.

Visionary employees will leave to start their own businesses. Once freed from the strictures of the previous firm, they can configure their offerings, revenue model and cost structure to suit the current environment and opportunities, rather than being stuck with a formation optimised for the past. This freshly minted organisation then begins its own journey around the cycle.

Meanwhile, if it is to survive, the old organisation must undergo a comprehensive transformation. Whilst it may retain its basic identity, divisions are sold off and board members replaced. New opportunities are pursued under fresh leadership that is not blinded by historic precedent. In some cases, the weakened company simply doesn't have the resources to turn itself around and is consigned to the history books. In others, the organisation may have a bright future ahead, possibly even exceeding all expectations as it enters new categories with a fresh, attacking spirit.

Conclusion: Maintaining Adaptability

The cycle I've just outlined reveals that two forces combine to rob a business of its adaptability. On the one hand, it experiences a change in mindset, becoming complacent and risk-averse. On the other, it accrues complexity and rigidity in its operations that become almost impossible to overcome.

To bring this final chapter to a close, I'll highlight some principles that might help you maintain adaptability, starting by exploring the psychological factors at work.

Beware of the ego

From start-up founders who insist that their vision is right even as the business crumbles around them, to managers whose sole concern is deflecting blame in other directions, an unchecked ego can crush your adaptability. You can't change direction if you refuse to accept something is wrong, and you can't learn from mistakes you refuse to acknowledge.[19]

The key to avoiding this fate is to learn to discern the difference between criticism of your work and of you as a person. When someone says 'I don't like this idea' people often hear 'You're a useless human being', but the two are not the same. Detaching yourself from your work, however hard it may be, means that you can overcome your instinctive impulse to get defensive.

If you can get into the habit of seeking critiques and honest feedback you will soon reap the benefits. Rather than reacting angrily to criticism, you will celebrate the potential to improve your plans through the input of others. With this kind of attitude, changing direction is much easier.

Question the optimism bias

A sense of optimism is valuable at any stage in an organisation's development – you must believe that you can succeed or you'd never try anything – but it's also dangerous.

In his bestseller *Thinking, Fast and Slow*, Daniel Kahneman explains: 'The chances that a small business will survive for five years in the United States are about 35%. But the individuals who open such businesses do not believe that the statistics apply to them . . . A common thread of boldness and optimism links businesspeople, from motel owners to superstar CEOs.'[20] One thing is for sure – a belief that one is the exception to the rule is a significant barrier, not only to adaptability, but to prudent decision-making in general.

If you are given credible advice and your impulse is to reject it, ask whether it's because there is a robust argument to the contrary, or because you think you're the exception to the rule. When using the grid, seeking an outside opinion – whether from an independent party or a member of a different team – can help keep individual biases in check.

Question your trajectory

The longer an approach has worked, the harder it becomes to conceive of any other. The danger is that you keep exaggerating your strengths until you succeed your way to failure. This is the central thesis of Danny Miller's excellent book *The Icarus Paradox*, where he outlines four common patterns.

Craftsmen – organisations who pride themselves on quality and attention to detail – become *tinkerers*. Obsessed with incremental improvement, they create perfect products that make no commercial sense.

Builders – who succeed though aggressive, entrepreneurial expansion – become *imperialists*. Overreaching into businesses they don't understand, they eventually bite off more than they can chew. (The Royal Bank of Scotland under Fred Goodwin is a great example.)

Pioneers – whose success came from big ideas and bleeding-edge innovations – become *escapists*. They turn off customers with inventions that are too far ahead of their time, too expensive or serve no practical need.

Finally, *salesmen* – organisations whose success was founded on brand creation and marketing – become *drifters*. Thinking they can sell anything, they end up with a jumbled portfolio of undifferentiated products and services.[21]

To nip these tendencies in the bud, question which trajectory you're on, if any. Are you overexpanding into businesses you don't understand? Are perfectionist tendencies getting the better of you? Are you building a viable product or a self-indulgent technological showcase? These are valuable questions to ponder and may help you course-correct before it's too late.

Consider Ruth Porat, Alphabet Inc's recently appointed chief financial officer, who is curbing the escapist tendencies of the tech giant's brilliant engineers. By improving their financial discipline, she is steering Alphabet towards the most viable opportunities and away from exciting but frivolous sideshows.[22]

Avoid the trap of the first version

People often ignore competitive threats until it is too late. The question is, with new technologies and products constantly emerging, how can you sort the real threats from the boondoggles? Two approaches can help.

First, if a new alternative appears on your radar, you should evaluate it in light of your customer's *super objective* – their highest-level goal (see pp. 69–70). Might it be a different means to the same end? This can stop you wrongly laughing off any solution that isn't identical to yours.

Second, you must avoid what Andy Grove called the 'trap of the first version' – ignoring early threats because of their inferior performance. The first version of anything usually leaves a lot to be desired, but if it can find early customers it will quickly improve. Grove suggests considering whether a '10 x' improvement to the first version might make it a threat. If it would, take it seriously – it may happen faster than you think.[23]

Spend time on the front line

In many organisations, management make decisions in a bubble. Rather than cultivating an empathic understanding of their customers' wants and needs, they rely on dashboards, spreadsheets and PowerPoint presentations to inform their judgement.

There is no substitute for spending time on the front line with customers, understanding their needs and experiencing your own products (and the alternatives) first-hand. These experiences will help keep you grounded and circumvent the inevitable 'news improvement' as information makes its way up the hierarchy.[24]

You can take the same approach with internal issues. The 'gemba walk' – visiting the actual place where work happens, observing a process and asking questions about it – is a foundational principle of the lean management approach and one that offers real benefits.[25]

Get to work on the next thing while the going is good

Eric Hoffer made a profound observation in his 1951 classic *The True Believer*:

> The powerful can be as timid as the weak. What seems to count more than possession of instruments of power is faith in the future. Where power is not joined with faith in the future, it is used mainly to ward off the new and preserve the status quo.

> Fear of the future causes us to lean against and cling to the present, while faith in the future renders us receptive to change . . . When the present seems so perfect that the most we can expect is its even continuation in the future, change can only mean deterioration. Hence men of outstanding achievement and those who live full, happy lives usually set their faces against drastic innovation.[26]

Every successful offering has a finite shelf life. If our organisation is to transcend the adaptive cycle it must pursue new opportunities before it is too late. As Hoffer makes clear, though, the crucial tipping point is *emotive*, not logical.

To maintain your adaptability and avoid suffocating conservatism, you must never allow the comfort of the present to outshine your excitement for the future. This means getting to work on something new before your current offering reaches its prime.

Peter Drucker expressed the same opinion as far back as 1957. In *Landmarks of Tomorrow*, he expounded timeless advice on this topic, with three recommendations in particular.

First, that if you wait until growth slows to pursue new opportunities you are already too late. Second, that organisations must experiment with multiple new opportunities simultaneously since the odds of any one plan succeeding are slim. Finally, that these exploratory activities must be undertaken with the knowledge that they are uncertain.

To use Drucker's words, you must 'perceive the as yet unknown' and 'do the as yet impossible' to safeguard your future.[27] Ideally, you need a business unit or offering at each of the key stages – outburst, steady growth and conservation.

Framestore, who created the visual effects seen in *Gravity* and the *Harry Potter* movies amongst others, have lived by these principles since their founding in 1986. Maintaining an entrepreneurial spirit and healthy appetite for risk, they have broken new ground creatively, whilst capitalising on wave after wave of technological developments.

They started out creating visual effects for TV and film. Then they successfully diversified into content creation, advertising and digital signage, opened a motion-capture facility and ventures division, and were amongst the first to launch a dedicated virtual-reality studio. By staying focused on tomorrow's technologies, they have never sacrificed their adaptability and have flourished as a result.[28]

As you pursue new opportunities, you must also be willing to let go of the old. You can ill afford to be sentimental about offerings that are struggling to generate a return, even if your brand has a close association with them.

There is nothing wrong with constructive abandonment. If an offering is not working out, find a way to turn it around, sell it off or shut it down. It is quite incredible, for example, that Sony allowed their television unit to incur more than $7 billion in losses – posting losses for ten years straight – before eventually splitting it off into its own subsidiary.[29]

Allow new opportunities to have new configurations

As I've repeatedly said, success emerges from the interplay of all the elements on the grid. All the parts must fit together to create a coherent whole.

When exploring new opportunities, you must give them enough structural freedom to succeed. Shackling a new offering to an old cost structure will not work, nor will trying to extract huge sales volumes from a nascent category. If an exciting opportunity would dilute your brand or confuse customers, creating a new brand may be a safer bet.

To be truly adaptable, every element must be free to respond to change. Whether it's your first venture or the latest in a long line, the rules remain the same – you must aim for the good of the whole, adjusting each and every element towards that end.

Key Questions

Cash position

- How might you improve your cash position?
- How can you reduce working capital?
- Are employees aware of how their decisions impact your cash position?

Scalability or capacity

- How easily can your business scale up or down?
- Is there enough slack in your operations to allow you to respond to change?

Complexity and rigidity

- What stage of the adaptive cycle is your business in?
- Does it look like you're heading to the next?

Maintaining adaptability

- Are you falling prey to one of the four dangerous trajectories of the Icarus Paradox? If so, which one?
- Have you fallen into the trap of the first version – dismissing new alternatives because they lack the polish of your own?
- Should you be working on the next big thing already? If not now, when?

Final Thoughts

As I write these concluding remarks, the dust is settling on another banking scandal, this one involving Wells Fargo.

Their strategy – to cross-sell products to existing customers – made perfect sense: the more services a customer uses, the higher the perceived switching cost and the more revenue each customer generates. CEO John Stumpf's mantra was 'Eight is great' – a reference to the number of products he wanted each customer to have.[1] To execute that strategy, employee compensation was linked to aggressive cross-selling targets. Here's where the problems began. If employees did not meet their quotas they risked being fired, and many staff struggled to cope.[2]

The *New York Times* reported employees having panic attacks and developing shingles from the stress. One even became addicted to drinking the office hand sanitiser in a bid to combat their anxiety.[3] Under intense pressure to meet targets, some employees began cutting corners by opening accounts and credit cards for customers without their consent or knowledge.

Over a five-year period, Wells Fargo employees opened approximately 1.5 million unauthorised accounts and half a million unauthorised credit cards, netting the bank $2.6 million in fees.[4] After a report by the *Los Angeles Times* exposed the scandal, regulators stepped in.[5]

Wells Fargo agreed to a $185 million fine and dropped the sales goals that led to the fraudulent behaviour.[6] Stumpf also agreed to forfeit $41 million in stock awards, but it wasn't enough.[7] After thirty-four years at the bank he stepped down as CEO with no severance pay and the bank's reputation badly damaged.[8]

This story, and the abundance of others like it, illustrates the main theme of the book: you cannot allow one or two elements of the grid to dominate the others without eventually facing adverse consequences. Prizing one or two metrics above all others – whether it be sales volumes, cash, costs or any other – creates an imbalanced enterprise that will eventually topple. Every box on the grid matters.

This story also demonstrates the second key theme of the book. Nobody can escape the law of cause and effect. The size or shape of your organisation makes no difference – you cannot change one element of your business without it impacting another. To make smart decisions you must consider their second-order effects – how other elements of the grid will be affected – and make the best trade-off you can.

Setting such aggressive targets at Wells Fargo may have driven up volumes but they had long-term consequences, damaging the brand, degrading the customer experience and incurring an extra $185 million cost that could have been avoided. As for John Stumpf, I'm sure it's not how he pictured ending his otherwise stellar career at the bank.

First and foremost, the grid is a thinking and communication tool – a means to bring structure to messy challenges, share perspectives and explore the implications of a course of action. Whilst I have high hopes that it will improve collaboration and decision-making, the grid cannot tell you what to do; it can only suggest what factors to consider.

Since every successful business is a unique configuration of the elements of the grid, every decision should be driven by its particular context. There is no guarantee that an approach that works for one firm will work for another.

I'm not the first to say it, and I won't be the last, but the truth is, there is no 'right' strategy, panacea or prescription for success. You must have the courage to plough your own furrow. To paraphrase the venture capitalist Ben Horowitz, there are no silver bullets, only lead ones.[9]

Working on this book has been a humbling experience that has heightened my admiration for entrepreneurs, leaders and decision-makers who steer their companies from strength to strength, and – perhaps surprisingly – for those who don't. Perhaps that is because it has been impossible for me to write the book without reflecting on my own weaknesses.

That said, while the grid has revealed many of my own short-comings, I've also never felt more confident tackling them. Launching, growing or turning a business around is a highly creative and demanding task, but ultimately a fulfilling one. I hope the grid will be a faithful companion on your unique business adventure.

Thank you, and good luck!

Matt Watkinson
mw@matt-watkinson.com

Deep Dives – Executive Summary

Wants and Needs (pp. 59–83)

To truly understand your customer there are three things you need to know:

- Who are they? *What are their values and beliefs?*
- What are they trying to achieve? *What are their goals?*
- What is standing in their way? *What barriers do they face?*

Values and beliefs

- You must start with the customer's values and beliefs, since these have the greatest influence on what they find desirable.
- Expressing their identity is often the factor that is most important to the customer, even more than the functional performance of a product or service.
- If your offering can reflect the customer's values and social group it can give it a magnetic appeal.
- In business-to-business markets, you must consider the behaviour that your customers are rewarded for, matching your offerings to the values of the organisation, rather than those of the individual.
- Customer beliefs are influenced by the brand, the category, their learned behaviours and past experiences, and what you tell them.

- Changing customer beliefs takes a two-pronged approach – first appealing to their existing desires, then providing them with reassuring evidence that your way is the future.

Goals

- Every product or service should be thought of as a means for the customer to achieve an objective.
- Start by considering the customer's *super objective* – the over-arching goal that drives their other behaviours.
- Customers often have a *subtext* – goals they don't feel comfortable discussing. Understanding this subtext can reveal opportunities.
- Defining the customer's intended *outcome* and *success criteria* gives you a reference point to keep the development of your offerings on track.

Barriers

- Barriers are obstacles that prevent or discourage a prospect from becoming a customer.
- Dismantling barriers that prevent a customer from achieving their goals can be a huge opportunity.
- Barriers fall into three categories: operational, experiential and financial.
- Common operational barriers include installation and compatibility issues, competing technologies, limited distribution, and the risk of the product failing.
- Experiential barriers are typically trialability, the training and expertise required, and strong fallback options.
- Lowering financial barriers involves making your price point accessible, or helping the customer feel comfortable paying it.
- Cutting the up-front cost, allowing the customer to spread the cost over time, and minimising any financial risk can help lower these barriers.

Rivalry (pp. 85–99)

Category

- Customers like to buy from established categories because it makes it easier for them to understand the products on offer.
- Track whether your category and complementary categories are growing or shrinking.
- Changing entry and exit barriers impact the profit potential of a category.
- Every category has baseline requirements – keeping an eye on how these are changing is essential to keeping your offerings competitive.

Territory

- Your chosen territory must have large enough demand to create a viable business.
- Different geographical territories will exhibit different characteristics across the rest of the grid.
- Your specific location within a territory is important.
- An inconvenient office location may mean that you struggle to attract the best employees, and clients may be reluctant to visit.
- A location can offer a cost advantage if it is close to key suppliers or customers.
- Your location can make you more convenient, improve awareness or help express your brand values.

Alternatives and substitutes

- Perceptions of desirability are relative rather than absolute. It's difficult to judge the value of anything without something to compare it to.
- It is essential to identify the reference points customers will use to judge your offerings and consciously position yourself amongst them.

- Desirability comes from making your offering the *obvious, easy choice* for the buyer. You can't do that unless you know what options they are choosing between.
- Rivals fall into three camps: alternatives, substitutes and your own range.
- Alternatives are direct rivals that customers use as a reference point to assess your desirability.
- Substitutes are offerings from outside your category that satisfy your customer's super objective.
- Offering a large range of products and services can hurt you if customers find it hard to choose between them.

Offerings (pp. 101–120)

- Every offering has three interdependent elements: the proposition, brand appeal and customer experience.
- There are consistent themes on which every successful brand, proposition and customer interaction are built.
- Anything that expresses our identity – our self-image, values, community or position in society – can be a source of value.
- The value of some products stems from utility – the goals they allow us to accomplish.
- Some offerings appeal for financial reasons: because they are cheap, will save us money, or because they will appreciate in value.
- A reputation for quality can be a great source of value, since high-quality products offer a more straightforward ownership experience.
- Some experiential characteristics are highly prized – less effort or stress, more sensory, social pleasure or control, and an emotional appeal can all make an offering valuable.

Proposition

- The bedrock of any successful business is a strong product or service proposition.

- You can express any proposition in this format: 'For (*target customer*) who has (*goals*), our product or service is a (*category*) that unlike (*specific alternative(s)*) provides (*compelling rationales*).'
- Rationales must be relevant to the customer.
- A strong proposition is distinctive.
- Your rationales should outperform rivals and industry norms.
- Rationales should be focused – you should emphasise just two or three.
- If you don't have a clear proposition, your team does not agree on a common version, or your customers don't buy into it, devote all your energy to resolving this issue before moving forward.

Brand appeal

- Branding is the process of attaching associations to a business that apply to all its products and services.
- Brand associations are formed in two ways: *inside out*, through marketing and communications, and *outside in*, through customers' real-world experiences and word of mouth.
- To build an appealing brand the first step is to choose a distinctive set of associations you will actively promote.
- These can relate to your sign value, category, quality, price point or experiential factors.
- Once you've identified these associations, you must express them consistently and ensure that the reality of the product is met by the image you portray.

Customer experience

- Your aim should be to improve the customer's *memory of the experience* – the basis for their satisfaction and their future decisions.
- Customers have two levels of expectation for their interactions: the *adequate* (the service level they find acceptable) and the *desirable* (the service they hope to receive).

- Between these points is a grey area known as the *zone of tolerance*, where events are satisfactory, yet unremarkable.
- Those interactions that are below what we find adequate or above what we find desirable have the greatest impact on our overall satisfaction.
- The most effective approach to improving satisfaction is to make sure each journey ends on a high. Next, you should eliminate any troughs. Finally, you should create the occasional positive peak by engineering in one or two interactions that are better than might reasonably be expected.
- You can improve most customer experiences by setting better expectations, or by applying simple design principles to improve those interactions.
- Reducing effort and stress, increasing sensory pleasure, social pleasure and control, and fine-tuning the emotional experience are powerful levers.

Revenues (pp. 123–43)

Revenue model

- A revenue model has two components. The *revenue stream* (the source of the income) and the *revenue mechanism* (how you charge for your goods).
- You should choose your revenue model based on what customers will find most desirable, rather than starting with a pre-existing model and retrofitting your offering onto it.
- Creating an offering that requires a change in revenue model is a powerful way to prevent rivals from imitating you.
- You must keep an eye on whether your revenue model is starting to limit the desirability of your offerings and, if so, summon the courage to change it.

Price

- Setting the right price for a product or service is the single most effective way to maximise profitability, and relatively minor changes can have a dramatic impact.
- The price must reflect the desirability of the offering. Customers don't care what your costs are. They care what represents value to them.
- Setting the price based on costs will lead you either to overprice and sacrifice volume, or underprice and sacrifice margin.
- When launching a new business or product you should start with the price you think customers will pay, then work backwards to the costs you can safely incur to generate a profit.
- Your market positioning reveals rough upper and lower price limits for your offering.
- The next best alternative, price sensitivity and what your price point says about you are all important considerations when setting the price.
- Consider running experiments to discover the optimum price for your product or service.
- Discounts adversely affect profit margins and often bring forward existing demand rather than increase it.
- Regular price cuts train customers to buy or stockpile goods when the price is low and can permanently devalue a product.
- Communicating the value of your proposition is crucial if you wish to avoid discounting.
- Sales people should be incentivised according to profitability, not revenue targets.

Volume

- Greater sales volume comes from increasing purchase frequency or quantity, and from new or existing customers – you should choose which you will target.
- A common way to increase sales volumes is to expand the territory.

- Introducing different versions of your product can increase sales by appealing to customers with a different willingness to pay.
- Improving the proposition or customer experience may generate more sales, as will increasing awareness.
- You can increase your sales volumes most effectively by looking at a broad sweep of metrics to see where the greatest opportunity lies.

Bargaining Power (pp. 145–66)

Customer and supplier power

- Relationships with suppliers and customers are both cooperative and competitive.
- Learning when to compete and when to cooperate is crucial to managing relationships.
- Whoever has the most bargaining power – your suppliers, your customers or you – gets to profit the most from the arrangement.
- The more you buy from a supplier, the more power you have.
- The harder it is for you to switch, the less power you have.
- The more important your product, the more power you have.
- The more rivals you have, the less power you have.
- The easier you are to imitate, the less power you have.

Rules and regulations

- Authorities shift the balance of power by direct intervention in the nine boxes of the grid.
- When starting a new business, you must thoroughly consider the regulatory environment.
- When regulations change, you must look beyond the obvious impact and consider how it might affect each element.

The power paradox

- It is extremely difficult to enrich yourself by using the power you have over people without accruing resentment that will bring you down again.
- The first step when making decisions that involve exerting leverage over buyers or suppliers is to consider how it might impact your reputation.
- If your buyers or suppliers are too powerful for you, you must look elsewhere, and improve your offerings to level the playing field.
- Be firm but fair. Being assertive will enhance your reputation, deterring those who would seek to exploit you.
- Whenever you make a decision where there is a risk of accruing resentment, you must carefully ponder not only the short-term consequences but the long-term ones as well.

Costs (pp. 169–88)

Fixed costs

- Fixed costs are those that don't change with your output; variable costs are ones that do.
- Headcount costs warrant particular attention since they are typically a large proportion of costs, they tend to go up over time and they are hard to reduce.

Variable costs

- Variable costs vary with your output.
- Target costing involves setting maximum costs the business can incur during product development.
- Persistence and accountability are key to reducing variable costs.
- Eliminating waste can help you reduce costs without compromising quality.

Cost structures

- You break even when the margin you make from your sales is enough to cover your fixed costs.
- The break-even equation helps you identify the costs you can safely incur to have a viable business.
- A firm with low fixed costs but high variable ones will break even sooner, but will typically have lower margins beyond that point.
- A firm with higher fixed costs but lower variable ones will take longer to break even, but past that point should make larger profits.
- You should use your estimated price and volumes as a basis for identifying the costs you can incur to make a profitable business, rather than working up to a price and volume from your costs.
- A business's *cost structure* is decided by the proportion of fixed and variable costs it incurs.
- The cost structure has a deep impact on the strategies that a business can follow, and how price or volume changes affect them.
- Your cost structure is affected by whether you do things yourself or pay suppliers to do them for you.
- Making things yourself typically increases fixed costs but decreases variable costs. Buying them increases your variable costs because suppliers must cover their overheads and make a profit too.

Cost reduction

- Good data and management accounts are vital to control costs.
- Prioritise opportunities based on their impact and ease of implementation.
- Consider the impact of a cost reduction on the rest of the grid, to prevent it adversely affecting the rest of the business.
- Start cost-reduction programmes as far away from the customer as possible.

Capital expenditure

- A capital expenditure is a long-term investment, like machinery, computer equipment or buying a factory.
- Every business or system has a constraint that limits its performance.
- Considering where the constraints are in your business can help you prioritise your expenditures and avoid investing in pointless improvements.
- When estimating the cash outlay for a capital expenditure, focus on the total cost, not just the obvious, up-front ones.
- Consider the benefits of an investment from a variety of perspectives using the grid.
- Be transparent and conservative with your estimates.
- The payback and net present value methods are the most common approaches to calculate return on investment for capital expenditures.
- The net present value method is more useful because it gives an estimated return and tells you whether it meets the business's minimum requirements.

Customer Base (pp. 191–208)

Awareness

- People cannot buy a product they don't know exists. Moreover, we instinctively prefer the familiar.
- Communications must have clear objectives, measurable success criteria and a clear target audience.
- A distinctive appearance will help get your product noticed and will make it easier to recognise in the future.
- Make sure your communications remind the customer of you: your product and your brand.
- Communications play a vital role in setting expectations.

- You must craft a simple message. If you can't sum up your product and rationale in a sentence or two you must go back to the drawing board.
- Considering the cues that trigger customers to act will help you deliver your message at the right time and in the right place.
- Communications with an emotional appeal are more engaging, since they encourage the customer to take action.
- Maintaining a consistent, continuous presence will cement your brand in the customer's mind.

Acquisition

- The growth potential from acquiring new customers is typically much larger than from improving retention.
- New customers can drive word of mouth more powerfully than existing ones.
- Acquiring new customers is essential not only to maintain your brand but to grow it.
- Reaching all kinds of potential buyers is important, especially light or infrequent buyers. They often constitute a large part of the overall customer base and need particular attention because they can easily forget about you.
- Marketing heavily to already loyal customers is pointless because their behaviour will not change much as a result.

Retention

- The cost of selling to an existing customer is typically much lower than acquiring a new one.
- Existing customers can be more likely to spend more when they do shop.
- Most customers are slightly loyal by default, since people are by nature both risk- and effort-averse.

- Customers do not have to be conscious loyalists to be retained or to repurchase from you. They just need to have better reasons to stay than to leave.
- Loyalty schemes can improve retention and increase repeat purchasing. They can also provide valuable data that can help you target promotions and improve your decision-making.
- Poorly executed rewards programmes can sap profits from heavy buyers. They are also expensive to set up and operate effectively.
- Specific contractual terms of business, building ecosystems, reducing interoperability with other products, and encouraging the customer to personalise the product can all reduce defection.
- Habit-forming products have high repeat usage and lower ongoing costs of promotion, but ethical considerations are paramount.
- Cross- and upselling are classic ways to sell more to existing customers.
- Just because I'm satisfied with one product, doesn't mean I wouldn't be more satisfied with another.
- Improving every aspect of the offering – not just satisfaction – is crucial to help retain customers.

Acquisition and retention metrics

- Keeping an eye on a diverse range of metrics can help you identify where to focus your efforts.
- Measuring the number of customers you have and how many you retain is a logical starting point.
- Calculating customer profitability and customer lifetime value can help you determine which customer groups to prioritise when it comes to acquisition and retention.
- Trying to gauge the cost of acquisition and retention can be immensely valuable.
- The Net Promoter Score is not without its shortcomings. Consider whether the Word of Mouth Index might work better for you.

Imitability (pp. 211–34)

A three-pronged approach can help keep imitators at bay. You can:

- Seek legal protection – patents, trademarks and copyrights.
- Build durable advantages – such as a unique cost structure or product ecosystem.
- Create competitor lag – staying out in front and forcing your rivals to catch up.

Legal protection

- Intellectual property rights fall into four broad categories: patents, trade secrets, copyright and trademarks.
- A patent excludes others from making, selling or using an invention, typically for fourteen or twenty years.
- To qualify for a patent, an invention must be new, non-obvious and must also have been kept a secret.
- Patents are best used in situations where an invention is highly valuable, visible, straightforward to imitate or likely to be discovered by another inventor.
- A trade secret is confidential information that gives a business an advantage.
- Keeping something a secret often costs less than a patent and can last indefinitely. However, if somebody discovers your solution independently and you don't have a patent, you have no protection.
- Copyright protects art, music, film, writing and other creative works, granting the owner exclusive rights to reproduce, distribute, perform or display them.
- The major challenge with copyright is enforcement.
- Trademarks prevent rivals from duping customers into buying a product that isn't the real deal, and reduce the risk of confusion about who makes a particular product.

- Trademarks typically cover names and logos, but can also include other distinctive features like a colour, shape or sound. The better known and more distinctive a brand is, the stronger their case is likely to be in court.
- If you don't carefully manage your intellectual property, you can put the business at risk or miss opportunities.
- There are three broad strategies for managing intellectual property – full exclusion, licensing (partial exclusion) and open access.

Durable advantages

- A competitive advantage is any benefit that allows a business to outperform rivals.
- Two tests determine whether you have a competitive advantage. First, you should be more profitable than your strongest competitor. Second, your relative market share should be stable (or growing) over time.
- Propositions requiring a unique combination of skills or activities to deliver can lead to a competitive advantage.
- Lower costs or economies of scale can be a source of competitive advantage.
- High customer retention can create a durable competitive advantage. Switching costs, force of habit, loyalty schemes or creating ecosystems of products can all help towards that goal.
- Network effects can lock customers in and lock competitors out at the same time, creating a durable advantage over rivals.
- Government action – whether through regulation or an official monopoly – can also give a business an advantage over rivals.
- Advantages become more durable when they are combined, for example economies of scale *and* retention, or network effects *and* government protection.

Competitor lag

- The only way to keep imitators at bay in the long run is to keep moving. If you're already on to the next big thing by the time rivals catch up, imitability isn't such a worry.
- You can gain a head start over rivals by exploiting their inertia and resistance to change. Forcing rivals to make trade-offs is the key to delaying them.
- Forcing a rival to change their revenue model to compete will often stop them in their tracks.
- Bringing a fundamentally different product to market will stop the current market leaders from attacking you in the short term.
- Bundling or unbundling can go against the grain of an incumbent's strategy, preventing them from copying you.
- Every technology creates a new problem in place of the one it solves. By looking at the problems current solutions are creating, you can identify opportunities for the future and get ahead of rivals.
- Creating offerings that use a different underlying technology to mainstream rivals can delay them indefinitely as they cling to old ways of doing things.

Network effects

- In some situations, the value of a product is dependent on the number of people who use it. To achieve this *network effect*, it is necessary to build a critical mass of customers.
- The more easily customers can get started with your product, the more likely they are to try it. This is critically important if network effects are to come into play.
- To grow your customer base as quickly as possible, turn customers into advocates who do your marketing for you. This requires an utterly compelling offering, and a referral marketing scheme.

- Building network effects is easier by targeting one community – a campus, office or city – at a time. This makes it easier for word of mouth to spread and for customers to experience the benefits of your offering. *Concentrate then replicate*, rather than trying to convert people *en masse*.

Adaptability (pp. 237–56)

Cash position

- If you run out of cash you cannot continue to operate the business. The more cash you have, the more options you can pursue.
- Cash acts as a buffer to insulate you from change, buying you time to figure out what to do, or allowing you to wait for the right opportunities.
- Cash and profit are not the same. Cash can come from other sources – selling shares or borrowing money.
- Free cash flow – the cash generated by the business minus any capital expenditures – is an important metric, shedding light on the company's cash position after it has made necessary investments to keep the business running.
- Working capital is the amount of cash tied up in day-to-day operations.
- Changing customer and supplier payment terms or inventory costs can dramatically impact the cash position of the business.
- Start-ups should estimate the cash-to-cash time between when they start spending money and when the first revenues will come in.
- A start-up's burn rate is the amount of cash it spends each month. The runway is the amount of cash you have divided by your burn rate. Both are important metrics to monitor.
- Producing a simple cash-flow forecast is helpful.
- When making a decision, consider how it will impact the business's cash position.

- If you are taking action to improve the cash position of the business, make sure it doesn't have adverse consequences for the rest of the grid.

Scalability or capacity

- You should be mindful of how easily your operations can scale, and consider whether your cash flow will cover expansion costs.
- Some businesses are inherently more scalable than others. Your ability to scale will be affected by your revenue model, brand appeal and your make or buy decisions.
- Your spare capacity fundamentally determines your adaptability because there is always a trade-off between efficiency and flexibility. Without slack in your operations it becomes impossible to change direction.

Complexity and rigidity

- As organisations grow they gain complexity and rigidity that reduce their adaptability. When market conditions change, they are unable to respond and suffer the consequences.
- Any business occupies one of six stages of an adaptive cycle.
- The *outburst* phase is characterised by aggressive entrepreneurs bringing fresh offerings to the market.
- Next comes *steady growth*. The organisation refines its offering, turns its attention to direct rivals, and matures operationally.
- As the market matures, organisations enter the *conservation* phase. They focus on defending their share of existing markets, often ignoring the big opportunities for the future.
- Next comes *high noon* – the organisation has surrendered its ability to adapt and the stage is set for decline.
- With the growth opportunities of the future captured by the next wave of entrepreneurial firms, *decline* sets in.

- The potential for renewal comes hand in hand with *reorganisation*. Each element of the grid is 'unseized' and reconfigured to suit the present environment.

Maintaining adaptability

- You can't change direction if your ego is always telling you you're right.
- Consider whether an optimism bias is colouring your judgement.
- Businesses often exaggerate their strengths until they become weaknesses. Four trajectories are common and should be actively avoided.
- *Craftsmen* become *tinkerers* – creating perfect products that make little commercial sense.
- *Builders* become *imperialists* – overexpanding into businesses they don't understand.
- *Pioneers* become *escapists* – creating technology showcases that nobody wants to buy.
- *Salesmen* become *drifters* – creating a jumbled portfolio of me-too offerings.
- If a '10 x' improvement to a new alternative would make it a threat, take it seriously.
- Explicitly consider the impact of decisions on the complexity and rigidity of the firm.
- Leaders should spend time on the front line with customers to avoid 'news improvement' as information makes its way up the hierarchy.
- The time to get to work on the next big thing is before the current offering reaches its prime.
- You should experiment with multiple new opportunities simultaneously to increase your odds of success.
- New opportunities should be treated as fresh configurations of the grid, to give them the best chance of success.

Recommended Reading

Wants and needs

Fixing the Game: Bubbles, Crashes, and What Capitalism Can Learn from the NFL by Roger Martin
Trying to maximise shareholder value is a daft idea. Instead, we should renew our focus on delighting customers and our shareholders will benefit as a result. That, in a nutshell, is Roger Martin's argument. *Fixing the Game* has valuable insights for any leader of a publicly traded business.

Buying In: The Secret Dialogue Between What We Buy and Who We Are by Rob Walker
Buying In is not a business book per se; it's more a journalistic exploration of the role brands play in expressing our identities. This book had a profound effect on me when I first read it many years ago and I have been recommending it since, not least because Rob Walker coined the term 'rationale thinking'.

The Biology of Belief: Unleashing the Power of Consciousness, Matter and Miracles by Bruce Lipton
A pioneering book by Bruce Lipton – a leading researcher into cellular biology – on the link between mind and body, exploring how our beliefs have a more dramatic impact on our well-being than our genes.

The Complete Stanislavsky Toolkit by Bella Merlin
I learned about the Stanislavsky system from this book. It's as far from a business book as you can get, but if the ideas about super objectives and subtext interested you, this is where to find out more.

Understanding Your Users: A Practical Guide to User Research Methods by Kathy Baxter and Catherine Courage
Although written primarily with user-experience professionals in mind, this compendium of research techniques should help anyone down the path to discovering their customers' wants and needs.

Strategic Market Research: A Guide to Conducting Research that Drives Businesses by Anne E. Beall
A well-written primer on how to approach market research with an overview of the most common techniques and when to use them. Short enough to be read during one soak in the bathtub. (Disclaimer: I'm a quick reader. Don't blame me if you turn into a prune.)

The Essential Persona Lifecycle: Your Guide to Building and Using Personas by Tamara Adlin and John Pruitt
In my experience, many firms struggle to segment their customers and communicate their different wants and needs effectively. This pragmatic guide is helpful if you want to produce useful customer profiles.

Rivalry

Understanding Michael Porter: The Essential Guide to Competition and Strategy by Joan Magretta
If you're new to Porter's work, or want an accessible primer, Joan Magretta's book is an excellent resource.

Positioning the Brand: An Inside-Out Approach by Rik Riezebos and Jaap van der Grinten
A rigorous, somewhat academic take on positioning, but full of practical techniques and real-world examples to help your brand stand out in a crowded market.

The Paradox of Choice: Why More Is Less by Barry Schwartz
Too much choice is worse than too little. This book might make you think twice before expanding your product range.

Offerings

Crossing the Chasm: Marketing and Selling High-Tech Products to Mainstream Customers by Geoffrey A. Moore
Although written with B2B offerings in mind, *Crossing the Chasm* has valuable guidance for those launching any kind of innovative product or service. Eminently readable and loaded with useful advice, the book deserves its cult status.

Positioning: The Battle for Your Mind by Al Ries and Jack Trout
Entertaining and thought-provoking, Ries and Trout's classic book on positioning reveals that the key to a successful brand is not just occupying a position in the market, but building one in the customer's mind.

Thinking, Fast and Slow by Daniel Kahneman
Few have contributed as much to our understanding of how we think as psychologist Daniel Kahneman and his long-term partner Amos Tversky. For a deeper understanding of the peak–end rule and other quirks of the human mind, look no further. It will change the way you think about your thinking.

Marketing Services: Competing Through Quality by Leonard L. Berry and A. Parasuraman
An oldie but a goodie. Full of timeless advice on customer experience for service businesses from before customer experience became the talking point it is today. The expectation model I espouse in this book can be found in Chapter Four.

The Ten Principles Behind Great Customer Experiences by Matt Watkinson
The research process and experience gained from my previous book informed a lot of the insights for the desirability column of the grid. It would be somewhat remiss of me not to mention it.

Revenues

The Business Model Navigator by Oliver Gassman, Karolin Frankenberger and Michaela Csik
This book describes fifty-five popular business models, making it a good primer to get the juices flowing. A slight criticism is that the term 'business model' is used somewhat loosely, at times referring more to a revenue

model, market position, product strategy or even channel. That said, it's still a great book.

Confessions of the Pricing Man: How Price Affects Everything by Hermann Simon
Excellent primer from an undisputed titan in the field. If you want to learn more about pricing, read this one first.

The 1% Windfall: How Successful Companies Use Price to Profit and Grow by Rafi Mohammed
Another excellent book on pricing. Easy to read and full of pragmatic guidance and examples.

The Strategy and Tactics of Pricing: A Guide to Growing More Profitably by Thomas Nagle and John Hogan
Far more academic and in-depth than the previous two recommendations, *The Strategy and Tactics of Pricing* is a more challenging read but has valuable insights for those prepared to persevere. Contains an excellent section on pricing and costs, with valuable guidance on performing advanced break-even calculations.

Bargaining power

Competitive Strategy: Techniques for Analyzing Industries and Competitors by Michael E. Porter
Porter's magisterial text on competitive strategy is worth reading not only for its enduring relevance to decision-making, but for its place in the history of management thinking – if you're into that kind of thing.

Friend and Foe: When to Cooperate, When to Compete, and How to Succeed at Both by Adam Galinsky and Maurice Schweitzer
Relationships often have cooperative and competitive elements simultaneously. As its title suggests, this book sheds light on which attitude is appropriate in a given situation. Includes a fascinating exploration of the toxic side effects of power.

The Power Paradox: How We Gain and Lose Influence by Dacher Keltner
Keltner spent twenty years researching power dynamics. Essential reading, not just for those at the top of the tree.

The Fairness Instinct: The Robin Hood Mentality and Our Biological Nature by L. Sun
A delightful book explaining how our innate sense of fairness came about, and how this instinct shapes our lives and society at large.

Costs

Financial Intelligence: A Manager's Guide to Knowing What the Numbers Really Mean by Karen Berman, Joe Knight and John Case
Light-hearted and accessible but rigorous, this is the best book bar none on finance for non-finance professionals. Should be mandatory reading for anyone in business.

Driving Down Cost: How to Manage and Cut Cost – Intelligently by Andrew Wileman
No-nonsense, pragmatic advice on how to reduce costs by a veteran in the field.

The Goal: A Process of Ongoing Improvement by Eliyahu M. Goldratt and Jeff Cox
If you want to learn more about the theory of constraints you may as well start at the source: Goldratt and Cox's classic text, *The Goal*. Written as a novel rather than as a business book, I'd judge it more as the latter than the former.

The Outsiders: Eight Unconventional CEOs and Their Radically Rational Blueprint for Success by William N. Thorndike
This book sheds light on the investment approaches and mentalities of eight iconoclastic CEOs, all of whom generated staggering returns for their shareholders. Highly recommended by none other than Warren Buffett himself.

Customer base

How Brands Grow: What Marketers Don't Know by Byron Sharp
Whilst I found his tone needlessly combative, if you work in marketing – especially at a large-scale commodity consumer brand – you need to read this book.

Contagious: Why Things Catch On by Jonah Berger
Berger's book is packed with wonderful insights into what makes things gain popularity, go viral and capture people's attention. If you're launching or marketing a product this is required reading.

Key Marketing Metrics: The 50+ Metrics Every Manager Needs to Know by Paul W. Farris, Neil Bendle, Phillip Pfeifer and David Reibstein
Using the grid is much easier if you're measuring the right things. To that end, look no further than this excellent reference book, which describes every marketing metric under the sun and how to use them.

Innovating Analytics: How the Next Generation of Net Promoter Can Increase Sales and Drive Business Results by Larry Freed
It's safe to say Larry Freed hasn't been on Bain's Christmas-card list since this came out. If you've niggling doubts or concerns about the validity of the Net Promoter Score, this book's for you.

Imitability

Intellectual Property Strategy by John Palfrey
In this well-written primer Palfrey argues strongly in favour of treating intellectual property as a flexible asset class that can be used in a variety of ways to create returns for the business. Well worth a read.

Guide to Intellectual Property: What It Is, How to Protect It, How to Exploit It by Stephen Johnson
If you want to understand a little more about each class of intellectual property, this book gives great nuts-and-bolts explanations.

The Curse of the Mogul: What's Wrong with the World's Leading Media Companies by Jonathan Knee, Bruce Greenwald and Ava Seave
Whilst the book is primarily an acerbic takedown of the leaders within the media industry, Chapter Two is a brilliant primer on real and sham sources of competitive advantage. The authors present a persuasive argument that brands are not a real source of competitive advantage, which – after much mental hand-wringing – ultimately convinced me to leave branding off my list of durable advantages.

Information Rules: A Strategic Guide to the Network Economy by Carl Shapiro and Hal Varian
Whilst it's getting a little long in the tooth and I've found some ideas defy practical application, this is still one of the few meaningful works tackling the challenging subject of network effects.

The Nature of Technology: What It Is and How It Evolves by W. Brian Arthur
Profound insights into how technologies change over time through a process of 'combinational evolution'. Arthur's book isn't just for technologists – anyone who wants to better understand the world they live in should find this a thought-provoking read.

Adaptability

Only the Paranoid Survive – How to Exploit the Crisis Points That Challenge Every Company by Andy Grove
A timeless guide to surviving 'strategic inflection points' – periods of intense change – written by one of the greatest managers of all time.

Self-Renewal: The Individual and the Innovative Society by John W. Gardner
A beautiful little book on the nature of change, growth and decay, and why we must safeguard our capacity for self-renewal. Inspirational and thought-provoking in equal measure.

Slack: Getting Past Burnout, Busywork, and the Myth of Total Efficiency by Tom DeMarco
A short book with a simple but powerful message about the downsides of our quest for efficiency. Should be required reading for anyone leading midsized businesses or larger.

The Innovator's Solution: Creating and Sustaining Successful Growth by Clayton Christensen
His prior work, *The Innovator's Dilemma*, may get the lion's share of the attention, but in my opinion this is a superior work. Packed with thought-provoking ideas, observations and guidance, for me this is Christensen's masterpiece.

The Icarus Paradox – How Exceptional Companies Bring About Their Own Downfall by Danny Miller
Probably the best business book you've never heard of. A powerful message delivered with a lively style, *The Icarus Paradox* is as relevant now as it was when it was written in 1991.

Panarchy Synopsis: Understanding Transformations in Human and Natural Systems by Lance H. Gunderson and C. S. Holling
A summary of a book that opened my eyes to the nature of complex adaptive systems; few books have been more influential on my thinking about how organisations grow and decay. Full disclosure – I've not read the synopsis version, only the original, which is not for the faint-hearted.

Thinking in Systems: A Primer by Donella Meadows
Once you understand how systems work, the world never looks the same again. This was one of the first books I read in researching the grid, and it was a life-changing read for me. These ideas should be taught in every school on earth.

References

Websites listed were accessed between January 2016 and April 2017.

Author's Note

1. Box, G. E. P., 'Robustness in the Strategy of Scientific Model Building', in R. L. Launer and G. N. Wilkinson, eds, *Robustness in Statistics* (New York: Academic Press, 1979), 201–36.

Introduction

1. See www.egoscue.com.
2. Myers, T. W., *Anatomy Trains* (London: Elsevier, 2009).
3. Watkinson, M., *The Ten Principles Behind Great Customer Experiences* (Harlow: FT Press, 2013).
4. See Arthur, W. B., *Complexity and the Economy* (Oxford: Oxford University Press, 2014).

Constructing the Grid

1. See Magretta, J., *Understanding Michael Porter: The Essential Guide to Competition and Strategy* (Boston: Harvard Business Review Press, 2012; Kindle edn), ch. 2.
2. Rumelt, R., *Good Strategy Bad Strategy: The Difference and Why It Matters* (New York: Crown Business, 2011; Kindle edn), ch. 8.
3. http://www.tetrapak.com/us/about/history.

The Elements of the Grid

1. Porter, M. E., *Competitive Strategy: Techniques for Analyzing Industries and Competitors* (New York: The Free Press, 1998; Kindle edn), ch. 5, section 3.
2. http://www.forbes.com/sites/joannmuller/2013/04/17/volkswagens-mission-to-dominate-global-auto-industry-gets-noticeably-harder/#354d5c2c1ab6.
3. http://www.caranddriver.com/news/vw-plans-to-triple-us-vehicle-sales-news.
4. https://www.nytimes.com/2015/10/05/business/engine-shortfall-pushed-volkswagen-to-evade-emissions-testing.html?_r=0.
5. Ibid.
6. Ibid.
7. Volkswagen stopped licensing Daimler's BlueTec solution in 2007 to save costs. Following the scandal, they settled on this strategic route again, adopting AdBlue, another alternative that was more expensive than their current defective system. See http://www.wsj.com/articles/vw-to-cut-investment-by-1-billion-a-year-1444728786.
8. https://www.nytimes.com/interactive/2015/business/international/vw-diesel-emissions-scandal-explained.html.
9. Ibid.
10. https://www.nytimes.com/2016/10/26/business/relief-at-last-for-us-owners-of-diesel-volkswagens.html.
11. http://www.wsj.com/articles/vws-dealers-fume-while-waiting-for-diesel-car-fix-1468604636.
12. https://www.bloomberg.com/news/articles/2016-08-25/vw-reaches-agreement-with-dealerships-over-diesel-cheat-losses.
13. http://www.thetruthaboutcars.com/2015/09/volkswagens-diesel-cars-sitting-u-s-ports-months/.
14. https://www.nytimes.com/2016/04/23/business/international/volkswagen-loss-emissions-scandal.html.
15. https://www.wired.com/2015/09/volkswagen-diesel-cheating-scandal-is-good-for-hybrid-cars/.
16. http://blogs.wsj.com/cfo/2015/09/23/volkswagen-financially-equipped-to-handle-diesel-emissions-scandal/?mg=id-wsj.

Using the Grid in Practice

1. DeMarco, T., Hruschka, P., et al., *Adrenaline Junkies and Template Zombies* (New York: Dorset House, 2008), pattern 86: 'Template Zombies'.
2. http://www.innocentdrinks.co.uk/us/our-story.

3. Segal, G. Z., *Getting There: A Book of Mentors* (New York: Abrams Image, 2015; Kindle edn), 30.

4. Burlingham, B., *Small Giants: Companies that Choose to Be Great Instead of Big* (2005; 10th anniversary edn, New York: Portfolio/Penguin, 2016; Kindle edn).

5. Rumelt, R., *Good Strategy Bad Strategy: The Difference and Why It Matters* (New York: Crown Business, 2011; Kindle edn), 77.

Deep Dives

1. See CB Insights, 'The Top Twenty Reasons Startups Fail' (7 October 2014), available at www.cbinsights.com. Noted venture capitalist Marc Andreesen also agrees that the number-one cause of start-up failure is a lack of market. See http://web.archive.org/web/20070701074943/http://blog.pmarca.com/2007/06/the-pmarca-gu-2.html.

Wants and Needs

1. http://www.economist.com/node/14857221.

2. Ibid.

3. Ibid.

4. https://www.revolution.watch/jean-claude-biver-on-record-part-1-of-3/.

5. See CB Insights, 'The Top Twenty Reasons Startups Fail' (7 October 2014), available at www.cbinsights.com.

6. Hankel, I., *Black Hole Focus* (Chichester: Capstone, 2014; Kindle edn), ch. 5.

7. Bloom, P., *How Pleasure Works* (London: The Bodley Head, 2010), xii.

8. Festinger, L., *A Theory of Cognitive Dissonance* (California: Stanford University Press, 1957).

9. Dobelli, R., *The Art of Thinking Clearly* (London: Sceptre, 2013), 23–8.

10. Hargittai, B., and Hargittai, I., *Wisdom of the Martians of Science: In Their Own Words with Commentaries* (New Jersey: World Scientific, 2015), 151.

11. Baudrillard, J., *For a Critique of the Political Economy of the Sign* (New York: Telos Press, 1981), 63–6.

12. http://www.coca-cola.co.uk/packages/history/share-a-coke/.

13. McDonald, M., and Dunbar, I., *Market Segmentation: How to Do It, How to Profit From It* (Chichester: John Wiley & Sons, 2012; Kindle edn), ch. 3, section 5.

14. http://newsroom.toyota.co.jp/en/detail/12077091/.

15. http://www.nytimes.com/2007/07/04/business/04hybrid.html?_r=0.

16. https://www.vitsoe.com/gb/about/ethos.

17. Bohlen, Joe M., and Beal, George M., 'The Diffusion Process', Special Report No. 18 (Cooperative Extension Service, Iowa State University,

1957), 5–6. Accessed online at http://www.soc.iastate.edu/extension/pub/comm/SP18.pdf.

18. Moore, G. A., *Crossing the Chasm: Marketing and Selling Disruptive Products to Mainstream Customers* (New York: Harper Business, 2014), 16–17.

19. See http://pmarchive.com/guide_to_startups_part5.html for a humorous and insightful take on this challenge by noted venture capitalist Marc Andreesen. His advice: 'First, don't do start-ups that require deals with big companies to make them successful. The risk of never getting those deals is way too high, no matter how hard you are willing to work at it. And even if you get the deals, they probably won't work out the way you hoped.'

20. Watkinson, M., *The Ten Principles Behind Great Customer Experiences* (Harlow: FT Press, 2013), 45–56.

21. https://www.shoreditchhouse.com/membership.

22. Riezebos, R., and van der Grinten, J., *Positioning the Brand: An Inside-Out Approach* (London: Routledge, 2012; Kindle edn), ch. 4, section: 'Brand-Product Class Connection'.

23. http://www.thisismoney.co.uk/money/cars/article-2451159/Aston-Martin-pulls-Cygnet-selling-fewer-150-years.html.

24. Reason, J., *Human Error* (New York: Cambridge University Press, 1990), 5.

25. Berry, L., and Parasuraman, A., *Marketing Services: Competing Through Quality* (New York: The Free Press, 1991; Kindle edn), part 2, ch. 2 and 3.

26. http://www.theatlantic.com/international/archive/2015/02/how-an-ad-campaign-invented-the-diamond-engagement-ring/385376/.

27. Asacker, T., *The Business of Belief* (Tom Asacker, 2013), 61.

28. Ibid., 70.

29. Ibid., 65.

30. Krychman, Michael L., *100 Questions & Answers About Women's Sexual Wellness and Vitality* (Sudbury: Jones & Bartlett Learning, 2010), 91–2.

31. Christensen, C., *The Clayton M. Christensen Reader* (Boston: Harvard Business Review Press, 2016), 46

32. Merlin, B., *The Complete Stanislavsky Toolkit* (London: Nick Hern Books, 2007), 219–26.

33. Ibid., 91–7.

34. https://onlinedoctor.lloydspharmacy.com/uk/mens-health.

35. https://onlinedoctor.lloydspharmacy.com/uk/info/about-us.

36. Watkinson, *The Ten Principles*, 80–83.

37. http://www.nytimes.com/2001/01/28/business/business-did-you-hear-the-one-about-the-superjumbo-that-ate-the-airport.html.

38. https://www.bloomberg.com/news/articles/2016-07-12/airbus-plans-to-cut-annual-a380-deliveries-to-12-as-of-2018.

39. McNish, J., and Silcoff, S., *Losing the Signal: The Untold Story Behind the Extraordinary Rise and Spectacular Fall of BlackBerry* (New York: Flatiron Books, 2015), 241.
40. https://www.statista.com/statistics/258749/most-popular-global-mobile-messenger-apps/.
41. Seba, T., *Winners Take All: The Nine Fundamental Rules of High Tech Strategy* (San Francisco: Tony Seba, 2006), 192–3.
42. http://www.wsj.com/articles/theranos-has-struggled-with-blood-tests-1444881901?mg=id-wsj.
43. http://www.vanityfair.com/news/2016/09/elizabeth-holmes-theranos-exclusive.
44. See note 42 above.
45. http://www.wsj.com/articles/u-s-regulator-bans-theranos-ceo-elizabeth-holmes-from-operating-labs-for-two-years-1467956064.
46. http://www.forbes.com/sites/matthewherper/2016/06/01/from-4-5-billion-to-nothing-forbes-revises-estimated-net-worth-of-theranos-founder-elizabeth-holmes/#2bf9da702f29.
47. http://www.wsj.com/articles/theranos-is-subject-of-criminal-probe-by-u-s-1461019055.
48. Rogers, E. M., *Diffusion of Innovations* (5th edn, New York: The Free Press, 2003), 258.
49. Ibid.
50. See www.goruck.com and http://www.goruck.com/gr1-explained.
51. Dr B. J. Fogg's behaviour-change model expands on this point. He makes the key point that the easier a target behaviour is to perform, the more likely a customer is to do it. Increasing training is a viable option, but less preferable to simplifying the task they must perform. See http://www.behaviormodel.org/for more details.
52. Loewy, R., *Never Leave Well Enough Alone* (New York: Simon & Schuster, 1950), 325–31.
53. Ibid.
54. https://www.netjets.com/AboutNetJets/Our-History/.
55. https://www.netjets.com/why-netjets/Largest-Finest-Fleet/.
56. Tony Seba suggests a similar approach. See note 43.
57. https://www.theguardian.com/business/2016/apr/18/dan-wagner-powa-technologies.
58. http://www.businessinsider.com/inside-the-crash-of-londons-payment-unicorn-powa-technologies-2016-4.

1. Credit to my neighbour Draža Janksy for pointing this out during the development of the manuscript.
2. For more detail on this topic I recommend: Magretta, J., *Understanding Michael Porter: The Essential Guide to Competition and Strategy* (Boston: Harvard Business Review Press, 2012; Kindle edn), ch. 1.
3. See Goddard, J., and Eccles, T., *Uncommon Sense, Common Nonsense: Why Some Organisations Consistently Outperform Others* (London: Profile Books, 2013). See section 'Losers Look to Competitive Benchmarks Rather than to Their Own Imagination for Their Model of Success.'
4. Adapted from Pfenning, D., and Pfenning, K., *Evolution's Wedge: Competition and the Origins of Diversity* (Berkeley: University of California Press, 2012), 2: 'Any direct or indirect interaction between species or populations that reduces access to vital resources or successful reproductive opportunities and that is therefore deleterious – on average – to both parties.'
5. Liddell Hart, B. H., *Strategy* (London: Faber & Faber, 1954), xx.
6. Darwin, C., *On the Origin of the Species: By Means of Natural Selection or The Preservation of Favoured Races in the Struggle for Life* (1859; New York: Cosimo, 2007), cited in Pfenning and Pfenning, *Evolution's Wedge*, 4.
7. McDonald, M., and Dunbar, I., *Market Segmentation: How to Do It, How to Profit From It* (Chichester: John Wiley & Sons, 2012; Kindle edn), ch. 3, section 4.
8. http://www.theregister.co.uk/2011/10/18/vodafone_kills_360/.
9. Riezebos, R., and van der Grinten, J., *Positioning the Brand: An Inside-Out Approach* (London: Routledge, 2012), ch. 4, section: 'Brand-Product Class Connection'.
10. See Thorndike, W. N., *The Outsiders: Eight Unconventional CEOs and Their Radically Rational Blueprint for Success* (Boston: Harvard Business Review Press, 2012; Kindle edn). A willingness to exit low-return businesses was a characteristic shared by the CEOs profiled in Thorndike's book.
11. Farris, P. W., Bendle, N. T., Pfeifer, P. E., and Reibstein, D. J., *Key Marketing Metrics: The 50+ Metrics Every Manager Needs to Know* (Harlow: Pearson Education, 2009), 23–4.
12. http://www.wsj.com/articles/is-the-tech-bubble-popping-ping-pong-offers-an-answer-1462286089?mg=id-ws.j.
13. Porter, M. E., *Competitive Strategy: Techniques for Analyzing Industries and Competitors* (New York: The Free Press, 1998; Kindle edn), ch. 1.
14. Ibid.

15. https://www.bloomberg.com/news/articles/2015-10-30/new-york-hotel-group-goes-on-offensive-against-airbnb-rentals.

16. http://news.bbc.co.uk/onthisday/hi/dates/stories/january/11/newsid_2520000/2520189.stm. For more details, see Gregory, M., *Dirty Tricks: British Airways' Secret War against Virgin Atlantic* (London: Virgin Publishing, 1994; revised edn, 2000).

17. Riezebos and van der Grinten, *Positioning the Brand*, 80.

18. McNish, J., and Silcoff, S., *Losing the Signal: The Untold Story Behind the Extraordinary Rise and Spectacular Fall of BlackBerry* (New York: Flatiron Books, 2015), 231.

19. Lafley, A. G., and Martin, R. L., *Playing to Win: How Strategy Really Works* (Boston: Harvard Business Review Press, 2013), ch. 3.

20. Knee, J. A., Greenwald, B. C., and Seave, A., *The Curse of the Mogul* (New York: Profile, 2009; Kindle edn), ch. 2, section 2.3: 'Real Competitive Advantages/Cost'.

21. Ries, A., and Trout, J., *Positioning: The Battle For Your Mind* (New York: McGraw-Hill, 2000), 196.

22. For Richard Huntington's Value Map see http://www.slideshare.net/adliterate/value-grid. For Ray Kordupleski's take, see his *Mastering Customer Value Management* (Cincinnati: Pinnaflex, 2003), 25–8.

23. http://www.luxottica.com/en/oakley-merge-luxottica-group-us2930-share.

24. https://www.wired.com/2008/08/ff-redcamera/.

25. Nagle, T. T., Hogan, J. E., and Zale, J., *The Strategy and Tactics of Pricing* (New Jersey: Prentice Hall, 2011), 181–2.

26. Porter, *Competitive Strategy*, ch. 1.

27. Christensen, C. M., *The Innovator's Solution: Creating and Sustaining Successful Growth* (Boston: Harvard Business Review Press, 2013; Kindle edn).

28. Schwartz, B., *The Paradox of Choice: Why More Is Less* (New York: Harper Perennial, 2004).

29. Isaacson, W., *Steve Jobs* (London: Little, Brown, 2011), 337.

30. Grove, A. S., *Only the Paranoid Survive: How to Exploit the Crisis Points That Challenge Every Company* (New York: Random House, 1999), 107.

31. Sung, E., *Customer Moat: How Loyalty Drives Profit* (Eddie Sung, 2016), ch. 2, section 3.

Offerings

1. Baudrillard, J., *For a Critique of the Political Economy of the Sign* (New York: Telos Press, 1981), 63–6.

2. Higgins, T., *Beyond Pleasure and Pain: How Motivation Works* (New York: Oxford University Press, 2012), 49.

3. Simon, H., *Confessions of the Pricing Man: How Price Affects Everything* (Switzerland: Springer, 2015; Kindle edn), ch. 3.
4. Pricken, M., *The Essence of Value* (Erlangen: Publicis, 2014), 36–58, 182.
5. I wrote about this topic at length in my previous book, *The Ten Principles Behind Great Customer Experiences* (Harlow: FT Press, 2013). My thinking on the subject was greatly inspired by Dr Thayer's research into mood management. See Thayer, R., *The Origin of Everyday Moods: Managing Energy, Tension and Stress* (New York: Oxford University Press, 1996).
6. See note 5.
7. Tiger, L., *The Pursuit of Pleasure* (New Jersey: Transaction Publishers, 2000), 53–4.
8. Ibid., 54–6.
9. Berger, J., *Contagious: Why Things Catch On* (New York: Simon & Schuster, 2013), ch. 4.
10. Deci and Ryan's influential *Self-Determination Theory* proposes that a feeling of autonomy is an innate psychological need. See Deci, I. L., and Ryan, R. M., *Intrinsic Motivation and Self-Determination in Human Behavior* (New York: Plenum Press, 1985). Psychologist Tory Higgins also supports the notion that a feeling of control is a fundamental human motivator. See Higgins *Beyond Pleasure and Pain*.
11. Moore, G. A., *Crossing the Chasm: Marketing and Selling Disruptive Products to Mainstream Markets* (New York: Harper Business, 2014), 186.
12. https://petapixel.com/2015/06/04/mirrorless-now-the-official-name-of-the-camera-market-dominated-by-sony/.
13. http://mashable.com/2015/08/02/google-plus-history/#bKf2Q3FnTPqx.
14. Paul Graham, co-founder of seed capital firm Y Combinator, makes a similar point, advising start-ups to launch when they have a 'quantum of utility' – the point where a potential customer can now do something they couldn't do before. https://news.ycombinator.com/item?id=542768.
15. https://www.tesla.com.
16. http://www.brandtags.com.
17. https://youtu.be/Vq9ap6JuXuc.
18. https://www.nytimes.com/2015/12/21/nyregion/unwrapping-mast-brothers-chocolatier-mythos.html.
19. http://dallasfood.org/2015/12/mast-brothers-what-lies-behind-the-beards-part-1-tastetexture/.
20. http://dallasfood.org/2015/12/mast-brothers-what-lies-behind-the-beards-part-3-ingredients/.
21. http://www.eater.com/2015/12/21/10634270/mast-brothers-scandal-admitted-chocolate.
22. http://www.vanityfair.com/culture/2015/02/mast-brothers-chocolate-wrappers.

23. http://www.businessinsider.com/mast-brothers-sales-tank-at-trendy-shops-2016-1.
24. https://www.theguardian.com/music/2013/sep/27/dr-dre-beats-1bn-carlyle-sale.
25. https://www.apple.com/pr/library/2014/05/28Apple-to-Acquire-Beats-Music-Beats-Electronics.html.
26. http://www.apple.com/shop/product/MHD02AM/B/urbeats-earphones-black.
27. Ibid.
28. Sharp, B., *How Brands Grow: What Marketers Don't Known* (South Melbourne: Oxford University Press, 2010) 195.
29. http://www.patagonia.com/company-info.html.
30. Kahneman, D., *Thinking, Fast and Slow* (London: Allen Lane, 2011), 378–80.
31. Ibid., 381.
32. Berry, L., and Parasuraman, A., *Marketing Services: Competing Through Quality* (New York: The Free Press, 1991; Kindle edn), ch. 4.
33. https://www.airnewzealand.com/press-release-2016-air-new-zealand-heads-to-hollywood-for-its-latest-safety-video.
34. http://www.airlineratings.com/awards.php.
35. http://www.nytimes.com/2009/04/16/business/media/16dominos.html.
36. http://www.fool.com/investing/general/2013/11/20/why-dominos-spent-millions-to-fix-its-pizza.aspx.
37. http://anyware.dominos.com.
38. http://www.cpbgroup.com/work/dominos/dominos-pizza-turnaround.
39. Ibid.

Revenues

1. https://www.bloomberg.com/features/2015-martin-shkreli-wu-tang-clan-album/.
2. http://www.rolls-royce.com/media/press-releases/yr-2012/121030-the-hour.aspx.
3. https://www.bloomberg.com/news/articles/2014-02-04/arm-chips-are-the-most-used-consumer-product-dot-where-s-the-money.
4. http://www.hpmuseum.net/exhibit.php?class=5&cat=20.
5. https://hbr.org/2013/01/burberrys-ceo-on-turning-an-aging-british-icon-into-a-global-luxury-brand.
6. https://www.theguardian.com/business/2013/jun/16/angela-ahrendts-burberry-chav-image.
7. Ibid.

8. Mohammed, R., *The 1% Windfall: How Successful Companies Use Price to Profit and Grow* (Harper Collins e-books, 2010; Kindle edn), introduction.

9. See 'Principle #2' in Sung, E., *Customer Moat: How Loyalty Drives Profit* (Eddie Sung, 2016).

10. Simon, H., *Confessions of the Pricing Man: How Price Affects Everything* (Switzerland: Springer, 2015; Kindle edn), ch. 5, section 6.

11. Nagle, T. T., Hogan, J. E., and Zale, J., *The Strategy and Tactics of Pricing* (New Jersey: Prentice Hall, 2011), 225.

12. See Mohammed, *The 1% Windfall*, ch. 1.

13. Ibid.

14. Nagle, Hogan and Zale, *The Strategy and Tactics of Pricing*, 132.

15. https://www.nytimes.com/2015/10/25/fashion/a-365-foam-roller-it-exists.html.

16. http://www.mckinsey.com/business-functions/marketing-and-sales/our-insights/pricing-new-products#0.

17. See note 10.

18. https://www.bloomberg.com/news/articles/2009-06-01/gm-files-for-bankruptcybusinessweek-business-news-stock-market-and-financial-advice.

19. https://www.vitsoe.com/us/news/black-friday-16.

20. Simon, *Confessions of the Pricing Man*, ch. 4: 'Premium Pricing'.

21. https://www.soul-cycle.com/our-story/.

22. Mohammed, *The 1% Windfall*, ch. 3.

23. Lovell, N., *The Curve: How Smart Companies Find High Value Customers* (London: Portfolio/Penguin Section, 2013; Kindle edn), preface.

24. http://www.red.com/news/red-dragon-begins-now.

25. https://articles.uie.com/three_hund_million_button/.

Bargaining Power

1. This came up in conversation with a friend, Draža Janksy.

2. Galinsky, A., and Schweitzer, M., *Friend and Foe: When to Cooperate, When to Compete, and How to Succeed at Both* (London: Random House Business, 2015; Kindle edn), introduction.

3. Porter, M. E., *Competitive Strategy: Techniques for Analyzing Industries and Competitors* (New York: The Free Press, 1998; Kindle edn).

4. http://www.newyorker.com/business/currency/why-are-there-so-many-shuttered-storefronts-in-the-west-village.

5. For more detail on factors underpinning buyer and supplier power, and strategies for buyer and supplier selection, see Porter, *Competitive Strategy*, chapters 1 and 6. For a lightweight introduction to the five forces

analysis see Magretta, J., *Understanding Michael Porter: The Essential Guide to Competition and Strategy* (Boston: Harvard Business Review Press, 2012; Kindle edn).

6. http://www.inc.com/magazine/201606/jason-fried/saying-no-to-large-enterprise-customers.html.
7. Christensen, C. M., Allworth, J., and Dillon, K., *How Will You Measure Your Life* (New York: HarperCollins, 2012; Kindle edn), ch. 7
8. https://www.hodinkee.com/articles/ftc-takes-major-action-against-shinola-demands-where-american-is-made-slogan-to-be-dropped-immediately.
9. https://www.colorado.gov/marijuana.
10. http://www.latimes.com/business/la-fi-drone-rules-20160829-snap-htmlstory.html.
11. http://www.reuters.com/article/us-eu-microsoft-IDUSBRE 92500520130306.
12. http://www.reuters.com/article/us-intel-court-eu-IDUSKBN0E N0M120140612.
13. https://www.law.cornell.edu/uscode/text/15/1052.
14. https://www.washingtonpost.com/local/judge-upholds-cancellation-of-redskins-trademarks-in-a-legal-and-symbolic-setback-for-team/2015/07/08/5a65424e-1e6e-11e5-aeb9-a4411a84c9d55_story.html?utm_term=.7a2ef382a7d5.
15. https://www.theguardian.com/environment/2016/jul/30/england-plastic-bag-usage-drops-85-per-cent-since-5p-charged-introduced.
16. http://www.pbs.gov.au/info/about-the-pbs#What_medicines_does_the_government_subsidise.
17. https://www.ofcom.org.uk/about-ofcom/latest/features-and-news/vodafone-fined-4.6-million?utm_source=Twitter&utm_medium=Twitter&utm_content=Vodafone.
18. http://www.nppaindia.nic.in/wh-new-2016/wh-new-29-2016.html.
19. http://abcnews.go.com/2020/Stossel/story?id=1954352&page=1.
20. https://www.theguardian.com/business/2016/aug/30/apple-pay-back-taxes-eu-ruling-ireland-state-aid.
21. https://www.treasury.gov/initiatives/financial-stability/TARP-Programs/Pages/default.aspx.
22. https://www.sec.gov/about/laws.shtml.
23. https://www.ft.com/content/5600f746-7f40-11e6-bc52-0c7211ef3198.
24. http://www.nytimes.com/2011/01/22/world/africa/22sidi.html?rref=collection%2Ftimestopic%2FBouazizi%2C%20Mohamed&action=click&contentCollection=timestopics&region=stream&module=stream_unit&version=latest&contentPlacement=8&pgtype=collection.

25. http://world.time.com/2013/08/21/mubarak-and-the-arab-springs-other-villains-where-are-they-now/.

26. For a detailed look at the biological and evolutionary origins of fairness and cooperation, see Sun, L., *The Fairness Instinct: The Robin Hood Mentality and Our Biological Nature* (New York: Prometheus Books, 2013; Kindle edn), and Ridley, M., *The Origins of Virtue* (London: Penguin, 1996; Kindle edn).

27. Galinsky and Schweitzer, *Friend and Foe*, ch. 2.

28. Keltner, D., *The Power Paradox: How We Gain and Lose Influence* (New York: Penguin Press, 2016; Kindle edn), ch. 4.

29. McNish, J., and Silcoff, S., *Losing the Signal: The Untold Story Behind the Extraordinary Rise and Spectacular Fall of BlackBerry* (New York: Flatiron Books, 2015), 166–75.

30. Ibid., 214.

31. https://www.bloomberg.com/news/articles/2015-09-23/how-marketing-turned-the-epipen-into-a-billion-dollar-business.

32. https://www.acep.org/content.aspx?id=104625.

33. https://obamawhitehouse.archives.gov/blog/2013/11/13/president-obama-signs-new-epipen-law-protect-children-asthma-and-severe-allergies-an.

34. See note 32.

35. http://abc.go.com/shows/the-view/video/pl5554876/VDKA0_opse6qzt.

36. http://www.in-pharmatechnologist.com/Processing/Sanofi-abandoning-Auvi-Q-after-dosage-problems-led-to-total-recall.

37. https://www.bloomberg.com/news/articles/2016-03-01/mylan-s-epipen-gets-boost-as-fda-spots-holes-in-teva-application?cmpid=yhoo.headline.

38. http://time.com/4465954/epipen-myland-cost-fix-problems/.

39. See note 32.

40. See note 32.

41. http://www.forbes.com/sites/emilywillingham/2016/08/21/why-did-mylan-hike-epipen-prices-400-because-they-could/#578fc668477a.

42. http://well.blogs.nytimes.com/2016/08/25/how-parents-harnessed-the-power-of-social-media-to-challenge-epipen-prices/?_r=0.

43. http://www.klobuchar.senate.gov/public/2016/8/klobuchar-calls-for-ftc-investigation-of-mylan-pharmaceuticals-for-possible-antitrust-violations-in-light-of-dramatic-price-increase-of-epipen-packs.

44. http://www.grassley.senate.gov/sites/default/files/constituents/upload/2016-08-24%20CEG%20PJ%20AK%20RB%20RJ%20to%20FDA%20(Mylan%20EpiPen)_Redacted.pdf.

45. http://www.wsj.com/articles/mylan-to-pay-465-million-in-epipen-settlement-1475874312?mg=id-wsj.

46. http://www.cnbc.com/2016/08/25/mylan-expands-epipen-cost-cutting-programs-after-charges-of-price-gouging.html.

47. http://www.nbcnews.com/business/consumer/mylan-execs-gave-themselves-raises-they-hiked-epipen-prices-n636591.
48. http://fortune.com/2016/09/21/mylan-stock-low/.
49. http://www.wsj.com/articles/mylan-launches-cheaper-generic-epipen-alternative-1481896300.
50. Keltner, D., *The Power Paradox*, epilogue.
51. http://taylorswift.tumblr.com/post/122071902085/to-apple-love-taylor
52. Apple vs GTAT paints an interesting picture of how the tech giant can deploy its bargaining power. See http://www.forbes.com/sites/chuckjones/2014/10/30/this-is-why-apple-did-not-want-its-gtat-contracts-made-public/#55eb5baa35a0.
53. http://www.bbc.com/news/entertainment-arts-33220189.

Costs

1. http://www.businessinsider.com/cost-cutting-at-dropbox-and-silicon-valley-startups-2016-5.
2. http://www.vanityfair.com/news/2016/05/dropbox-is-keeping-its-chrome-panda-statue-to-remind-itself-about-the-importance-of-frugality.
3. http://www.bizjournals.com/sanfrancisco/morning_call/2016/06/dropbox-is-in-the-post-unicorn-era-says-ceo.html.
4. See note 1.
5. Wileman, A., *Driving Down Cost: How to Manage and Cut Costs – Intelligently* (London: Nicholas Brealey Publishing, 2010), 55–7.
6. http://www.businessinsider.com/inside-the-crash-of-londons-payment-unicorn-powa-technologies-2016-4.
7. Vance, A., *Elon Musk: How the Billionaire CEO of SpaceX and Tesla Is Shaping our Future* (London: Ebury Publishing, 2015; Kindle edn), ch. 6.
8. Ibid., ch. 9
9. Robertson, D. C., *Brick By Brick: How LEGO Rewrote the Rules of Innovation* (London: Random House Business Books, 2013), 202.
10. Ibid., 23.
11. Ibid., ch. 7.
12. http://time.com/4253546/ingvar-kamprad-ikea-billionaire-frugal-clothes/.
13. Kamprad, I., *The Testament of a Furniture Dealer* (Inter IKEA Systems BV, 1976).
14. Ibid., 207.
15. The Toyota Production System distinguishes between seven sources of waste. I have included the four that are most prevalent in my experience. For more detail, see: Liker, J. K., *The Toyota Way* (New York: McGraw-Hill, 2004), 28–9.

16. https://www.fastcompany.com/3025315/fast-feed/shaving-startup-harrys-buys-razor-factory-for-100-million.

17. Bragg, S. M., *Cost Management* (Centennial: Accounting Tools Inc., 2014; Kindle edn), ch. 1.

18. Ibid., 124.

19. Ibid., 48–9.

20. http://www.wsj.com/articles/SB10355929943494003751?mg=id-wsj.

21. http://www.nytimes.com/2002/07/22/us/worldcom-s-collapse-the-overview-worldcom-files-for-bankruptcy-largest-us-case.html?_r=0.

22. http://www.washingtonpost.com/wp-dyn/content/article/2005/07/13/AR2005071300516.html.

23. The theory of constraints became well known after the success of Goldratt's book *The Goal* – see Goldratt, E. M., and Cox, J., *The Goal: A Process of Ongoing Improvement* (1984; 30th anniversary edn, Great Barrington: The North River Press Publishing Corporation, 2014). William Dettmer also provides a thorough introduction – see Dettmer, H. W., *Breaking the Constraints to World-Class Performance* (Milwaukee: ASQ Quality Press, 1998). The theory's application to capital expenditure is mentioned in Techt, U., *Goldratt and the Theory of Constraints: The Quantum Leap in Management* (Stuttgart: Ibidem Press, 2015), ch. 6, and Bragg, *Cost Management*, ch. 7.

24. For an excellent primer on capital expenditure calculations, see Berman, K., Knight, J., and Case, J., *Financial Intelligence: A Manager's Guide to Knowing What the Numbers Mean* (Boston: Harvard Business Review Press, 2013), part 6.

Customer Base

1. Grove, A. S., *Only the Paranoid Survive: How to Exploit the Crisis Points That Challenge Every Company* (New York: Random House, 1999), 65.

2. http://www.forbes.com/sites/ryanmac/2013/03/04/the-mad-billionaire-behind-gopro-the-worlds-hottest-camera-company/#5bb00b435a75.

3. http://marcbarros.com/build-brand-awareness-first-distribution-second/.

4. Ries, L., *Visual Hammer* (Laura Ries, 2015).

5. Suggestion from conversation with Catrina Funk.

6. As note 5.

7. http://www.businessinsider.com/most-expensive-apple-watch-2015-3.

8. https://www.marinelayer.com.

9. https://www.headspace.com.

10. https://www.apple.com/pr/library/2001/10/23Apple-Presents-iPod.html.

11. https://www.bloomberg.com/news/articles/2016-09-08/death-of-apple-s-17-000-gold-watch-leaves-swiss-rivals-smiling.

12. Berger, J., *Contagious: Why Things Catch On* (New York: Simon & Schuster, 2013), ch. 2.

13. Grimm, K., 'Communications', in N. Gallagher and L. Myers, eds, *Patagonia Tools for Grassroots Activists* (Ventura: Patagonia Books, 2016), 101.

14. http://www.martinagency.com/clients/geico.

15. https://www.geico.com/about/corporate/at-a-glance/.

16. http://www.independent.co.uk/news/business/news/transferwise-valued-at-1bn-by-top-silicon-valley-venture-capital-fund-10002618.html.

17. Sharp, B., *How Brands Grow: What Marketers Don't Know* (South Melbourne: Oxford University Press, 2010), 210.

18. Ibid., 32–4.

19. Ibid., 35.

20. Ibid.

21. Ibid., 110.

22. Ibid., 23.

23. Ibid., 41–5.

24. Ibid., 13.

25. Humby, C., Hunt, T., and Phillips, T., *Scoring Points: How Tesco Continues to Win Customer Loyalty* (London: Kogan Page, 2008), 30–32.

26. Ibid., 11–12.

27. http://www.forbes.com/sites/johnellett/2014/09/14/sephoras-winning-formula-highly-relevant-personalized-data/#21de7aa42459.

28. Humby, Hunt and Phillips, *Scoring Points*, 19–24.

29. Capgemini Consulting, *Fixing the Cracks: Reinventing Loyalty Programs for the Digital Age* (Capgemini, 2015).

30. Ibid., ch. 11.

31. http://adage.com/article/datadriven-marketing/starbucks-data-pours/240502/.

32. Kordupleski, R., *Mastering Customer Value Management* (Cincinnati: Pinnaflex, 2003), xv.

33. Ibid., xvi.

34. Ibid., xviii.

35. Farris, P. W., Bendle, N. T., Pfeifer, P. E., and Reibstein, D. J., *Key Marketing Metrics: The 50+ Metrics Every Manager Needs to Know* (Harlow: Pearson Education, 2009), 132–7.

36. Ibid., 134.

37. Ibid., 142–50.

38. Ibid., 151–3.

39. Reichheld, F., and Markey, R., *The Ultimate Question 2.0* (Boston: Harvard Business School Publishing, 2011), 4–6.

40. Ibid., 62.
41. Freed, L., *Innovating Analytics: How the Next Generation of Net Promoter Can Increase Sales and Drive Business Results* (Hoboken: John Wiley & Sons, 2013; Kindle edn), ch. 3.
42. Ibid.
43. Ibid., ch. 4.
44. Ibid.
45. Ibid., ch. 6.

Imitability

1. https://www.bloomberg.com/news/articles/2015-03-26/meerkat-gets-14-million-as-livestreaming-becomes-tech-fad-again.
2. Data sourced from https://www.appannie.com.
3. http://www.recode.net/2016/3/4/11586696/meerkat-is-ditching-the-livestream-and-chasing-a-video-social-network.
4. http://sprudge.com/exclusive-aeropress-inventor-alan-adler-selling-company-111887.html.
5. Palfrey, J., *Intellectual Property Strategy* (Cambridge: The MIT Press, 2011), introduction.
6. Johnson, S., *Guide to Intellectual Property: What it is, How to Protect It, How to Exploit It* (London: Profile, 2015; Kindle edn), ch. 2.
7. Sherman, A. J., *Harvesting Intangible Assets* (New York: Amacom, 2012; Kindle edn), ch. 5.
8. See Note 6.
9. http://www.nytimes.com/2005/12/17/world/americas/an-unlikely-trendsetter-made-earphones-a-way-of-life.html.
10. http://www.telegraph.co.uk/news/uknews/1368860/Dyson-cleans-up-in-patent-battle-with-rival-Hoover.html.
11. See note 7.
12. http://www.nytimes.com/2007/09/13/sports/13iht-prix.5.7500107.html.
13. http://theweek.com/articles/457529/blurred-lines-5-other-popular-songs-sued-copyright-infringement.
14. http://www.autocar.co.uk/car-news/guangzhou-motor-show/land-rover-complain-about-chinese-copy-range-rover-evoque.
15. http://www.bbc.com/news/technology-23530337.
16. Johnson, *Guide to Intellectual Property*, ch. 3.
17. See note 7.
18. https://www.hodinkee.com/articles/can-you-guess-how-many-fake-watches-were-seized-last-year.
19. Johnson, *Guide to Intellectual Property*, ch. 8.
20. Ibid., ch. 4.

21. http://www.bbc.com/news/technology-28525440.

22. Roland, A., *Model Research Volumes 1 & 2* (Washington DC: National Aeronautics and Space Administration, 1985), ch. 2: 'The Cross-Licensing Agreement', accessed at: https://history.nasa.gov/SP-4103/ch2.htm.

23. http://www.hollywoodreporter.com/thr-esq/warner-music-pays-14-million-863120.

24. http://www.hollywoodreporter.com/news/george-lucas-star-wars-288513.

25. http://theweek.com/articles/575363/star-wars-isnt-movie-franchise-toy-franchise.

26. http://americanhistory.si.edu/collections/search/object/nmah_630930.

27. https://www.tesla.com/blog/all-our-patent-are-belong-you.

28. Knee, J. A., Greenwald, B. C., and Seave, A., *The Curse of the Mogul* (New York: Profile, 2009; Kindle edn), ch. 2.

29. Rumelt, R., *Good Strategy Bad Strategy: The Difference and Why It Matters* (New York: Crown Business, 2011), 122.

30. https://www.youtube.com/watch?v=PBg90zYM-pk.

31. Simon, H., *Confessions of the Pricing Man: How Price Affects Everything* (Switzerland: Springer, 2015; Kindle edn), ch. 4.

32. https://www.american-giant.com/our-story.html.

33. http://www.inc.com/ilan-mochari/2015-30-under-30-casper.html.

34. See note 28.

35. http://www.saudiaramco.com/en/home/about.html.

36. https://www.theguardian.com/business/2016/jun/16/zara-profits-uk-sales-profits.

37. Kiechel III, W., *Lords of Strategy: The Secret Intellectual History of the New Corporate World* (Boston: Harvard Business School Press, 2010; Kindle edn), ch. 13.

38. Grove, A. S., *Only the Paranoid Survive: How to Exploit the Crisis Points That Challenge Every Company* (New York: Random House, 1999), 48, 50, 68.

39. Magretta, J., *Understanding Michael Porter: The Essential Guide to Competition and Strategy* (Boston: Harvard Business Review Press, 2012; Kindle edn), ch. 5.

40. https://dealbook.nytimes.com/2010/09/23/blockbuster-files-for-bankruptcy/.

41. Christensen, C. M., *The Innovator's Solution: Creating and Sustaining Successful Growth* (Boston: Harvard Business Review Press, 2013; Kindle edn), ch. 6.

42. https://hbr.org/2014/06/how-to-succeed-in-business-by-bundling-and-unbundling.

43. Quammen, D., *The Song of the Dodo* (New York: Scribner, 1996), 11–12.

44. http://fortune.com/2014/06/23/telecom-companies-count-386-billion-in-lost-revenue-to-skype-whatsapp-others/.

45. https://www.bloomberg.com/ukinnovators/innovators/graze/.

46. Arthur, W. B., *The Nature of Technology: What It Is and How It Evolves* (New York: The Free Press, 2011; Kindle edn), ch. 10.

47. Ibid., ch. 7.

48. https://dealbook.nytimes.com/2012/01/19/eastman-kodak-files-for-bankruptcy/.

49. Arthur, W. B., *Complexity and the Economy* (Oxford: Oxford University Press, 2014), 69–70.

50. Shapiro, C., and Varian, H. R., *Information Rules: A Strategic Guide to the Network Economy* (Boston: Harvard Business Review Press, 1998; Kindle edn), ch. 7.

51. Seba, T., *Winners Take All: The Nine Fundamental Rules of High Tech Strategy* (San Francisco: Tony Seba, 2006), 184.

52. http://www.slideshare.net/gueste94e4c/dropbox-startup-lessons-learned-3836587.

53. http://www.huffingtonpost.com/2013/07/02/tinder-app-college-kids_n_3530585.html.

54. https://www.cnet.com/news/why-sxsw-doesnt-need-another-twitter-moment/.

55. See note 50.

56. https://www.theguardian.com/technology/2016/apr/27/how-uber-conquered-london.

57. http://www.businessinsider.com/airbnbs-summer-reach-has-grown-by-353-times-in-5-years-2015-9.

Adaptability

1. Butt, T., *Surf Science: An Introduction to Waves for Surfing* (2002; 3rd edn, Cornwall: Alison Hodge, 2014), ch. 2–7.

2. Netflix Q2 2016 Letter to Shareholders. Accessed at: http://files.shareholder.com/downloads/NFLX/2902023149x0x900152/4D4F0167-4BE2-4DC1-ACC7-759F1561CD59/Q216LettertoShareholders_FINAL_w_Tables.pdf.

3. Munger, C. T., *Poor Charlie's Almanack: The Wit and Wisdom of Charles T. Munger* (Virginia Beach: PCA Publication, 2008), 102.

4. Blank, S., *The Startup Owner's Manual* (Pescadero: K. & S. Ranch, 2012; Kindle edn), ch. 1.

5. Ries, E., *The Lean Startup: How Today's Entrepreneurs Use Continuous*

Innovation to Create Radically Successful Businesses (New York: Crown Publishing, 2011), 160.

6. http://www.slate.com/articles/technology/technology/2012/12/american_giant_hoodie_this_is_the_greatest_sweatshirt_known_to_man.html.

7. http://www.bbc.com/news/business-21680884.

8. https://www.crossfit.com/.

9. DeMarco, T., *Slack* (New York: Dorset House, 2001).

10. Goddard, J., and Eccles, T., *Uncommon Sense, Common Nonsense: Why Some Organisations Consistently Outperform Others* (London: Profile Books, 2013), part 1: 'Winners and Losers'.

11. Grove, A. S., *Only the Paranoid Survive: How to Exploit the Crisis Points That Challenge Every Company* (New York: Random House, 1999), 3.

12. Although the phases I describe deviate from it, my thinking on this topic was heavily influenced by the adaptive life cycle proposed by Gunderson and Holling, who use the terms 'exploitation', 'conservation', 'release' and 'reorganisation' to describe the stages in the evolution of a complex adaptive system. See Gunderson, L. H., and Holling, C. S., *Panarchy: Understanding Transformations in Human and Natural Systems* (Washington DC: Island Press, 2001; Kindle edn), ch. 2.

13. John Glubb uses this term – 'the outburst' – to describe the aggressive expansion of a small conquering nation, whose characteristics resemble that of a successful start-up. See Glubb, J., *The Fate of Empires and Search for Survival* (Edinburgh: William Blackwood & Sons, 1976), 4.

14. Ibid., ch. 8.

15. Arthur, W. B., *The Nature of Technology: What It Is and How It Evolves* (New York: The Free Press, 2011; Kindle edn), ch. 7.

16. Christensen, C. M., *The Innovator's Solution: Creating and Sustaining Successful Growth* (Boston: Harvard Business Review Press, 2013; Kindle edn), ch. 1.

17. Meadows, D., *Thinking in Systems: A Primer* (White River Junction: Routledge, 2009), ch. 3.

18. Ibid., 124.

19. Holiday, R., *Ego is the Enemy* (New York: Portfolio/Penguin, 2016), part 2.

20. Kahneman, D., *Thinking, Fast and Slow* (London: Allen Lane, 2011), 256–9.

21. Miller, D., *The Icarus Paradox: How Exceptional Companies Bring About Their Own Downfall* (New York: Harper Business, 1991).

22. http://fortune.com/google-cfo-ruth-porat-most-powerful-women/.

23. Ibid., 112–14.

24. DeMarco, T., Hruschka, P., et al., *Adrenaline Junkies and Template Zombies* (New York: Dorset House, 2008), pattern 45: 'News Improvement'.

25. For more details see Womack, J., *Gemba Walks* (expanded 2nd edn, Cambridge: Lean Enterprise Institute, 2013; Kindle edn).

26. Hoffer, E., *The True Believer* (1951; New York: HarperCollins e-books, 2010), 10.

27. Drucker, P. F., *Landmarks of Tomorrow* (Oxford: Heinemann, 1996), 50–54.

28. https://www.framestore.com/about-us.

29. https://www.bloomberg.com/news/articles/2014-02-06/sony-ceo-credibility-takes-hit-with-1-1-billion-loss-forecast.

Final Thoughts

1. http://www.forbes.com/sites/maggiemcgrath/2016/09/23/the-9-most-important-things-you-need-to-know-about-the-well-fargo-fiasco/#54667ddc7dcb.

2. http://www.latimes.com/business/la-fi-wells-fargo-sale-pressure-20131222-story.html.

3. https://www.nytimes.com/2016/10/21/business/dealbook/voices-from-wells-fargo-i-thought-i-was-having-a-heart-attack.html.

4. https://www.nytimes.com/2016/09/09/business/dealbook/wells-fargo-fined-for-years-of-harm-to-customers.html.

5. See note 2.

6. http://www.wsj.com/articles/wells-fargo-to-pay-185-million-fine-over-account-openings-1473352548?mg=id-wsj.

7. https://www.bloomberg.com/news/articles/2016-09-27/wells-fargo-ceo-forfeits-more-than-41-million-amid-board-review.

8. http://www.forbes.com/sites/maggiemcgrath/2016/10/12/embattled-wells-fargo-ceo-john-stumpf-is-retiring-effective-immediately/#5e2be52f46c4.

9. Horowitz, B., *The Hard Thing About Hard Things: Building a Business When There Are No Easy Answers* (New York: HarperCollins, 2014; Kindle edn), ch. 4, 'Lead Bullets'.

Complete Bibliography

The following texts have been instrumental in developing my thinking whilst researching the grid. Although most were not directly cited in the text, they merit acknowledgement.

Adlin, T., and Pruitt, J., *The Essential Persona Lifecycle: Your Guide to Building and Using Personas* (Burlington: Morgan Kaufmann, 2010).

Alvesson, M., and Spicer, A., *The Stupidity Paradox* (London: Profile Books, 2016).

Arthur, W. B., *Increasing Returns and Path Dependence in the Economy* (Ann Arbor: University of Michigan Press, 1994).

——, *The Nature of Technology: What It Is and How It Evolves* (New York: The Free Press, 2011).

——, *Complexity and the Economy* (Oxford: Oxford University Press, 2014).

Asacker, T., *The Business of Belief* (Tom Asacker, 2013).

Augustine, N. R., *Augustine's Laws* (New York: American Institute of Aeronautics and Astronautics, 1983).

Axelrod, R., *The Evolution of Cooperation* (New York: Basic Books, 1984).

Beall, A. E., *Strategic Market Research: A Guide to Conducting Research that Drives Businesses* (Bloomington: iUniverse, 2010).

Berger, J., *Contagious: Why Things Catch On* (New York: Simon & Schuster, 2013).

Berkun, S., *The Myths of Innovation* (Sebastopol: O'Reilly Media, 2007).

Berman, K., Knight, J., with Case, J., *Financial Intelligence: A Manager's Guide to Knowing What the Numbers Mean* (Boston: Harvard Business Review Press, 2013).

Berry, L., and Parasuraman, A., *Marketing Services: Competing Through Quality* (New York: The Free Press, 1991).

Beyer, H., and Holtzblatt, K., *Contextual Design: Defining Customer-Centered Systems* (San Fransisco: Morgan Kaufmann, 1998).

Blank, S., *The Startup Owner's Manual* (Pescadero: K. & S. Ranch, 2012).

Blau, K., Franco, Z. E., and Zimbardo, P. G., *Heroism: A Conceptual Analysis and Differentiation Between Heroic Action and Altruism* (Washington DC: Review of General Psychology, 2011).

Bloom, P., *How Pleasure Works* (London: The Bodley Head, 2010).

Bragg, S. M., *Cost Management* (Centennial: Accounting Tools Inc., 2014).

Brandt, R. L., *One Click* (London: Penguin Group, 2011).

Buffett, W. E., and Olson, M., *Berkshire Hathaway Letters to Shareholders 1965–2015* (Mountain View: Explorist Productions, 2015).

Burlingham, B., *Small Giants: Companies that Choose to Be Great Instead of Big* (2005; 10th anniversary edn, New York: Portfolio/Penguin, 2016).

Byman, J., *Andrew Grove and the Intel Corporation* (Greensboro: Morgan Reynolds, 1999).

Caldwell, L., *The Psychology of Price: How to Use Price to Increase Demand, Profit and Customer Satisfaction* (Richmond: Crimson Publishing, 2012).

Chouinard, Y., *Let My People Go Surfing* (New York: The Penguin Press, 2005).

Christensen, C. M., *The Innovator's Dilemma* (Boston: Harvard Business Press, 1997).

——, *The Innovator's Solution: Creating and Sustaining Successful Growth* (Boston: Harvard Business Review Press, 2013).

——, *The Clayton M. Christensen Reader* (Boston: Harvard Business Review Press, 2016).

Christensen, C. M., Allworth, J., and Dillon, K., *How Will You Measure Your Life* (New York: HarperCollins, 2012).

Chwe, M. S. K., *Jane Austen, Game Theorist* (Princeton: Princeton University Press, 2013).

Cokins, G., *Activity-Based Cost Management: An Executive's Guide* (New York: John Wiley & Sons, 2001).

Collins, J., *Good to Great* (London: Random House, 2001).

——, *Built to Last* (London: Random House, 2005).

Cooper, A., Reimann, R., and Cronin, D., *About Face 3* (Indianapolis: Wiley Publishing, 2007).

Cope, N., *The Seven Cs of Consulting* (Harlow: Financial Times/Prentice Hall, 2003).

Courage, C., and Baxter, K., *Understanding Your Users* (San Francisco: Morgan Kaufmann, 2005).

Cowen, T., *The Great Stagnation* (Boston: Dutton, 2011).

Csikszentmihalyi, M., *Flow: The Psychology of Optimal Experience* (New York: HarperCollins, 1990).

Davidson, N., *Don't Just Roll the Dice: A Usefully Short Guide to Software Pricing* (Cambridge: Simple Talk Publishing, 2009).

De Botton, A., *Status Anxiety* (London: Penguin Books, 2005).

Deci, I. L., and Ryan, R. M., *Intrinsic Motivation and Self-Determination in Human Behavior* (New York: Plenum Press, 1985).

DeMarco, T., *Slack* (New York: Dorset House, 2001).

DeMarco, T., Hruschka, P., et al, *Adrenaline Junkies and Template Zombies* (New York: Dorset House, 2008).

Dettmer, H. W., *Breaking the Constraints to World-Class Performance* (Milwaukee: ASQ Quality Press, 1998).

Dobelli, R., *The Art of Thinking Clearly* (London: Sceptre, 2013).

Drucker, P. F., *Landmarks of Tomorrow* (Oxford: Heinemann, 1996).

——, *The Daily Drucker* (Oxford: Butterworth-Heinemann, 2005).

——, *Innovation and Entrepreneurship* (Oxford: Butterworth-Heinemann, 2007).

——, *The Five Most Important Questions You Will Ever Ask About Your Organization* (San Francisco: Jossey-Bass, 2008).

Ekman, P., *Emotions Revealed* (London: Weidenfeld & Nicolson, 2003).

Evans, D., *Emotion: A Very Short Introduction* (Oxford: Oxford University Press, 2001).

Farris, P. W., Bendle, N. T., Pfeifer, P. E., and Reibstein, D. J., *Key Marketing Metrics: The 50+ Metrics Every Manager Needs to Know* (Harlow: Pearson Education, 2009).

Festinger, L., *A Theory of Cognitive Dissonance* (California: Stanford University Press, 1957).

Fleming, N., *Evergreen: Cultivate the Enduring Customer Loyalty that Keeps Your Business Thriving* (New York: Amacom, 2015).

Freed, L., *Innovating Analytics: How the Next Generation of Net Promoter Can Increase Sales and Drive Business Results* (Hoboken: John Wiley & Sons, 2013).

Fried, J., and Heinemeier Hansson, D., *ReWork* (London: Vermilion, 2010).

Galinsky, A., and Schweitzer, M., *Friend and Foe: When to Cooperate, When to Compete, and How to Succeed at Both* (London: Random House, 2015).

Gallagher, N., and Myers, L., eds, *Patagonia Tools for Grassroots Activists* (Ventura: Patagonia Books, 2016).

Gardner, J. G., *Self-Renewal and the Innovative Society* (New York: W. W. Norton and Co., 1995).

Gassmann, O., and Frankenberger, K., *The Business Model Navigator: 55 Models That Will Revolutionise Your Business* (London: FT Publishing, 2015).

Gawande, A., *The Checklist Manifesto* (London: Profile Books, 2010).

Glubb, J., *The Fate of Empires and Search for Survival* (Edinburgh: William Blackwood & Sons, 1976).

Gobé, M., *Emotional Branding* (New York: Allworth Press, 2009).

Goddard, J., and Eccles, T., *Uncommon Sense, Common Nonsense: Why Some Organisations Consistently Outperform Others* (London: Profile Books, 2013).

Goldratt, E. M., and Cox, J., *The Goal: A Process of Ongoing Improvement* (1984; 30th anniversary edn, Great Barrington: The North River Press Publishing Corporation, 2014).

Greene, R., *The Concise 48 Laws of Power* (London: Profile Books, 1998).

——, *The Concise Art of Seduction* (London: Profile Books, 2003).

——, *Mastery* (London: Profile Books, 2013).

Gross, D., *Forbes Greatest Business Stories of All Time* (Hoboken: John Wiley & Sons, 1996).

Grove, A. S., *High Output Management* (New York: Vintage Books, 1983).

——, *Only the Paranoid Survive: How to Exploit the Crisis Points That Challenge Every Company* (New York: Random House, 1999).

Gunderson, L. H., and Holling, C. S., *Panarchy: Understanding Transformations in Human and Natural Systems* (Washington DC: Island Press, 2001).

Hankel, I., *Black Hole Focus* (Chichester: Capstone, 2014).

Higgins, T., *Beyond Pleasure and Pain: How Motivation Works* (New York: Oxford University Press, 2012).

Hoekman Jr, R., *Designing the Obvious* (Berkeley: New Riders, 2007).

Hoffer, E., *The True Believer* (1951; New York: HarperCollins e-books, 2010).

Holden, R. K., and Burton, M. R., *Pricing With Confidence: 10 Ways to Stop Leaving Money on the Table* (Hoboken: John Wiley & Sons, 2008).

Holiday, R., *The Obstacle Is the Way: The Ancient Art of Turning Adversity to Advantage* (London: Profile Books, 2014).

——, *Ego Is the Enemy* (New York: Portfolio/Penguin, 2016).

Horowitz, B., *The Hard Thing About Hard Things: Building a Business When There Are No Easy Answers* (New York: HarperCollins, 2014).

Humby, C., Hunt, T., and Phillips, T., *Scoring Points: How Tesco Continues to Win Customer Loyalty* (London: Kogan Page, 2008).

Iacocca, L., with Novak, W., *Iacocca: An Autobiography* (New York: Bantam, 1984).

Isaacson, W., *Steve Jobs* (London: Little, Brown, 2011).

——, *The Innovators* (London: Simon & Schuster, 2014).

Ittelson, T. R., *Financial Statements* (Franklin Lakes: Career Press, 2009).

Jenson, S., *The Simplicity Shift* (Cambridge: Cambridge University Press, 2002).

Johnson, S., *Guide to Intellectual Property: What It Is, How to Protect It, How to Exploit It* (London: Profile Books, 2015).

Jones, D., *Who Cares Wins* (London: Pearson Education, 2012).

Kahneman, D., *Thinking, Fast and Slow* (London: Allen Lane, 2011).

Kamprad, I., *The Testament of a Furniture Dealer* (Inter IKEA Systems BV, 1976).

Kasparov, G., *How Life Imitates Chess* (London: William Heinemann, 2007).

Kiechel III, W., *Lords of Strategy: The Secret Intellectual History of the Corporate World* (Boston: Harvard Business School Press, 2010).

Keltner, D., *The Power Paradox: How We Gain and Lose Influence* (New York: Penguin Press, 2016).

KesselsKramer, *Advertising For People Who Don't Like Advertising* (London: Laurence King Publishing, 2012).

Knee, J. A., Greenwald, B. C., and Seave, A., *The Curse of the Mogul* (New York: Profile Books, 2009).

Knight, P., *Shoe Dog: A Memoir by the Creator of Nike* (London: Simon & Schuster, 2016).

Kordupleski, R., *Mastering Customer Value Management* (Cincinnati: Pinnaflex, 2003).

Krishna, A., *Sensory Marketing* (New York: Routledge, 2010).

Krug, S., *Don't Make Me Think* (Indianapolis: New Riders, 2000).

Lafley, A. G., and Martin, R. L., *Playing to Win: How Strategy Really Works* (Boston: Harvard Business Review Press, 2013).

Lanning, M. J., *Delivering Profitable Value* (Cambridge: Basic Books, 1998).

Lehrer, J., *How We Decide* (New York: First Mariner Books, 2009).

Liddell Hart, B. H., *Strategy* (London: Faber & Faber, 1954).

Lidwell, W., Holden, K., and Butler, J., *Universal Principles of Design* (Gloucester, Massachusetts: Rockport Publishers, 2003).

Liker, J. K., *The Toyota Way* (New York: McGraw-Hill, 2004).

Lipton, B. H., *The Biology of Belief: Unleashing the Power of Consciousness, Matter and Miracles* (2005; new edn, London: Hay House, 2015).

Livingston, J., *Founders at Work* (Berkeley: Apress, 2007).

Loewy, R., *Never Leave Well Enough Alone* (New York: Simon & Schuster, 1950).

Lovell, N., *The Curve: How Smart Companies Find High-Value Customers* (London: Portfolio/Penguin, 2013).

Maeda, J., *The Laws of Simplicity* (Cambridge, Massachusetts: The MIT Press, 2006).

Magretta, J., *Understanding Michael Porter: The Essential Guide to Competition and Strategy* (Boston: Harvard Business Review Press, 2012).

Martin, R. L., *Fixing the Game: Bubbles, Crashes, and What Capitalism Can Learn from the NFL* (Boston: Harvard Business School Publishing, 2011).

Matthews, G., Davies, D. R., et al., *Human Performance: Cognition, Stress and Individual Differences* (Hove: Psychology Press, 2000).

McDonald, M., and Dunbar, I., *Market Segmentation: How to Do it and How to Profit from it* (Chichester: John Wiley & Sons, 2012).

McJohn, S. M., *Examples & Explanations: Intellectual Property* (New York: Wolters Kluwer, 2015).

McNish, J., and Silcoff, S., *Losing the Signal: The Untold Story Behind the Extraordinary Rise and Spectacular Fall of BlackBerry* (New York: Flatiron Books, 2015).

Meadows, D., *Thinking in Systems: A Primer* (White River Junction: Chelsea Green Publishing, 2009).

Merholz, P., Schauer, B., et al., *Subject to Change* (Sebastopol: O'Reilly Media, 2008).

Merlin, B., *The Complete Stanislavsky Toolkit* (London: Nick Hern Books, 2007).

Miller, D., *The Icarus Paradox: How Exceptional Companies Bring About Their Own Downfall* (New York: Harper Business, 1991).

Mitchell, M., *Complexity: A Guided Tour* (Oxford: Oxford University Press, 2009).

Moore, G. A., *Crossing the Chasm: Marketing and Selling Disruptive Products to Mainstream Customers* (New York: Harper Business, 2014).

Mohammed, R., *The 1% Windfall: How Successful Companies Use Price to Profit and Grow* (New York: HarperCollins e-books, 2010).

Morgan, G., *Images of Organisation* (Newbury Park: Sage Publications, 1986).

Mulder, S., and Yaar, Z., *The User Is Always Right* (Berkeley: New Riders, 2007).

Munger, C. T., *Poor Charlie's Almanack: The Wit and Wisdom of Charles T. Munger* (Virginia Beach: PCA Publication, 2008).

Musashi, M., *The Book of Five Rings*, tr. T. Cleary (Boston: Shambhala Productions, 1993).

Myers, T. W., *Anatomy Trains* (London: Elsevier, 2009).

Nagle, T. T., Hogan, J. E., and Zale, J., *The Strategy and Tactics of Pricing* (New Jersey: Prentice Hall, 2011).

Neumeier, M., *The Brand Flip: Why Customers Now Run Companies – and How to Profit From It* (San Francisco: Peachpit, 2015).

Niedenthal, P. M., Krauth-Gruber, S., and Ric, F., (2006) *Psychology of Emotion* (New York: Psychology Press, 2006).

Norman, D. A., *Emotional Design* (New York: Basic Books, 2004).

Osterwalder, A., and Pigneur, Y., *Business Model Generation* (New Jersey: John Wiley & Sons, 2010).

Palfrey, J., *Intellectual Property Strategy* (Cambridge: The MIT Press, 2011).

Parkinson, C. N., *Parkinson's Law* (New York: Buccaneer Books, 1957).

Patnaik, D., and Mortensen, P., *Wired to Care* (New Jersey: FT Press, 2009).

Perez, C., *Technological Revolutions and Financial Capital: The Dynamics of Bubbles and Golden Ages* (Cheltenham: Edward Elgar Publishing, 2002).

Pfenning, D., and Pfenning, K., *Evolution's Wedge: Competition and the Origins of Diversity* (Berkeley: University of California Press, 2012).

Phillips, G. D., *Stanley Kubrick Interviews* (Jackson: University Press of Mississippi, 2001).

Pink, D. H., *Drive: The Surprising Truth About What Motivates Us* (New York: Canongate Books, 2009).

Poltorak, A. I., and Lerner, P. J., *Essentials of Intellectual Property* (Hoboken: John Wiley & Sons, 2011).

Porter, M. E., *Competitive Advantage: Creating and Sustaining Superior Performance* (New York: The Free Press, 1985).

——, *Competitive Strategy: Techniques for Analyzing Industries and Competitors* (New York: The Free Press, 1998).

Poundstone, W., *Priceless: The Hidden Psychology of Value* (Oxford: Oneworld Publications, 2010).

Pricken, M., *The Essence of Value* (Erlangen: Publicis, 2014).

Quammen, D., *The Song of the Dodo* (New York: Scribner, 1996).

Rams, D., *Less But Better* (Hamburg: Jo Klatt Design + Design Verlag, 1995).

Ratneshwar, S., Mick, D. G., and Huffman, D., *The Why of Consumption* (New York: Routledge, 2000).

Read, L., *I, Pencil* (Atlanta: Foundation for Economic Education, 2010).

Reason, J., *Human Error* (New York: Cambridge University Press, 1990).

——, *The Human Contribution: Unsafe Acts, Accidents and Heroic Recoveries* (Farnham: Ashgate Publishing, 2008).

Reichheld, F., and Markey, R., *The Ultimate Question 2.0* (Boston: Harvard Business School Publishing, 2011).

Reisman, D., *The Lonely Crowd* (New Haven: Yale University Press, 1961).

Rich, B. R., and James, L., *Skunk Works* (London: Sphere, 1994).

Ridley, M., *The Origins of Virtue* (London: Penguin, 1996).

Ries, A., and Trout, J., *Positioning: The Battle For Your Mind* (New York: McGraw-Hill, 2000).

Ries, E., *The Lean Startup: How Today's Entrepreneurs Use Continuous Innovation to Create Radically Successful Businesses* (New York: Crown Publishing, 2011).

Ries, L., *Visual Hammer* (Laura Ries, 2015).

Robertson, D. C., *Brick by Brick: How LEGO Rewrote the Rules of Innovation* (London: Random House Business Books, 2013).

Rogers, E. M., *Diffusion of Innovations* (5th edn, New York: The Free Press, 2003).

Rumelt, R., *Good Strategy Bad Strategy: The Difference and Why It Matters* (New York: Crown Business, 2011; Kindle edn).

Schumacher, E. F., *Small Is Beautiful: A Study of Economics as if People Mattered* (London: Vintage Books, 1973).

Schwartz, B., *The Paradox of Choice: Why More Is Less* (New York: Harper Perennial, 2004).

Scruton, R., *Beauty* (Oxford: Oxford University Press, 2009).

Seba, T., *Winners Take All: The Nine Fundamental Rules of High Tech Strategy* (San Francisco: Tony Seba, 2006).

Segal, G. Z., *Getting There: A Book of Mentors* (New York: Abrams Image, 2015).

Shapiro, C., and Varian, H. R., *Information Rules: A Strategic Guide to the Network Economy* (Boston: Harvard Business Review Press, 1998).

Sharp, B., *How Brands Grow: What Marketers Don't Know* (South Melbourne: Oxford University Press, 2016).

Shaw, C., *The DNA of Customer Experience: How Emotions Drive Value* (Basingstoke: Palgrave Macmillan, 2007).

Sherman, A. J., *Harvesting Intangible Assets* (New York: Amacom, 2012).

Silver, N., *The Signal and the Noise* (London: Allen Lane, 2012).

Simon, H., *Confessions of the Pricing Man: How Price Affects Everything* (Switzerland: Springer, 2015).

Sun, L., *The Fairness Instinct: The Robin Hood Mentality and Our Biological Nature* (New York: Prometheus Books, 2013).

Sung, E., *Customer Moat: How Loyalty Drives Profit* (Eddie Sung, 2016).

Taleb, N. N., *Fooled by Randomness: The Hidden Role of Chance in Life and the Markets* (New York: Random House, 2005).

——, *Antifragile: Things that Gain from Disorder* (London: Penguin, 2012).

Taylor, F. W., *The Principles of Scientific Management* (New York: Harper & Bros, 1911).

Techt, U., *Goldratt and the Theory of Constraints: The Quantum Leap in Management* (Stuttgart: Ibidem Press, 2015).

Thaler, R. H., *Misbehaving: The Making of Behavioural Economics* (London: Allen Lane, 2015).

Thayer, R., *The Origin of Everyday Moods* (New York: Oxford University Press, 1996).

Thorndike, W. N., *The Outsiders: Eight Unconventional CEOs and Their Radically Rational Blueprint for Success* (Boston: Harvard Business Review Press, 2012).

Tiger, L., *The Pursuit of Pleasure* (New Jersey: Transaction Publishers, 2000).

Tsu, S., *The Art of War* (Boston: Shambhala Classics, 2001).

Tufte, E., *Envisioning Information* (Connecticut: Graphics Press, 1990).

Turke, S., *Evocative Objects* (Cambridge, Massachusetts: The MIT Press, 2007).

Vance, A., *Elon Musk: How the Billionaire CEO of SpaceX and Tesla Is Shaping our Future* (London: Ebury Publishing, 2015).

Vinjamuri, D., *Accidental Branding: How Ordinary People Build Extraordinary Brands* (Hoboken: John Wiley & Sons, 2008).

Vogelstein, F., *Battle of the Titans: How the Fight to the Death Between Apple and Google Is Transforming our Lives* (London: William Collins, 2013).

Watkinson, M., *The Ten Principles Behind Great Customer Experiences* (Harlow: FT Press, 2013).

Watzlawick, P., Erickson, M. H., et al., *Change: Principles of Problem Formulation and Problem Resolution* (New York; London: W. W. Norton and Co. 2011).

White, F., *The Overview Effect* (New York: American Institute of Aeronautics and Astronautics, 2014).

Wickens, C. D., and Hollands, J. G., *Human Psychology and Engineering Performance* (New Jersey: Prentice Hall, 2000).

Wileman, A., *Driving Down Cost: How to Manage and Cut Costs – Intelligently* (London: Nicholas Brealey Publishing, 2010).

Winograd, T., *Bringing Design to Software* (New York: ACM Press, 1996).

Womack, J., *Gemba Walks* (expanded 2nd edn, Cambridge: Lean Enterprise Institute, 2013).

Index

About the Author

Matt Watkinson is an internationally renowned author, speaker and business consultant. His first book, *The Ten Principles Behind Great Customer Experiences*, won the CMI's Management Book of the Year Award in 2014.